HALDANE'S BEST
RESUMES FOR PROFESSIONALS

Books in the Haldane's Best Series...

HALDANE'S BEST
RESUMES FOR PROFESSIONALS

Bernard Haldane Associates

IMPACT PUBLICATIONS
Manassas Park, Virginia

Library of Congress Cataloging-in-Publication Data

Haldane's best resumes for professionals / Bernard Haldane Associates.
   p. cm.
Includes bibliographical references and index.
ISBN 1-57023-109-5 (alk. paper)
1. Resumes (Employment). I. Title. Best resumes for professionals.
HF5383.H183 1999
808'.06665—dc21   99-14867
                                                          CIP

Publisher: For information on Impact Publications, including current and forthcoming publications, authors, press kits, bookstore, and submission requirements, visit Impact's Web site: *www.impactpublications.com*

Publicity/Rights: For information on publicity, author interviews, and subsidiary rights, contact the Public Relations and Marketing Department: Tel. 703/361-7300 or Fax 703/335-9486.

Sales/Distribution: Bookstore sales are handled through Impact's trade distributor: National Book Network, 15200 NBN Way, Blue Ridge Summit, PA 17214, Tel. 1-800-462-6420. All other sales and distribution inquiries should be directed to the publisher: Sales Department, IMPACT PUBLICATIONS, 9104-N Manassas Dr., Manassas Park, VA 20111-5211, Tel. 703/361-7300, Fax 703/335-9486, or *haldane@impactpublications.com*

Book design by Kristina Ackley

CONTENTS

PREFACE

Welcome to Bernard Haldane Associates. We're pleased you have decided to join us on what may well become an exciting journey, as well as a defining moment, in your career and your life—writing and distributing a targeted, employer-centered resume that clearly communicates your career goals, major strengths, and patterns of accomplishments.

Like other books in the "Haldane's Best" series, this is not your typical job search book. ***Haldane's Best Resumes For Professionals*** represents the collective efforts of hundreds of career professionals who have successfully worked with more than 600,000 clients for over 50 years. Experienced in the day-to-day realities of finding jobs and changing careers, our work continues to represent the cutting edge of career counseling. Indeed, our innovative Career Strategy 2000 program, which interfaces with the Internet, provides our clients with quick access to today's new job search frontier.

Based on the career management principles of Dr. Bernard Haldane, the father of modern career counseling, this is much more than just another resume book filled with "dos" and "don'ts" and packed with examples of so-called "winning resumes." Consistent with Haldane's career management principles, this book takes you step-by-step through the building blocks that are so essential for creating a powerful Haldane resume and an effective job search. Focusing on the "unique you," these principles will help you focus your resume around what you do well and enjoy doing—your major strengths. You will begin to clearly communicate to employers what it is you want to do, can do, and will do for them. Employers, in turn, should invite you to job interviews because your Haldane resume speaks their language loudly and clearly—they are looking for people who can add *value* to their operations. They want to hire your *pattern of accomplishments*.

The book is organized into two major parts. The first nine chapters outline the key principles for developing a Haldane resume. They present, for example, one of the most important assessment devices used in career counseling—Success Factor Analysis. Chapters 10 and 11 include numerous examples of resumes drawn from our client files. They incorporate the many principles outlined in the previous chapters. The names, addresses, and employers have been changed to maintain the confidentiality of our clients.

Bernard Haldane Associates consists of a network of more than 80 career management offices in the United States, Canada, and the United Kingdom (see pages 220-225) that work with thousands of clients each day in conducting effective job searches based upon the many principles outlined in this book.

So join us as we celebrate our more than 50 years of experience in helping professionals realize their career dreams. Whatever you do, make sure you navigate the job market with a Haldane resume. Such resumes really stand out from the crowd because they speak directly to the needs of employers.

HALDANE'S BEST
RESUMES FOR PROFESSIONALS

WELCOME TO 21ST CENTURY EMPLOYERS AND RESUMES

You're a stranger; I really don't know much about you; and I might make a hiring mistake that could cost me dearly. So, tell me why should I interview and maybe hire you? What can you really do for me?

I understand where you're coming from and why you may be reluctant to interview and hire me for this job. Knowing what I do about both you and the job, I feel I'm a perfect fit for this position because:

- *I share your vision; this is my objective.*
- *I have the experience and qualifications you desire; these are my accomplishments.*
- *I have a track record of adding value to employers' operations.*
- *I love to do what you need done.*
- *I'm an enthusiastic team player who focuses on the bottom line.*
- *I'm very predictable in what I'll do for you.*

If only resumes could talk, they might engage in interesting and insightful conversations with employers. But they can't talk—only communicate clues to future performance that get talked about in job interviews.

WHAT'S YOUR RESUME I.Q.?

But resumes do speak a language of their own. They say things to strangers that make the difference between being called or passed over for a job interview. Just how well prepared are you to write a resume that grabs the attention of employers who will call you for job interviews? Let's begin answering this question by responding to the statements on page 2.

1

YOUR RESUME I.Q.

SCALE: 1 = strongly disagree   3 = maybe, not certain   5 = strongly agree
            2 = disagree   4 = agree

1. I have a clear idea of what I do well and enjoy doing and know how to communicate it on my resume.	1	2	3	4	5
2. I can state an employer-centered objective that reflects exactly what I want to do.	1	2	3	4	5
3. I know what should and should not be included on a resume.	1	2	3	4	5
4. I know which resume format works best for my level of experience.	1	2	3	4	5
5. I know how to write an electronic resume.	1	2	3	4	5
6. I know how to write an e-mail resume.	1	2	3	4	5
7. I can select an appropriate language for a conventional resume.	1	2	3	4	5
8. I can select an appropriate language for an electronic resume.	1	2	3	4	5
9. I know when I should and should not fax or e-mail my resume.	1	2	3	4	5
10. I know the name and position of the person who should receive my resume.	1	2	3	4	5
11. I have a clear strategy for distributing my resume to the right people.	1	2	3	4	5
12. I know how and when to use my resume to network and conduct referral interviews.	1	2	3	4	5
13. I know how to get my resume into the databases of online employment and headhunter sites.	1	2	3	4	5
14. I know how to write an appropriate cover letter to accompany my resume.	1	2	3	4	5
15. I know how to conduct an effective resume follow-up.	1	2	3	4	5

TOTAL:

Add the numbers you circled to the right of each statement in order to get a total cumulative score. If your total is 60 or more, you are well on your way to producing an excellent resume that incorporates many principles of successful resumes. If your score is below 50, you should benefit greatly from this book. In fact, once you finish this book, you should be able to score 65 points or higher on this resume I.Q. test.

THE HALDANE WAY

Does your resume have wings? Is it both candidate- and employer-centered? Does it clearly present an appealing pattern of accomplishments? Does it soar high above the competition by communicating key messages about your past, present, and future performance loudly and clearly to potential employers?

> *A Haldane resume is based on key principles that have literally defined the field of career management for more than 50 years.*

If you have a Haldane resume, it's a perfect fit for both you and the employer. This type of resume is based on key principles or rules that have literally defined the field of career management for more than 50 years. Such a resume can give both you and your career renewed and life-long direction.

Best of all, if you write and distribute the type of resume outlined in this book, you may quickly join thousands of professionals who have gone on to extremely rewarding jobs and careers because they incorporated our tested career management principles in every phase of their job search. They know the rules, and these rules continue to guide them in rewarding careers. Above all, they know how to better take control and manage their careers for the new millennium.

Welcome to the resume world of Bernard Haldane Associates. Join us as we take you on a well-focused journey to renewed career success. Let us share with you proven rules for job and career success honed over five decades in working with more than 600,000 clients. We'll incorporate these rules into writing, producing, and distributing a powerful Haldane resume—a document that may well become your most important calling card in the years ahead!

Client Feedback

"I am ecstatic that I have received a position that is more meaningful than I had ever expected, and paying $200,000 in salary, much more than I expected . . . . I also learned that once I quit trying to do things my way and 'Just Do It' the Haldane way, that I began to make so many contacts that led me to this position."

—D.C.

FINDING JOBS IN A TALENT-DRIVEN, VALUE-ADDED ECONOMY

We indeed live in interesting, unprecedented, and highly unpredictable times. While the booming American economy in the final half of the 1990's created more than 3 million new jobs each year, attained a historical low unemployment rate of 4.2 percent, and generated new career vocabularies in employee-scarce high-tech fields, this was not business as usual. Fundamental restructuring of both the economy and job market also meant the economy destroyed thousands of jobs each day. Seeking new opportunities, facing increased competition, and focusing on the bottom line, companies continue to downsize, rationalize, and economize their operations through the application of technology, out-sourcing, and mergers. In such an environment, thousands of people both find and lose jobs each day as companies restructure their workforces to position themselves better in the volatile new economy. While young, inexperienced, and low-wage workers have little difficulty finding entry-level positions in such a rapidly transforming economy, on the other hand, older, experienced, and high-wage professionals face special difficulties in making job and career transitions. And it's this latter group of experienced professionals who disproportionately seek the career management assistance of Bernard Haldane Associates.

One thing is certain as we start a new millennium: jobs, careers, skill-sets, and employer-employee relations are increasingly unpredictable. The employment game has significantly changed from seeking greater security and minimizing risks to seeking greater opportunities and taking on more risks. Indeed, the job you have today may disappear tomorrow. Between now and when you retire, you may have 10 to 15 different jobs and work in two or three different careers. And the skills you use today

> *Throughout your work life, you may have 10 to 15 different jobs and work in two or three different careers.*

may become obsolete in another few years. As a result, individuals must increasingly take responsibility for their own career management—from acquiring new skills and marketing themselves to alternative employers to taking greater on-the-job initiative. They must view themselves as self-directed economic entities who offer unique skill-sets that make significant contributions to employers' bottom lines. They must view employment situations as sets of client-professional relationships rather than traditional employer-employee relationships. They must present themselves as professionals who enthusiastically take charge and produce results.

So, can you write a resume that responds to the needs of employers in this new talent-driven, value-added economy? Whether you like it or not, to get a job in today's economy, you must initially communicate your qualifications to employers in the form of a one- to two-page resume. Indeed, you will write and rewrite your resume several times in the years ahead as you navigate this brave new job market. The question is how well will you communicate your qualifications to employers? If your resume is based on the career management principles of Bernard Haldane Associates, it will clearly communicate your major strengths to employers who, in turn, will invite you to many job interviews.

Today's economy is a highly competitive, talent-driven economy. While it is uncertain whether this economy has shed its traditional recessionary boom and bust cycles (high employment followed by high unemployment), one thing is certain: the best jobs—those that pay well and have a bright future—go to those who are intelligent, well educated, skilled in the technologies of today and tomorrow, and behave like entrepreneurs. In the talent-driven economy, technology is king; it both defines and drives workplace skills. Individuals must constantly train and retrain in order to survive and prosper in today's fast-paced job market and demanding workplace. Since the talent-driven economy is very competitive, it's driven by highly entrepreneurial professionals who constantly focus on contributing to employers' bottom lines. Be-ing employer- and job-centered, these individuals un-derstand what skills are required to do their job and they acquire and use them accordingly. Knowing that jobs and employers change frequently, savvy profes-sionals compile a solid record of *accomplishments* which they can articulate to their boss and to other employ-ers. Best of all, they are capable of writing terrific re-sumes that are rich in the language of skills, experi-ence, and accomplishments. Being talent-driven em-ployees, they exude the very principles that are the basis for Haldane resumes—a pattern of success that can be expressed as a predictable, recurring set of employer-centered behaviors. Put in its simplest form, these in-dividuals communicate again and again—especially on resumes and letters as well as in job interviews—the famous Haldane principle of career success: *do what you do well and enjoy doing.* This principle is the basis for identifying your *motivated skills and abilities* that enable you and others to predict your future performance.

> *The best jobs go to those who are intelligent, well educated, skilled in the technolo-gies of today and tomorrow, and behave like entre-preneurs.*

RESUME POWER AND YOUR JOB SEARCH

Employers in this talent-driven economy are very responsive to Haldane resumes. These resumes are employer-centered calling cards that clearly communicate a *past pattern of success.* This pattern of success should appear both predictable and applicable to the needs of a potential employer. In essence, it says *"I am a person of significant accomplishments who can do for you what I have done for others."* In today's new economy and workplace, this employer-centered principle is more relevant than ever. It clearly speaks the language of employers who seek increasing value from their employees.

Only a few years ago some career experts were predicting the death of resumes. Confusing the purpose of a job interview with the purpose of a resume, these sages felt resumes were at best obsolete and at worst damn lies. In fact, some studies show that over 30 percent of all resumes include false information; many are deliberately fraudu-lent. However, the fact that most resumes are poorly written or that many contain false information are not good reasons to believe that resumes are obsolete or that they are less than useful. On the contrary. These negative aspects of resumes reflect failures on the part of employers to both demand better resumes and do more thor-ough reference and background checks on candidates. Indeed, poor hiring practices tend to beget poor resumes.

As the economy and workplace have undergone dramatic changes during the past decade, so too have the job search and candidate screening processes. Surprising to many people, the resume is playing an increasingly important role in the hiring pro-cess. Employers are demanding better quality resumes as well as using the latest technology to screen candidates via resumes. The job search, which traditionally was a paper and pencil exercise conducted by mail and telephone, now has important electronic components involving faxes, e-mail, and online employment sites. Consequently, today's job seekers are well advised to sharpen their Internet and e-mail skills to supplement the more traditional job search activities involving the mailing of resumes and letters and doing interpersonal networking.

> **Client Feedback**
>
> *"Haldane Associates helped me the most by refining my resume and helping me pinpoint my skills and achievements."*
> —S.J.
>
> *"My enhanced (Haldane) resume and letter got me the interview."*
> —M.F.

Despite problems associated with resumes, they are here to stay and in a very big way. Resumes are one of the most important elements in a job search. For employers, resumes are important time and money savers: they give employers critical information for screening candidates—in or out—for a job interview. For candidates, resumes are important calling cards for opening the doors of employers.

If you want to open the doors of employers, you simply must have a first-class resume that responds to the needs of employers. Over the years, employers have been especially responsive to resumes that incorporate the job search principles of Bernard Haldane Associates. These principles speak the language of employers who seek individuals who have the right experience, skill-sets, and a pattern of performance that fit well within their organization.

WHY RESUMES ARE MORE IMPORTANT THAN EVER

Resumes play a significant communication role in linking candidates to employers. Depending on whether you are the resume writer or recipient, resumes take on increasing importance in today's employment process for two reasons. First, resumes have become the major medium through which job seekers first communicate their interests and qualifications to employers and by which employers initially screen candidates. This medium, whether in paper or electronic form, serves the best interests of both job seekers and employers. Second, as the job search increasingly moves online and employers use the latest scanning technology to screen candidates, the resume has taken on renewed importance. A well-crafted resume designed for the latest technology is the key to unlocking employers' doors. Indeed, in addition to conventional resumes that get mailed or faxed to employers, Internet and electronic resumes are increasingly playing a major role in recruitment. Neglect the importance of crafting a first-class resume and you may effectively eliminate yourself from today's highly competitive, resume-driven job market.

DEVELOPING RESUME POWER THE HALDANE WAY

Only a few people can write a Haldane resume that both reflects the "unique you" and speaks the language of employers. As we will see in the following pages, a Haldane resume is not just another resume that summarizes one's work history or presents the canned language of a professional resume writer who may have only a superficial knowledge of your interests, skills, accomplishments, and goals. A Haldane resume is a very special document that reflects proven principles of job and career success. Writing such a resume begins with an analysis of you, the job seeker (Chapters 6 and 7), and ends with a well-crafted document that clearly communicates what you do well and enjoy doing (Chapters 10 and 11). The underlying principles of a Haldane resume are based upon years of counseling hundreds of thousands of job seekers who have gone on to very satisfying and rewarding careers. If you write and distribute a Haldane resume, you will be benefiting from the experience of many job seekers and the expertise of the best career counseling in the field of career management.

Do both yourself and your next employer a favor by writing a first-class resume. If you enter today's job market with a Haldane resume, chances are you will join thousands of others who have landed jobs that truly reflect what they want to do with the rest of their lives.

JOIN AN EXCLUSIVE CLUB

Anyone can write a resume, but only a few can write powerful Haldane resumes. Our task in the next ten chapters is to provide expert guidance so you can produce a resume that truly reflects your "best self" to employers. In so doing, you should learn a great deal about yourself and what you want to do with the rest of your life. And if you are like many others who have benefited from the Haldane approach to career success, you will be embarking on an exciting journey of self-discovery that will enrich both your personal and professional lives.

2

What Employers Expect On Resumes Today

How do employers hire and what do they expect from candidates during the hiring process? It's well worth taking a few minutes to identify key information employers seek from candidates. In so doing, you'll have a better understanding of what to include or exclude on your resume as well as how to best prepare yourself for today's increasingly demanding employers who seek greater value from employees.

Expect the Best, Forget the Rest

Employers are increasingly picky in the hiring process. They are getting more demanding and smarter in how they hire and fire. Indeed, many employers know they've made bad and costly hiring decisions in the past, and they are determined to avoid repeating such mistakes in the future. Many employers ask the wrong questions, fail to do adequate background checks, get into legal problems, and make decisions based upon first impressions and wishful thinking rather than on demonstrated job performance. Not surprisingly, in such situations, candidates who manage to craft impressive resumes and talk their way effectively through interviews tend to get hired. Unfortunately, within a few weeks of hiring such "impressive" individuals, many employers discover the job performance they thought they had hired was not what they got. Instead, what they got was a terrific role player—a well coached job search candidate who made all the right resume and interview moves to get the job. Good writers, good talkers, but not much in the way of adding value to the employer's operations. These employers also learn that replacing such a new hire can be both costly and time consuming.

While many employers used to hire fast and fire slow, savvy employers have discovered it's often best to hire slow and fire fast. As a result, today's employers spend more time examining resumes, verifying credentials, testing, and interviewing candidates than ever before. Instead of interviewing a candidate only twice and then offering a position, employers may now interview a candidate five, six, or seven times before extending an offer. Employers want to make sure they are making the right decision. Hiring mistakes tend to be very costly mistakes.

> *While many employers used to hire fast and fire slow, savvy employers have discovered it's often best to hire slow and fire fast!*

SMART HIRING AND RETENTION

Call it what you may, but employers like to refer to their decisions on candidates as "smart hiring." Times are changing as employers are getting smarter in the hiring process. Hiring the right people with the right motivations, attitudes, and skills is extremely important. Employees are increasingly seen as a company's most important asset, and companies that hire well and maintain a low turnover tend to have a competitive advantage. Consequently, hiring and retention tend to be two very big issues with employers today. Human resources departments are increasingly under pressure to help recruit, train, and retain the company's most valuable asset—their employees. Hire right and maintain low turnover, and you may have a competitive advantage. Hire wrong and experience high turnover, and you may be out of business soon.

In fact, numerous books have recently flooded the market to help employers make the right hiring decisions. These books are high on employers' reading lists:

- *Love 'Em or Lose 'Em: Getting Good People to Stay* (Kaye & Jordan-Evans)
- *Hire With Your Head: A Rational Way to Make a Gut Decision* (Adler)
- *Smart Staffing: How to Hire, Reward, and Keep Top Employees For Your Growing Company* (Outlaw)
- *Finding and Keeping Great Employees* (Harris & Brannick)
- *High-Impact Hiring: A Comprehensive Guide to Performance-Based Hiring* (Rosse & Levin)
- *45 Effective Ways For Hiring Smart: How to Predict Winners and Losers in the Incredibly Expensive People-Reading Game* (Mornell)
- *Smart Hiring: The Complete Guide to Finding and Hiring the Best Employees* (Wendover)
- *The Essential Book of Interviewing* (Kanter)
- *Unofficial Guide to Hiring and Firing Employees* (Horowitz)
- *96 Great Interview Questions to Ask Before You Hire* (Falcone)
- *The Manager's Book of Questions: 751 Great Interview Questions For Hiring the Best Person* (Kador)
- *Getting Employees to Fall in Love With Your Company* (Harris)

- *The Complete Reference Checking Handbook* (Andler)

- *Verify Those Credentials* (Earnst & Sankey)

- *Adams Streetwise Hiring Top Performers: 600 Ready-to-Ask Interview Questions and Everything Else You Need to Hire Right* (Adams & Veruki)

- *Fair, Square, and Legal: Safe Hiring, Managing, and Firing Practices To Keep You and Your Company Out of Court* (Weiss)

- *Don't Hire a Crook! How to Avoid Common Hiring (and Firing) Mistakes* (LeMey and Flowers)

Be assured that the next employer you meet has probably read some of these books and prepared for you accordingly! The message is clear: employers have higher expectations in today's hiring process; they are increasingly suspicious of exaggerated performance claims and more alert to possible misrepresentation and outright dishonesty on resumes and in job interviews. They've become gun-shy of employees who often misrepresent themselves and their qualifications. Indeed, more and more employers conduct behavior-based interviews, check references, do background investigations, require drug testing, put employees through a battery of psychological and aptitude tests, and require lengthy probationary periods.

> *Employers are looking for the right type of be-havior for their organizations. Your resume should be designed to help them pre-dict your perfor-mance in their organization.*

Employers are looking for the right type of *behavior* for their organizations. Not only do they want to know your work history, they want to know if you have the right combination of skills and attitudes to "fit into" their organization. They are looking for indicators of such behavior on resumes and in interviews. Since more and more employers are conducting behavior-based interviews, it's safe to assume they are also looking for *behavior-based resumes*. Such resumes tell them what you will most likely do for them based upon a knowledge of your *past patterns of behavior* with other employers. In other words, your resume should be designed to help them *predict your performance* in their organization. Can you do their work, fit into the culture of the organization, and exceed performance expectations?

Candidate screening is becoming more and more an art and a science. No longer will a slick resume and canned answers to interview questions get you far with many employers who now know better ways of hiring. Your resume is only one of many presentation elements required in today's new hiring world. Above all, employers want specific *examples* of your past performance in order to predict your future performance in *their* organization. They want you to tell them about your major *accomplishments*, especially those that are likely to be transferred to their organization, and they expect to verify your background and performance claims. Your performance claims begin with your resume.

The Employer's Value-Added Perspective

It's safe to assume that most employers hire individuals they hope will add greater value to their organization. Their value-added perspective is one you should incorporate in your job search and particularly in your resume. You do this by making your resume employer-centered rather than self-centered. In fact, one of the major errors found in most resumes is that they tend to be self-centered—communicate what the candidate *wants from* the employer rather than what added-value he or she is prepared to *give to* the employer. Each section of your resume should address the needs of the employer. If you know what you want to do, can clearly express your major skills and accomplishments, and keep focused on the employer's needs, your resume should be well received by employers. It will communicate many of the Haldane principles outlined in this book.

Resumes as Advertisements and Screening Devices

One of the major difficulties individuals have in writing resumes starts at the very beginning—defining a resume. Because resumes tend to be intensely personal documents and thus very ego involved, many job seekers mistakenly think a resume is a summary of work history. They believe it should summarize what a person has done in the past on the assumption that employers are primarily interested in learning about an individual's work history. Such a perspective leads to creating resumes that are literally summaries of past jobs. These resumes disproportionately emphasize inclusive employment dates, names of employers, and specific job duties and responsibilities. They also include other standard descriptive elements often found on resumes: educational background, professional affiliations, and personal information. Such resumes are often viewed as "obituaries" since they provide summaries of one's history. The ultimate example of self-centered resumes, these resumes say little or nothing about career goals, interests, skills, or accomplishments.

If you shift the focus to the goals of both job seekers and employers, a resume takes on different meaning and the elements become better focused on the purpose of your job search. For the job seeker, the main purpose of writing and distributing a resume is to get a job interview with an employer. A resume also may have several pre-interview purposes, such as to inform people of your interest in finding a new job and to uncover job leads. But these other purposes should not distract you from the main purpose of your resume—getting in the door for a job interview. Your resume, in essence, is your *calling card* to meet with company representatives about a job. Like a good advertisement, your resume should provide just enough information to entice the reader to contact you for a job interview. If you keep this single purpose in mind, the structure and content of your resume should

> *The main purpose of writing and distributing a resume is to get a job interview. Like a good advertisement, your resume should provide just enough information to entice the reader to contact you for an interview.*

easily come together. Your resume will take on a very different form from other resumes that are much less focused on the ultimate outcome of a resume—the job interview.

For employers, resumes have similar purposes but from a somewhat different perspective. For them, resumes are screening devices—they screen you in or out of a job interview. Screened by human eyes or optical scanners, resumes indicate whether or not candidates meet employers' standards of acceptance. Screening is both positive and negative. Most employers sort resumes into three piles: yes, maybe, or no. The goal is to move as few resumes as possible into the "yes" category and as many resumes as possible into the "no" category so that the interview process can be made most manageable. In other words, the goal of employers is to screen candidates both "in" and "out" of consideration. Because employers receive so many resumes, many of which are unsolicited and include less than accurate information, they invariably are suspicious of "paper strangers" and thus look toward the negative—any indicators that you might be a bad "fit" for their position. These negative indicators can be anything from unexplained time gaps to spelling and grammatical errors. Remember, employers are trying to answer the question *"Why should I hire you?"* In so doing, they also raise a parallel question: *"Are there reasons I shouldn't hire you?"*

> *Employers are trying to answer the question "Why should I hire you?" In so doing, they also raise a parallel question: "Are there reasons I shouldn't hire you?"*

ACCEPTABLE AND PREFERRED RESUME FORMATS

Resumes can be written in many different formats. Which one you choose to best showcase your qualifications reflects how well you've focused your job search as well as how quickly employers are likely to respond to you. The six basic formats are chronological, functional, combination or hybrid, curriculum vitae, portfolio, and resume letter. While not equally effective, all of these formats are acceptable depending on your level of experience, the position for which you are applying, and your goals. The most widely used format is the reversed chronological resume which primarily summarizes work history by inclusive employment dates. But one format stands out as superior to all others: an achievement-oriented combination or hybrid resume. This resume can best showcase one's objective, experience, and accomplishments in reference to an employer's hiring needs. It's the most widely used and successful resume format for clients of Haldane Associates.

Let's look at each of these formats in terms of their strengths and weaknesses. In so doing, you'll get a better idea of which format might best work for you.

Chronological Resumes

A chronological resume is the most popular format used by resume writers. Organized with the most recent position listed first, this type of resume emphasizes dates, employers, and positions. By quickly reviewing dates of employment, the employer gets some initial indications of your patterns of behavior: (1) your level of experience and skills, (2) how long you normally stay with an employer, and (3) whether or not your career history demonstrates a pattern of career advancement. If your employment history is one of stability and advancement, this type of resume will tend to showcase your career progression. However, individuals with little work experience, who change jobs frequently, who go from one type of job to another, or who have employment gaps, may be handicapped by a chronological resume. If you have such an employment history, this type of resume may raise negative questions in the mind of employers: "Only worked for two years? Why three employers in two years? Does a two-year time gap between jobs mean unemployment, hospitalization, or imprisonment? No clear career goals or advancement with three different jobs in three different career fields over a five year period." For individuals with such backgrounds, chronological resumes will emphasize what may be patterns of employment problems and the lack of appropriate experience and skills.

However, not all chronological resumes are the same. There are many types of chronological resumes, ranging from outstanding to the good, the bad, and the ugly. Unfortunately, most chronological resumes are less than outstanding; many are simply bad, if not ugly. The typical chronological resume over-emphasizes dates and names and catalogs official duties and responsibilities rather than communicates goals and accomplishments.

Functional Resumes

The functional resume format de-emphasizes employment dates, employers, and responsibilities. Organized primarily to communicate qualifications, skills, and accomplishments sought by employers, this resume may or may not reference particular jobs or employers. In fact, many of the skills may be acquired through educational, volunteer, or parenting experiences. Focusing on abilities and transferable skills, this type of resume is often used by individuals with little direct work experience or those seeking to make a major career change.

Functional resumes are double-edged swords and tend to raise red flags amongst employers who have learned to read between the lines. While the major strength of functional resumes is the focus on skills and accomplishments, this strength also becomes a weakness when it is not accompanied by reference to specific employers, job titles, and inclusive employment dates. In fact, many employers are very suspicious of functional resumes—candidates using this type of resume are probably hiding their lack of direct work experience, an unstable employment history, or a less than stellar pattern of career advancement. They may have the requisite skills, but chances are they lack the necessary experience required for the position. This suspicion is usually a correct assessment of the situation because most individuals choosing this format are deliberately de-emphasizing their lack of direct work experience in the hope that the employer is primarily attracted to their skills. Our advice: use this format only as a last resort. Remember, at this initial screening stage, in addition to learning about your skills and accomplishments, employers want to know where you have worked and for how long. They do want information on your work history.

Combination or Hybrid Resumes

A combination or hybrid resume format combines the best elements of both the chronological and functional formats. This type of resume primarily emphasizes objectives, skills, and accomplishments but it also includes a section on employment history. The skills and accomplishment section immediately follows an objective and/or summary of qualifications and it may be variously entitled "Experience," "Achievements," "Career Highlights," "Abilities," "Areas of Effectiveness," or "Qualifications Summary." The employment history section is usually called "Work History," "Employment History," or "Experience" and includes a single line for each employer: title of position, name of employer, location of employment, and inclusive employment dates.

Haldane resumes are achievement-oriented hybrid resumes. They are focused around an employer-centered objective and emphasize accomplishments.

Haldane resumes are achievement-oriented hybrid resumes. They are focused around an employer-centered objective and emphasize accomplishments relevant to an employer's needs. Both goal-oriented and behavior-based, these resumes clearly communicate to employers that you understand their needs and are capable of solving their problems.

Curriculum Vitae (CV)

A curriculum vitae or CV is a type of resume you probably will not be writing, unless you are seeking an academic position or a job with a foreign employer. The term "curriculum vitae" usually refers to a special type of resume required by educational institutions and many non-American employers. CVs tend to be lengthy work history documents that reflect the work cultures of educational institutions and the hiring cultures of non-American employers. These are very inclusive documents that can run from 10 to 30 pages, depending on both your work history and how much you document your professional background and activities. In addition to including one's educational background and work history, CVs usually include detailed listings of teaching specialties, courses taught, publications, presentations, public appearances, committee memberships, leadership positions, professional affiliations, recommendations, and other types of information one would normally not include on the standard one- to two-page resume. The goal in writing a CV is to reaffirm your professional status by documenting your accomplishments as much as possible. The most impressive CVs tend to be the longest CVs.

CVs also are highly prized among many non-American employers who tend to be impressed by the weight of the resume rather than by the brevity and language of one's writing. Indeed, in many countries, the one- to two-page American-style resume is viewed as inappropriate. If you send such a resume to one of these employers, they may feel insulted; you obviously are not a serious candidate because you could only write one or two pages on your whole life! To be taken seriously in such hiring cultures, you need to write a lengthy CV, similar to what is acceptable to American academic institutions. In such a situation, you need to go for volume rather than demonstrate your parsimony. At the same time, many European employers will require you to handwrite a cover letter to accompany your CV. The reason for this is that many European employers still use handwriting analysts to screen candidates' personality and behavioral characteristics. You should be aware of such differences in hiring cultures before sending a resume or CV to an employer overseas.

Portfolio

Portfolios are normally associated with the presentation of work samples. They are most frequently used by artists, writers, models, actors, and others who can easily showcase their body of work in a booklet or folder form. If, for example, you are a graphic artist, you definitely should consider sending samples of your work to a prospective employer. Within the past few years, some career experts have popularized portfolios as substitutes for the traditional resume. In this case, the portfolio usually consists of a one- or two-page chronological resume followed by examples of one's work or press materials relating to one's accomplishments. These examples might be in the form of articles, photos, certificates, awards, letters, or models. The real strength of the portfolio is showcasing examples of one's accomplishments rather than just summarizing accomplishments in the language of resumes. If you have received a great deal of press coverage for your work or if you have received awards and letters of commendation, a portfolio presentation prefaced with a hybrid resume may work especially well in your situation. However, portfolios are not for everyone. Some things, especially presentation of work samples, are best left to the interview stage.

Resume Letters

A resume letter is sometimes used in lieu of a formal resume and cover letter. This is basically a cover letter that incorporates the "Experience," "Qualifications Summary," or "Career Highlights" section of a resume into the body of the letter. You may want to use such a letter when networking for job information, advice, and referrals. It should never substitute for a formal resume that would be requested as part of a resume-cover letter application package.

At Bernard Haldane Associates, our clients often use "T" letters and Focus Pieces that either accompany a resume or are sent in lieu of a resume. Both "T" letters and Focus Pieces are excellent substitutes for resumes. They emphasize the near perfect fit between an employer's hiring needs (skills and experience required) and the candidate's specific skills and accomplishments. Many of our clients regularly use these letters to get interviews. We outline the principles for writing such letters as well as include numerous examples of "T" letters and Focus Pieces in our companion volume, **Haldane's Best Cover Letters For Professionals.**

The Haldane Choice

Whenever possible, we prefer a powerful hybrid resume that clearly showcases your goals, skills, and accomplishments as well as satisfies employers' "need to know" about your employment history. Written as a behavior-based resume that will most likely lead to a behavior-based interview, your Haldane resume should be employer-oriented. It should reflect your professional goals, clearly showcase your major skills and accomplishments, and document a strong history of career achievement and advancement. It should motivate the employer to contact you for a job interview.

BEING EFFECTIVE THROUGH DISTRIBUTION AND FOLLOW-UP

In many respects, writing a resume is one of the easiest job search tasks. Once you know what should and should not be included on your resume, and you've gathered all the necessary information about yourself to include in the resume, the writing exercise should not be difficult. Within a few hours, you should be able to complete your resume. The result should be a first-class resume that both looks and sounds good. But looking and sounding good tells you nothing about *effectiveness*. Resume effectiveness is measured by the number of resulting job interviews. In other words, does your nice looking resume have the power to move employers to invite you to job interviews?

The major difficulties with resumes come at two different stages: (1) gathering information on your skills, accomplishments, and goals, and (2) deciding on what to do with the resume once it's completed. In Chapters 6 and 7, we'll examine the back-end work that needs to be done in order to generate critical data on yourself—your skills, accomplishments, motivations, and goals. In Chapter 8, we'll examine the front-end work—what to do with your resume once the writing and production exercises are completed. As Haldane clients quickly learn, a resume is only as good as its distribution and follow-up. To be effective, you must get your resume into the right hands that result in invitations to job interviews. Where, for example, should you send your resume? Do you only send it in response to job announcements or should you broadcast it to hundreds of potential employers? What about including your resume in online resume databases? Are there other things you should do with your resume that may be more effective for your job search? What are the best methods for distributing your resume?

> *Resume effectiveness is measured by the number of resulting job interviews.*

Unlike most resume books that primarily focus on the writing exercise, Haldane Associates recognize the importance of being effective at every stage of your job search. Our many years of experience confirm that the most effective job seekers are those who write their resumes according to Haldane's career management principles and then distribute them through the right channels and regularly follow-up. Most important of all, they follow-up, follow-up, and follow-up. Without a well developed distribution and follow-up system, your first-class resume writing may be for naught. Whatever you do, you must do more than just write a good looking and nice sounding resume. Your resume must get into the right hands whose fingers will dial your telephone number for an interview.

Whatever you do, don't forget to pay particular attention to resume distribution and follow-up. Behind each of the resume examples presented in this book is Haldane's attention to the details of distribution and follow-up. In many respects, your effectiveness will be determined by this key job search principle: your resume is only as good as the quality of your distribution and follow-up activities.

3

HALDANE BEHAVIOR-BASED RESUMES

Haldane resumes are different from most other resumes—they are behavior-based resumes. They focus on what's important to both the job seeker and employer. These resumes are perfectly designed to prepare you for excelling in today's new behavior-based job interviews. Above all, they are based upon a clear set of principles that have largely defined the career management movement for more than 50 years. This set of principles has proved effective for millions of job seekers who have either used the career management services of Bernard Haldane Associates or those of other career counselors who directly or indirectly incorporate Haldane principles in their day-to-day practices. These principles also are the basis for some of today's most popular self-directed career planning and job search books.

ALWAYS DO FIRST THINGS FIRST

Most job seekers both enter and exit the job market by accident or at least in a less than stellar manner. An ultimate exercise in serendipity, their job search meanders in one direction and then another, and yet another, until they land a job they hope will be a good one. Armed with a traditional helter-skelter resume that lacks a clear focus, many job seekers don't know what they are good at doing or what they really want to do. Conducting a rudderless job search, their self-centered resume merely summarizes their past work history and education without giving a hint of what they are really good at doing nor what they most enjoy doing; their resume gives little evidence of potential future performance—a key concern of employers.

Job seekers typically know what they don't like to do, but they find it difficult to specify exactly what they want to do. They often look for a variety of jobs they think they might like to do—regardless of their interests, skills, and experience. Like most other job seekers, they look for jobs they hope to fit into rather than one that fits well with their particular mix of interests, skills, and abilities. They may significantly alter their resume for each job in order to achieve such a "fit." During job interviews, they often give canned answers to questions, focus on benefits, appear uncertain about their career goals, or seem desperate for a job. Not knowing what they do well and enjoy doing, they are ill-prepared for today's new behavior-based interviews that require them to provide details on their accomplishments. Most important of all, they lack clear goals that would help direct their job search into fruitful directions and inform employers of their potential to perform.

Not surprisingly, many of these people end up with jobs that are less than satisfying. These job seekers accumulate lots of work experience but little in the way of career intelligence. They eventually get jobs but not particularly good ones for their long-term career development.

One of the foundation principles of Haldane Associates is that job seekers should always do first things first. And two of the first things they need to do are:

1. assess their interests, skills, and abilities.
2. set clear career goals.

For to conduct a job search without first knowing what it is you do well and enjoy doing will most likely result in an unfocused, self-centered job search. You are likely to communicate the wrong messages to employers—you

> **Client Feedback**
>
> *"I took the time to interview most of the Management Recruiting companies in the St. Louis market and, I can honestly say that Bernard Haldane Associates proved to be in a league of their own. With access to an extensive database of companies and an extremely educated, professional staff, there was a support structure beyond comparison."*
>
> —J.G.

don't know what you want other than a job and its attendant benefits. Since employers want to know what you want to do, can do, and will do for them, you must be prepared to clearly communicate your strengths and goals to them. You should initially do this on your resume. In so doing, you will direct your job search into the most fruitful directions and eventually land a job that is right for you.

BENEFIT FROM THE HALDANE COACHING AND SUPPORT NETWORK

While most of the information provided in this book can be used for developing a resume and conducting a job search on your own, at the same time, you may want to take advantage of the Bernard Haldane Associates' network of support services which consists of hundreds of career professionals, called Career Advisors, in more than 80 offices in the United States, Canada, and the United Kingdom (see the Appendix on pages 220-225 for a complete listing of offices). Anyone can conduct a job search on their own and find a job. But we assume you don't want to find just any job. You want a high quality job that is the right "fit" for both you and the employer—one you really enjoy doing and one that benefits both you and the employer. Unfortunately, the novice do-it-yourself approach often results in taking shortcuts rather than doing first things first. For example, most job seekers begin their job search by first

Client Feedback

"Most valuable to me was the support given me by you and your staff. As you know, it is easy to get anxious and depressed during a career search, especially if you are unemployed. The positive reinforcement really helped keep me 'up.' The Haldane system works if you stay positive, stay focused, and believe that your dreams can come true. . . Your clients need to keep their chins up, work hard on their search, and keep the Faith. God helps those who help themselves."

—R.R.

writing their resume rather than doing the necessary foundation work that should be the basis for their resume and other key job search activities, such as networking, interviewing, and negotiating. After all, they say, isn't that what you're supposed to do first, because that's what others always do? Some, as indicated by the popularity of resume example books, even go so far as to creatively plagiarize others' resumes. By following the crowd, they literally put the horse before the cart and thereby immediately handicap their job search with an ill-fitting resume that may communicate all the wrong messages!

You owe it to yourself to present your very best self to employers. That means taking the time and spending some money to do first things first when conducting a job search. The prerequisite foundation work involves self-assessment and goal setting—two activities that may be best done with the assistance of a professional career counselor or career coach. If you fail to do this foundation work and go directly to writing your resume, you will most likely join thousands of other do-it-yourself job seekers who wander through the job market trying to find a job they can fit into. You will find a job but chances are it will not be a good fit. You may be well advised to work with a professional career counselor or career coach to identify what it is you do well and enjoy doing.

The Haldane approach, which is known as Success Factor Analysis and is outlined in Chapter 6, has helped thousands of clients who use Haldane's career management services for coaching them through the job search process. With the assistance of a professional career coach who helps them with assessment, goal setting, and resume writing, these individuals go on to find jobs that are excellent fits. While these same individuals could conduct a job search on their own, they choose to work with a professional who can assist them every step of the way. The professional does not find them a job. Instead, their career coach provides important career services, advice, and structure that enables the individual to become successful on his or her own terms. In the process, they acquire important long-term career development skills that will serve them well throughout their worklife.

The prerequisite foundation work involves self-assessment and goal setting—two activities that may be best done with the assistance of a professional career counselor or career coach.

Let's talk truth about what we're dealing with in the world of self-help and enlightenment. It can be very lonely and depressing out there in the job market. Our experience, as well as that of most career counselors, is that very few job seekers conduct this process well on their own. Not that they can't; it's just that they won't and thus they don't. Understanding, yes; action, some, but not enough sustained, purposeful action to make things happen the way they should. Most job seekers can cognitively understand what's involved in conducting a successful job search, but the actual process of putting it all together, finding time, implementing each step properly, remaining focused, and maintaining a high level of motivation and energy in the face of no responses or ego-wrenching rejections is something that is very difficult to do on their own. Not surprisingly, people normally used to being effective all of a sudden feel ineffective when conducting their own job search. Nothing seems to work according to expectations, or perhaps expectations are either too high or are misplaced. They procrastinate, find excuses, get depressed, and give up in what is often a cycle of good intentions and dashed expectations with sustained action conspicuously absent. Indeed, very few people ever do it right on their own. Accordingly, most people can benefit tremendously by using the services of professional career counselors. A career management professional can save you a great deal of time, money, and headaches because they combine expertise with a structure for implementing a job search campaign. This expertise comes in many forms:

> *Very few job seekers conduct this process well on their own. A career management professional can save you a great deal of time, money, and headaches because they combine expertise with a structure for implementing a job search campaign.*

1. testing and assessing
2. developing and targeting a job search plan
3. assisting with writing resumes and letters
4. honing networking skills
5. implementing an action plan
6. coaching for job interviews and negotiations

Most important of all, a professional can serve as a mentor who helps you maintain your focus and motivation as well as provides a critical structure for routinely implementing each phase of your job search.

At the same time, you need to be cautious in using so-called professional career services. This is a big business fraught with snake-oil salesmen and varying levels of competence. Professional career services come in many different forms, from testing and assessment centers to full-blown career marketing operations. Some individuals and companies offer career services at an hourly rate while others charge a flat contract price. If you work with someone who charges by the hour, be sure to know exactly what you need. Otherwise, you may be putting together a piecemeal job search that will most likely produce less than desirable outcomes. We prefer a contract arrangement that covers the complete job finding process, from start to finish. This type of arrangement avoids the chaos and excuses attendant with piecemeal activities; it focuses on every element in a successful job search. Most important of all, it commits the individual to seeing the process through at each step and doing everything possible to ensure success. Individuals use their time efficiently, remain focused, and handle well the psychological ups and downs of finding a job. Without such a long-term commitment and structure to move through the process expeditiously, individuals tend to conduct a haphazard job search, experience lots of psychological downs, and short-change their future by conducting a relatively ineffective job search.

Client Feedback

"I signed on with your organization several months ago, feeling lower than the algae that lives underneath pond scum. I now have more confidence and self-assurance than I've ever had in my life, and I couldn't have done it without the assistance of these fine people (at Haldane Associates)."

—B.R.

Unfortunately, some career operations also are fraudulent. They take your money in exchange for broken promises. The promises usually come in the form of finding you a job. Many of these firms promise to do all the work for you—write your resume, broadcast it to hundreds of employers, and schedule interviews. All you have to do is write a check for this service and then sit back for the phone to ring. While this may sound good, because it appears to be a quick and easy way to find a job, such an approach is antithetical to the more than 50 years of Haldane experience.

At Haldane we believe in doing first things first and coaching job seekers to do their very best. You team up with an experienced Career Advisor who literally takes you step-by-step through the complete career planning and job search process, from assessment, goal setting, researching, and resume and letter writing to networking, interviewing, and negotiating salary. Our clients also have access to Haldane's new Career Strategy 2000 electronic program. Designed specifically for Haldane's clients, this rich and powerful electronic program uses the Internet for conducting research, networking, distributing resumes, and targeting employers. We do not find you a job. That's not what we do nor should be doing for you. Instead, we help you find your own job through a well structured process. This is an important distinction often lost in the job search business. It's a distinction that is central to writing a Haldane resume that should ultimately represent the "unique you"—rather than the expertise of a professional resume writer—to employers.

FOCUS ON THE UNIQUE AND FUTURE YOU

Haldane resumes are not your typical historical summaries of work history. They are designed from the bottom-up—based on attention to the details of assessment and goal setting. Sensitive to the needs of employers and reflecting the requirements of today's workplace, Haldane's best resumes represent the unique and future you. They integrate goals with skills and accomplishments that are the basis for predicting future performance. They are an accurate representation of what you do well and enjoy doing. They clearly communicate to employers your past, present, and future:

1. What it is you have done in the past.
2. What you can do at present.
3. What you will most likely do in the future.

By focusing on the past, present, and future, your resume provides employers with a complete picture of your capabilities.

Reflecting the overall purposes of an effective job search, a Haldane resume has three major purposes:

1. Present a positive and unique objective that relates to both your greatest strengths and the needs of the employer.
2. Provide evidence that indicates your objective is realistic and supported by your experience and accomplishments.
3. Focus a job interview around key points of reference on the resume.

Unlike many other resumes, Haldane resumes emphasize the importance of *objectives* in relationship to accomplishments that eventually help set the agenda for the job interview. The resume objective guides other elements on the resume as well as provides important direction to your overall job search, including the job interview.

A Haldane resume serves as a personal brief or an advertising brochure. As your calling card, it says:

1. This is what I want (your Objective).
2. This is why the objective is reasonable; these are my capabilities (your Qualifications).
3. This is proof of my capabilities (your Achievements).
4. This is the environment where I gained these capabilities (your Experience and/or Education).

In the end, your resume should clearly communicate who you are in terms of your goals and capabilities. It should say you are uniquely qualified to join the employer's team, because you have the capabilities to bring increased value to the employer's operations. By emphasizing the unique you and the future, your Haldane resume should be well received by employers who are looking for someone with your particular capabilities. They should immediately know whether or not you are likely to fit into their organization. When invited to an interview, your Haldane resume should provide a solid basis from which to discuss your objectives, qualifications, accomplishments, and future performance. If faced with a behavior-based interview, which is the interview of preference for more and more of today's employers, your behavior-based Haldane resume should help focus the questioning around your patterns of behavior that have consistently added value to previous employers' operations.

CONDUCT YOUR SUCCESS FACTOR ANALYSIS

The key transformational element in the Bernard Haldane approach to career success is what we call "Success Factor Analysis." As we will explore in greater depth in Chapter 6, Success Factor Analysis is a Bernard Haldane developed assessment technique that results in identifying your *motivated* skills and abilities. These also are known as your *strengths*—those things that employers want to hire. Based on a thorough analysis of your major *achievements*, your motivated skills and abilities are those things you both enjoy doing and do well. For example, you may be very talented in developing Web pages, but you might hate having a job that requires you to design Web pages eight hours a day. In this case, you do something very well (your Web design skill) but you're not motivated to do it constantly. Therefore, designing Web pages would not qualify as one of your motivated skills nor would it appear as part of your Success Factor Analysis.

> *Based on a thorough analysis of your major achievements, your motivated skills and abilities are those things you both enjoy doing and do well.*

Once you conduct your own Success Factor Analysis, you may be amazed at the picture it presents of you and your strengths. Indeed, if you are like many of our clients, this picture may be worth a thousand words multiplied by thousands of dollars in future earnings! It may change your life forever as you begin pursuing jobs that you really love. Through your Success Factor Analysis, you should have a clear picture of where you have come from and where you are going. You'll express this picture in words and phrases on your Haldane resume as well as in Haldane job interviews. When an employer you really want to work for says "You're hired!", you'll know this outcome is in part directly attributable to how well you conducted your Success Factor Analysis and subsequently incorporated the results of this analysis into resume content and interview responses.

TARGET INDIVIDUAL EMPLOYERS

Your Haldane resume also should be designed to target individual employers. While it is tempting to broadcast your resume to hundreds of potential employers in the belief that you might be able to snag an employer through such a direct-mail operation, we see limited value in such a throw-your-resume-to-the-wind approach. While such a direct-mail campaign does involve taking action, the results are more often than not disappointing. Few employers will contact you for an interview based on sending them an unsolicited resume. And why would they? Chances are they do not at present have a job opening for someone with your experience. Furthermore, many employers are already overwhelmed with unsolicited resumes, many of which come from firms that sell their resume broadcast services to job seekers. Many of these firms claim results that are hard to believe. Many employers have two quick and easy ways of handling unsolicited resumes: throw them away or scan them into an electronic database for future reference. The more thoughtful employers may even send you a personalized thank-you form letter indicating they are keeping your resume on file for future reference.

This is not to say that resume broadcasting never works. Indeed, at Bernard Haldane Associates, we use a very targeted broadcast approach that focuses on key employers and headhunters who are interested in receiving resumes from our clients. We also include electronic broadcast elements in our Career Strategy 2000 program.

Armed with a Haldane resume, your goal should be to align the "unique you" with a specific employer who is attracted to your particular goals and accomplishments. You do this primarily through a one-on-one marketing campaign that puts your resume in the hands of the right people rather than in anyone's hands who happens to open their mail. Our advice: be cautious in using resume distribution services or schemes that promise to fast-track your job search through what is nothing more than the lazy way to job search success. Our experience with thousands of clients is that there is no substitute for developing a well-targeted job search campaign that strategically places your resume in the right hands—with employers who can use someone with your experience and qualifications. While the Haldane approach takes time and effort, the payoffs are well worth it. You'll eventually connect with a job that is right for both you and the employer.

EMBRACE THE INTERNET

Within the past five years, the Internet has increasingly played an important role for both job seekers and employers as more and more job search and recruitment activities have moved online. In fact, the whole job finding process lends itself well to today's fast growing electronic medium, the Internet. If you have not incorporated the Internet in your job search, it's time that you do so, and the sooner the better. Indeed, you should integrate the Internet into your job search. It will enable you to engage in four critical job search activities:

1. Network for information, advice, and referrals.
2. Enter resumes into online commercial databases.
3. Search for online job listings.
4. Transmit resumes to employers via e-mail.

For starters, you may want to visit today's three largest online employment sites—*www.monster.com*, *www.careerpath.com*, and *www.careermosaic.com*—as well as acquire a copy of one of the best books on using the Internet in your job search, Pam Dixon's ***Job Searching Online For Dummies*** (IDG Books). If you are a Haldane client who uses our Career Strategy 2000 program, you will have instant access to hundreds of Web sites that offer everything from key data on companies to numerous online employment sites. Rather than access each site individually, you can search many sites simultaneously through our unique search engine.

As you may quickly discover, the currency of Internet job searching is the resume. Without an Internet resume, you will not be an active player in the Internet job search game.

Today's savvy job seekers use two key online skills: access information on the Internet and transmit their resume through e-mail. If you can use the Internet and send e-mail, you are well on your way to embracing the Internet. If you haven't done so, don't worry. Using the Internet and sending e-mail are not formidable tasks. You should be able to get up and running after a couple of hours of orientation and practice. Embracing the Internet may be one of the easiest things you can do to enhance your job search. Best of all, you can embrace the Internet 24 hours a day!

Embracing the Internet means different things to different players in the employment game. For **employers**, the Internet is a cost effective and efficient way to recruit individuals. Rather than spend $10,000 to place classified ads or pay a headhunter $25,000 to locate an employee, employers can now go online to place job listings on their home pages or contract with high traffic and/or specialized commercial employment sites to place ads and conduct online searches of resume databases for as little as $150. At the same time, employers can cast a much wider recruitment net and attract more highly qualified candidates (Internet users tend to be viewed by most employers as more technically competent and current in their skills than non-Internet users) by recruiting online. In fact, the Internet has quickly become the employer's best friend. As a job seeker, you'll want to visit employers' Web sites to gain information about their companies and survey current job listings as well as post your resume on various sites that attract employers in your field.

> *Today's savvy job seekers use two key online skills: access information on the Internet and transmit their resume through e-mail.*

The Internet also has become the best friend of **headhunters** which are also known as executive search firms. Headhunters work for employers; they recruit talent that employers choose not to recruit by other means. Primarily working with individuals who make in excess of $60,000 a year, headhunters are normally paid a percent of an employee's first year salary—usually 25-30 percent—by the employer. Today, most headhunters are avid users of the Internet. Using commercial employment sites that enable them to search resume databases by "keywords," they go online to find candidates to include in their resume pools. They, in turn, present these candidates to employers who pay them their regular fees. Employers who incorporate the Internet in their recruitment efforts can probably locate the same candidates, using the same sites, at a fraction of the cost involved in using the headhunter. However, many employers still prefer using headhunters for recruiting candidates for certain positions. Therefore, you are well advised to get your resume in the hands of headhunters. One of the best ways of doing this is to make sure your resume is posted on as many online employment sites as possible. If you have the experience and skills headhunters need, chances are they will find you online. Indeed, many job seekers who use the Internet are surprised to find that many of the "hits" they receive online come from headhunters who wish to market them to their clients.

For **job seekers**, the Internet opens up new possibilities for conducting research and contacting potential employers. It's a huge marketplace for showcasing skills and experience before employers and headhunters. Best of all, most of it is free to job seekers—paid for by employers and headhunters. Since employers who use the Internet do so for posting job listings (the electronic equivalent of the paper classified ad) and for searching resume databases for candidates, you are well advised to periodically check online job listings and enter your resume in online resume databases. Your resume must be designed for the databases which usually means it must be (1) e-mailed to the site, and (2) filled with keywords, which are usually nouns, that are the basic elements employers and headhunters use to conduct a resume search. If you don't design a resume to be both e-mailed and accessed by keywords in an electronic database, you may miss out on many new opportunities available on the Internet. As you will see in subsequent chapters, today's Haldane resumes are designed to be both e-mailed and accessed by keywords.

> *You are well advised to periodically check online job listings and enter your resume in online resume databases.*

With more than 3,000 employment sites now functioning, conducting an online job search can be a daunting and extremely time-consuming task for most job seekers. Our unique Career Strategy 2000 program, which includes thousands of dollars of proprietary online services, brings together key Internet sites to help clients efficiently and effectively use the Internet in their job search. If you are not a Haldane client, we recommend that you select a group of 25 key Internet sites that best represent your occupational interests and level of experience and regularly monitor these sites. Keep in mind that many sites tend to be geared toward recent college graduates or individuals making less than $50,000 a year. Assuming you are experienced and seek jobs that pay more than $50,000 a year, you may be able to eliminate most of the largest and more general sites. You need to hone in on sites that best represent your level of experience and income expectations. Your professional association, for example, may be the perfect place to start since it may have its own employment site which employers turn to for resumes.

For **Internet employment sites**, the Internet is potentially a big and lucrative business. It means an initial influx of venture capital followed by advertising revenues, user fees, and the potential to go public with another wild IPO ride on the Internet. Most sites are based on a very well defined and competitive advertising model: employers pay for job listings, resume database searches, and advertising buttons and banners. In most cases, job seekers pay nothing to use the site. Individuals usually can post a resume in a resume database for free. They are encouraged to visit a site as frequently as possible. Indeed, they are encouraged to do this because the size of a site's resume database largely determines how much they will charge an employer or headhunter to access that database. The amount of traffic, or "hits," a site receives largely determines their advertising rates—how much they will charge for buttons and banner ads. As long as this advertising model continues to keep venture capitalists, stockholders, employers, and headhunters happy, the services of online commercial employment sites should remain free for job seekers.

WRITE, DISTRIBUTE, AND FOLLOW-UP THE HALDANE WAY

At Haldane Associates we're very picky about how our clients conduct their job search. While we want them to be Internet savvy, first of all we want them to know how to write, distribute, and follow-up their resume. We're not new at this business. We do not offer some quick and easy new success formulas nor do we pump you up on lots of positive thinking. We focus on the details of achieving success the old fashioned way—lots of hard work that is often exhilarating and always rewarding. We've successfully shown the way to hundreds of thousands of clients. And we think our way is still the best way to career success. Guided by the Bernard Haldane philosophy, we're set in our ways: you should be looking for jobs that are good fits with your interests, skills, accomplishments, and goals. Our focus is on *quality jobs* that reflect our quality candidates. The measure of our success is when clients go on and prosper in their careers. Most need not return for more coaching and counseling because they've learned how to manage their own career success. They've developed the capacity to continue being successful throughout their work life. At Haldane Associates, what we do is all about building new capabilities to be successful throughout your work life.

Client Feedback

"In the end, Haldane does NOT get jobs for any-one—THEY provide us with the right tools! WE have to do the work! Have you ever tried accomplishing something without the right tools?"

—G.O.

If you are just looking for any job, then our way may not be the best way and the remainder of this book may not be for you. Anyone can find a job with or without this book or the help of a career professional. In fact, in a booming economy, you would be hard pressed not to a find job! But chances are it won't be the right job for you. And that's where Haldane comes in and invites you to explore a different approach to finding jobs and managing your career.

Join us as we show you the Haldane way to career success by focusing on one of the most important elements in your job search—your resume. For some, this may be an exciting trip of self-discovery. For others, it should result in improving what may be a weak and rudderless resume and job search. For everyone, this should result in renewed career success. By focusing on the resume, we'll reveal many of the secrets of successful job seekers who have gone on to prosper in their careers and change their lives. Focusing on what's really important in their job search, they write powerful resumes that clearly communicate their goals and accomplishments to potential employers. They distribute their resume so it gets in the right hands through a combination of mail, fax, e-mail, and electronic databases. Most important of all, they know how to effectively follow-up their job search communication so that employers take action. In other words, we don't just write pretty resumes that may please you or a professional resume writer. Bernard Haldane clients write powerful resumes that see the light of day with the people that really count—hiring managers.

4

MYTHS, REALITIES,
AND MISTAKES

M any of the problems job seekers face in conducting an effective job search— or preventing them from taking effective action—relate to a series of myths about various aspects of the job search and resumes. For example, should you put personal information on your resume? Should you keep your resume to one page? What color paper should you use? When should you fax or e-mail a resume? Is it best to send your resume to the personnel office? Should you follow-up with a letter, phone call, fax, or e-mail?

Job seekers frequently ask these and hundreds of other questions about the "do's" and "don'ts" of resume writing, production, distribution, and follow-up. Let's examine some of the major myths and corresponding realities facing today's job seekers. In so doing, you should get a good overview of how to write, produce, distribute, and follow-up your resume.

FIVE RESUME STAGES

Any discussion of resume effectiveness must address five distinct resume development stages: assessment, writing, production, distribution, and follow-up. **Assessment**, the first stage, is the foundation upon which all resume stages as well as other job search activities are based. Once you have conducted a thorough assessment of your interests, skills, and abilities, know your key strengths, and can articulate a clear objective based upon your major accomplishments, you should be well prepared to move into the next resume stage.

Unfortunately, most examinations of resumes only focus on **resume writing** which is the second stage. They offer advice on how to best write each section of the resume so that it conforms to preconceived notions of what constitutes a good resume. In today's job market, this means two types of resumes: conventional and electronic. Each type has different rules that define what goes into creating a good resume. A conventional resume, for example, is rich in action verbs that describe performance and is intended to be read with human eyes. On the other hand, an electronic resume is designed with a rich combination of keywords or nouns so it can be machine transmitted and read—electronically scanned, e-mailed, or entered into and retrieved from a resume database. Most resume writing discussions focus on resume language, layout, style, and length and are often topped off with numerous examples of what are claimed to be "effective resumes." The end result should be a resume that looks good and will be well received by resume recipients, whether human or electronic. Nearly 90 percent of resume guides focus exclusively on this second resume stage. Most say little or nothing about the remaining three stages that largely determine resume effectiveness.

The third stage, **resume production**, focuses on how to produce your resume. Here the major concerns are decisions about paper color and quality, who should produce it, and the equipment used in making copies of the resume. For example, what's the best color ink and paper to use? Should your resume be produced on high quality paper or would regular 20 pound paper be sufficient? Should you use a word processor or have your resume typeset? Should you do the design and production work yourself or is it better to hire a professional designer who has a keen eye for visual design and who can create a unique professional style? Is it okay to make photocopies of your resume or should you have them professionally printed? How you produce your resume can make a major difference in the overall quality of your resume which, in turn, affects your professional image. If, for example, you have no talent for layout and design, you may produce a terrible looking resume that screams "unprofessional" and "amateur." Production alternatives also affect your job search costs. Top quality production costs can be expensive, especially if you hire the services of a professional designer or artist, or decide to have your resume professionally typeset and put on a press. At the same time, production concerns encompass nonconventional resumes, such as the video or multimedia resume and HTML resumes designed for Web pages. Should you go to the expense of producing these types of resumes?

> *Failure to follow-up ranks as one of the major job search sins. It is a major reason why so many "good resumes" never see the light of day.*

The fourth stage, **resume distribution**, is the key to resume effectiveness. In the end, your resume is only as good as the quality of your distribution. If you don't get it in the right hands, you won't get desired responses. Distribution covers everything from targeting specific audiences (network contacts, personnel offices, hiring officials, headhunters, resume databases) to distribution mediums (hand, mail, fax, e-mail) and carriers (postal system, UPS, FedEx, courier).

The final stage, **resume follow-up**, may be the most important, yet neglected stage in determining resume effectiveness. To distribute a resume without following it up is largely a waste of time, effort, and money. In fact, most job seekers do little or no follow-up because they are either shy or afraid of getting bad news; many simply don't know that they *should* follow-up. Indeed, they assume it's incumbent upon the resume recipient to contact them. If they don't hear from them, then the employer must not be interested in their qualifications. Time and again successful job seekers report it was their follow-up telephone call that made the difference in getting the job interview. Failure to follow-up ranks as one of the major job search sins; it is the single most important reason why so many job seekers experience rejections in their job search. It is a major reason why so many "good resumes" never see the light of day. If you learn only one thing from this book, it should be this: *resume effectiveness requires resume follow-up.* Like the early bird that gets the worm, the "follow-upper" often gets the job interview and the job!

Numerous myths surround each resume stage. Let's examine each of these in order to get a better understanding of how to write, produce, distribute, and follow-up your resume. From the very beginning, you must approach your job search and resume with a clear understanding of certain realities. By examining the following myths, we should be able to shed some unnecessary baggage that could interfere with your job search effectiveness.

APPROACHING THE JOB MARKET

MYTH #1:   **The best qualified individual gets the job.**

REALITY: "Qualifications" mean different things to different people. It could translate as experience, talent, or chemistry. Employers hire for all kinds of reasons. While employers want new employees to be technically competent to do the job, they also look for other indicators of success: enthusiasm, energy, attitude, honesty, integrity, and social behavior—the ability to adjust to their organizational culture. These personal characteristics or qualities, or what some call "chemistry," will largely determine whether or not an employer will like you. In the end, "likability" will largely determine whether or not you will be hired. Indeed, studies show that subjective "likability" often outranks more objective indicators of qualifications, such as education, skills, and experience. All things being equal, the candidate that gets hired is the one the employer likes the most. That candidate is viewed as someone who can both do the job and work well with the boss and co-workers. He or she is a "good fit" for both the job and the organization. Consequently, you need to do more than just present your qualifications to employers. You need to present an all-encompassing "unique you" that goes beyond education, skills, and experience. While easier to communicate in face-to-face interviews, these other qualities can be expressed on resumes through the tone of your language and writing style. For example, does your resume sound like it's coming from someone who is enthusiastic, energetic, engaging, and honest—someone who is very interesting both professionally and personally? If you can capture these qualities in your resume, you should be well on your way to getting an interview and the chance for a job offer.

MYTH #2: Most people learn from their mistakes. Knowing your weaknesses will help you redirect your career.

REALITY: Knowing your mistakes and your weaknesses is interesting information that may help you avoid future errors, but such knowledge seldom translates into positive action and greater initiative. Indeed, it may lead to being more cautious because of the fear of making more mistakes. Most people are better able to change their behavior and redirect their careers if they examine their strengths. If you study your successes—those things that are right about you and constitute the "unique you"—you will have a much clearer idea of where you should channel your career energies in the future. Knowing that you have a particular pattern of successes will help you redirect your career in the direction of greater successes. Failures tend to breed an extreme form of realism that can lead to cynical attitudes and self-defeating behaviors. Success tends to breed success and a positive, proactive attitude. Always try to focus on understanding and building upon your successes.

MYTH #3: The Internet is the key to getting a job. You should spend most of your time "surfing the Net" for job opportunities.

REALITY: The Internet is a wonderful resource for conducting a job search. Embrace it, but don't fall in love with it! The Internet is only one of many potentially fruitful avenues for getting a job in today's job market. All job seekers are well advised to incorporate an Internet component in their job search. They also are cautioned not to go to extremes in devoting too much time on the Internet. While the Internet has the potential to increase one's job search effectiveness, it's also a deceptive double-edged sword: it can be extremely addictive, time-consuming, disorienting, and fruitless—a big electronic search and retrieval hole that can suck up valuable job search time. In fact, only a few job seekers at present get interviews based upon using the Internet. A well-balanced job search should integrate Internet job search activities with other important job search initiatives. Use the Internet to conduct research on employers by visiting their Web sites; gather information and advice by joining chat groups and using message boards; post your resume in online resume databases; survey job listings; and e-mail your resume in response to vacancies. But make sure you relate these online activities to key off-line interpersonal job search activities: networking by telephone, conducting face-to-face referral interviews, and responding to print and/or word-of-mouth vacancies.

> A well-balanced job search should integrate Internet job search activities with other important job search initiatives.

MYTH #4: **Individuals over 40 have difficulty finding jobs in today's youth-oriented job market. If you're over 50, you're in real trouble.**

REALITY: It's true that many employers prefer hiring younger workers, and for two good reasons—most are cheaper and more highly skilled in today's technologies than older workers. In other words, they may represent better *value* to employers than older workers.

Expect to encounter resistance from employers if you emphasize your age, if you lack current skills, and if your salary expectations are too high. Indeed, today's employers tend to equate the lack of current skills, high salary expectations, high insurance premiums, and lack of drive and energy with age. Not surprisingly, they are afraid of hiring individuals who both lack appropriate skills and expect to be paid more than individuals who have newer skills, who may work harder, and who cost much less. To hire such individuals, who invariably are older workers, means getting less value for your money. An employer would be paying top dollar for experience but would be getting less value in terms of skills and work output. But here's the dilemma: employers also want experience—the more the better. If you are over 40 or 50, you have advantages over younger individuals: lots of experience and a pattern of accomplishments which should be a good predictor of your future performance. You should emphasize these advantages as *strengths* you bring to the job. At the same time, you need to address possible *objections* that may be raised to your age. These objections usually come in three forms: lack of current skills, high salary expectations, and less energy and drive than younger employers.

Under no circumstances should you emphasize your age alone as a strength because age, in and of itself, is not a positive. It's what comes with age—experience—that is viewed as a plus for employers. If your salary expectations are too high for employers, you may need to lower your expectations. Better still, be prepared to offer pay-for-performance options, such as bonuses and incentivized pay schemes, that should effectively neutralize objections to high salary expectations.

While you can deal with the age objection during the job interview, you should at least anticipate this objection at the initial resume screening stage. If, for example, your resume indicates you graduated from college 25 years ago, be sure to include recent education and training experiences that suggest that you are in a constant learning mode. Make sure your resume communicates loudly and clearly that you (1) have current and appropriate skills, (2) approach your work with energy and drive, and (3) demonstrate a certain depth of experience, evidenced in an attractive pattern of accomplishments, that is likely to continue for a new employer. If you can do this, age should be no barrier to getting a job. Instead, it may become one of your greatest assets!

MYTH #5:   **The resume is the key to getting a job.**

REALITY: A resume is extremely important to getting a *job interview* which hopefully leads to a job offer and a job. In fact, during the past five years, the resume has become even more important because of the role of the Internet, resume databases, and optical scanners in the job search. The problem for employers is how to better manage the resume in-take process as well as screen the large number of resumes in order to identify a highly qualified pool of candidates from which to interview. A resume is a unique calling card for opening the doors of employers. While a resume is important to the job search, the job interview is the most critical to getting the job. How well you do in the job interview will determine whether or not you will be offered the job. The resume may help structure the interview questions, but it does not get you a job.

MYTH #6:   **The best way to get a job is to respond to classified ads, complete applications, send your resume to human resources offices, enter your resume in a resume database, and wait to be called.**

REALITY: Do you like standing in long lines? That's what you're doing when you focus on these highly formalized job search activities. Lots of people do get jobs using these methods, but these are not the most effective methods for getting a job. Most of them relate to mass application processes that attract hundreds and thousands of job seekers. The best way to get a job is to target specific jobs and employers through networking. The best jobs—high level and high paying— are not advertised nor recruited in the same manner as lower level and lower paying jobs. Your best job will most likely be found through word-of-mouth, a headhunter, sponsorship, or direct application. If you organize your job search toward jobs through these channels, your resume distribution and follow-up activities will follow a different pattern from that of most job seekers who operate according to this myth. You'll custom-design your resume and use it as part of your networking activities for uncovering and targeting key employers as well as for contacting headhunters. As for waiting to hear from employers, he who waits may wait forever. Waiting is simply not a good job search strategy. Effective job seekers follow-up at every stage of their job search. Tenacious yet professional, they make phone calls; they write thank-you letters; they send e-mail; they basically do whatever they feel is appropriate to get a response from a potential employer. They assume employers are busy and thus do not feel obligated to respond to every job seeker. Therefore, it is incumbent upon the job seeker to follow-up.

MYTH #7:	Hiring a professional to help you with the job search is a waste of time and money. Anyone can do this on their own by reading self-help books and using the Internet.
REALITY:	Many people can benefit from using the career planning and job search services of a professional—if they know what they are doing and shop around for the services that best meet their needs. Most people, for example, need to do a skills assessment that is really the foundation for the whole job search. While such an assessment can be done on your own by completing a series of self-directed exercises, the assessment is best done with the assistance of a career professional who can both administer and interpret the appropriate tests. Moreover, many individuals can benefit from the structure and guidance provided by a professional. Those who waste their time and money on a professional most likely don't know how to best select or use a professional. Many hire the wrong person for the wrong purpose. Some even get involved in fraudulent operations. At the same time, some people can do the job search on their own with great success by following a few self-help books and using the Internet. But their numbers are very few. Whatever you do, don't be afraid to seek out a career professional for assistance.

> *Many individuals can benefit from the structure and guidance provided by a career professional.*

WRITING AND RESUME CONTENT

MYTH #8:	You should always write your own resume.
REALITY:	In a perfect world, where everyone is an expert on conducting each phase of a job search, you would write your own resume. Indeed, if you follow each of the chapters in this book, you should be able to write a resume on your own. However, many job seekers can benefit by working with a professional resume writer. But it's extremely important how you use these people. The quick and easy way to get a resume done is to hire someone to write it for you. If you do this, the professional may produce a pretty resume with all the bells and whistles, but it may not represent the "unique you" because it's not based upon a thorough assessment of your major strengths. Our advice is to write at least the first draft of your resume on your own based on the advice presented in this book. At that stage, decide whether or not you need the services of a professional resume writer by evaluating your draft according to the criteria outlined in Chapter 8.

MYTH #9: **A resume should not include an objective.**

REALITY: This is an old debate that continues between different schools of thought and approaches to career planning and job search. Many so-called resume experts advise you to dispense with an objective since it is either meaningless or too confining. Instead, they advise you to include your objective in a cover letter or discuss it during an interview. Not surprisingly, individuals who follow this advice tend to write resumes that are essentially highlights of experience. They often have no central focus nor purpose that clearly communicates what it is they do well and enjoy doing. Moreover, they simply don't know how to write a thoughtful objective based upon a thorough assessment of their skills and achievements. The resume reader must infer goals from interpreting the contents of your resume: *"Maybe this person wants to . . . It's not really clear what he really wants to do other than get this job."* Also, by advising you to include an objective in a cover letter, rather than in your resume, you are being told that you will have greater job search flexibility by doing this; it's okay to change your objective for each job and employer! Such an approach may satisfy people who really don't know what they want to do; they wait for a job to come by and then see if it's something they might want to fit into. Our philosophy is just the opposite: first identify what it is you do well and enjoy doing, formulate this knowledge into an employer-oriented objective, and then target jobs and employers that appear to be excellent fits. Your objective should guide you to your perfect job. It clearly communicates to an employer exactly what it is you want to do as well as demonstrates that you have the requisite skills and experience to accomplish great things for the employer. Without a well thought-out objective, both you and your resume may look rudderless to employers.

MYTH #10: **Your resume should include employment dates followed by the employer and your duties and responsibilities.**

REALITY: How you describe your experience is extremely important to employers. While most employers are interested in inclusive employment dates, they are most interested in your *accomplishments.* Everyone has duties and responsibilities as outlined in their formal job descriptions. But such duties and responsibilities convey nothing about what you really did. If, for example, you were responsible for overseeing a budget of $10 million dollars and supervising 40 people, what exactly did you accomplish? Did you save the company $500,000 by introducing new budgetary procedures? Did you increase productivity within your division by reorganizing operations and automating various functions? These questions relate to accomplishments or outcomes rather than assigned duties and responsibilities.

MYTH #11:	**It's okay to include references and salary expectations on your resume.**

REALITY: Never include references and salary expectations on your resume, unless expressly asked to do so by the employer. These two pieces of information should be reserved for a job interview. Take with you to the interview a list of references should you be asked to supply them, which usually will be at the end of the job interview. Be prepared to talk about salary expectations which also should occur near the end of the job interview. If you reveal your salary expectations early on—before the interview or early in the interview, you will place yourself at a disadvantage when you finally negotiate your compensation package. Above all, don't confuse what information needs to be included on a resume versus information that should be revealed in a job interview. Remember, your resume should be designed to get the job interview; your job interview should lead to a job offer.

MYTH #12:	**Employers read resumes. Put as much information on your resume as possible to help your reader understand who you are.**

REALITY: Few resumes are actually read word-for-word and line-by-line. Most are quickly scanned by either humans or machines. For human readers, your resume must be immediately eye-catching. Indeed, the typical employer spends fewer than 30 seconds scanning a resume. The more you can make your resume reader-friendly or scannable, the better. This means highlighting major skills and accomplishments, using emphasizing techniques, incorporating keywords, and writing short sentences. Always give your resume a 20-second test—can it be quickly scanned and still command the attention of the reader? Separate writing rules apply to electronic resumes that will be scanned into a database and retrieved by keywords.

> *The typical employer spends fewer than 30 seconds scanning a resume.*

MYTH #13:	**Employers prefer a short one-page resume.**

REALITY: The length of your resume will largely depend on your level of experience. If you have fewer than five years of workplace experience, you'll probably want to keep your resume to one-page. Individuals with at least ten years of work experience should write a two-page resume. Individuals with extensive work experience and impressive accomplishments may want to go to three pages. However, it's best to keep your resume to two pages simply because resume recipients lose interest after one or two pages, especially if they are quickly screening numerous resumes.

MYTH #14: **You should only write one resume.**

REALITY: You may need to write more than one version of your resume. However, do not continually change the content of your resume in response to different positions. To do so indicates you don't know what you really want to do; you need to do first things first by focusing on the basics of your job search. Expect to write three different versions of your resume: conventional, electronic, and e-mail. A conventional resume is designed to be read by humans and thus is rich in action verbs that describe your accomplishments. An electronic resume is designed for optical scanners that "read" resumes for keywords which are primarily nouns. An e-mail resume is designed to be e-mailed. It can be written as either a conventional or electronic resume. If you know your e-mailed resume will be included in a resume database or scanned, be sure to convert your electronic resume into an e-mail version.

MYTH #15: **You should never include personal information or statements on your resume.**

REALITY: Most personal information, such as age, height, weight, marital status, and political and religious affiliations, is inappropriate for a resume for a U.S. employer. However, other personal information, including personal statements, may be appropriate in certain situations, especially if it relates to the job, the employer, and/or your skills. If, for example, you are applying for a high-energy position, or you know your age may appear to be a negative, you might want to include a personal statement or list special hobbies or activities that indicate your high-level of energy, such as the fact that you run in the Boston Marathon, play soccer, or climb mountains. Select only those things that communicate your uniqueness in relationship to the employer's position. Avoid personal statements that say nothing about your ability to perform the job, such as the fact that you have three children ages 7, 10, and 14. If a job requires extensive travel, this information may raise questions about your willingness to leave your family for extended periods.

MYTH #16: **Writing a resume is the first thing you should do when starting your job search.**

REALITY: Resume writing should only occur after you have had a chance to assess your skills, develop an objective, and explore employment options. You want to write a powerful resume that truly reflects who you are and what you want to do. If you start your job search by writing your resume, chances are you will conduct a haphazard and disoriented job search.

MYTH #17: **A resume should include all of your work history.**

REALITY: It depends on your experience. Employers are most interested in the last ten years of work experience. Be sure to provide details on your accomplishments during this period. Include information on employers you worked for fifteen, twenty, or twenty-five years ago, but do so very briefly: position, employer, location, and inclusive dates of employment. You can drop altogether very old jobs that may be irrelevant to your current career, such as worked as a bartender or waitress while attending college twenty-five years ago. Several of these jobs can be summarized under a general category: Temporary and Part-Time Jobs.

> *Remember, employers want to hire your future performance, not your past work history.*

MYTH #18: **Only include direct work experience on your resume.**

REALITY: The concept of "experience" covers both paid work and non-paid work experience. If you do not have a lengthy record of paid work experience, be sure to include volunteer and other non-paid experience. Remember, your goal is to communicate your major skills and accomplishments to employers. Skills and accomplishments cross-cut all types of experiences.

MYTH #19: **Education should appear at the end of your resume.**

REALITY: The positioning of resume categories depends on your level of work experience and the significance of education to your objective. If you have little experience and your education is most relevant to the position for which you are applying, then put education near the beginning of your resume. The basic principle for ordering categories is this: always put the most important information first. If education is your most important qualification, put it first, immediately following your objective.

MYTH #20: **It's best to start writing a resume from the very beginning and complete each section in consecutive order.**

REALITY: Always complete your objective first because all other sections need to be related to your objective. However, the order in which you complete the remaining sections is not important. Many people find it's much easier to write from the bottom up.

MYTH #21: Your choice of resume language should be simple and straight-forward.

REALITY: Pay particular attention to the details of your resume language. If you are writing a conventional resume, be sure to incorporate lots of action verbs and use the active voice in your descriptions of experience (*"Increased profits by 24%"* or *"Improved first quarter performance by nearly 50 percent"*). If you are writing an electronic resume, incorporate lots of keywords which should be nouns (*"public relations, C++, customer service"*). Be succinct. Keep your sentences and paragraphs short. Do not refer to yourself as "I", an awkward, inappropriate, and self-centered reference on resumes. Always use the language of accomplishments and achievements rather than duties and responsibilities. Remember, employers want to hire your *future performance*, not your past work history.

MYTH #22: Include both your home and work telephone numbers on your resume.

REALITY: To maximize confidentiality, it's best to only include your home telephone number. If you include a work number, you could receive an embarrassing phone call from a prospective employer that inadvertently announces to others in your office that you are conducting a job search on your current employer's time. Also, include your e-mail address, assuming you have private e-mail, along with a street mailing address and fax number, if you have one. Avoid post office box numbers which do not engender confidence in your degree of permanent residence.

MYTH #23: Put your full name at the top of your resume.

REALITY: It's not necessary to use your full formal name, including your middle name or initial. Use whatever name you normally use and which is most flattering. Individuals who include their middle name or initial on their resume tend to be seen as formal and academic individuals, people who may like to keep their social distance. Avoid nicknames which may not be too flattering (James "Shooter" Jones). Your name should appear simple and inviting to strangers.

MYTH #24: Center your name, address, and contact information at the very top of your resume.

REALITY: There is no hard and fast rule here. The header information can take on several forms, from center and off center to flush right or flush left. It depends on what visual effect you would like to achieve.

MYTH #25:   **The experience section should be rich with action verbs.**

REALITY: Yes, in the case of conventional resumes. However, electronic resumes include few action verbs because they need to be rich in keywords which are usually nouns.

MYTH #26:   **You should try to get as much information as possible on your resume.**

REALITY: You should be very selective in what you include or exclude on your resume. Remember, employers are primarily interested in your last ten years of work experience. They want to know what it is you will do for them based upon knowledge of what you did for others. Your resume also should be inviting to read. Make generous use of white space. Avoid a cramped and cluttered look that often comes with trying to include too much information in a one- or two-page resume. Remember, you're not trying to write your history. You're trying to provide just enough information on your achievements to get invited to a job interview.

MYTH #27:   **You should not use more than three emphasizing techniques, such as all caps, bold, italicizing, underlining, bullets, boxes, and asterisks, in your resume.**

REALITY: This rule is generally applicable to conventional resumes. But when you write electronic and e-mail versions of your resume, many of these standard emphasizing techniques will work against you. In these cases, limit your use of emphasizing techniques to all caps and asterisks. Other emphasizing techniques create problems when scanning or transmitting these types of resumes.

MYTH #28:   **It's okay to include pictures and graphics on your resume.**

REALITY: Avoid pictures and graphics unless you are in an occupational field where they are appropriate, such as film, modeling, or graphic arts. Regardless of what you think of your good looks, photos are double-edged swords: some people will be attracted to you whereas others will be turned off by your photo. The problem is in knowing who will like you. Simple graphic elements, such as an attractive border around the text, can add a nice touch to a conventional resume. But if your resume is likely to be scanned, the graphic element may interfere in the scanning process.

MYTH #29:   **You should be as honest as possible on your resume.**

REALITY: While it's important to be honest throughout your job search, honesty does not mean you should volunteer negative information about yourself nor confess your weaknesses. Indeed, honest people some-

> *Honesty does not mean you should volunteer negative information about yourself nor confess your weaknesses. There's a difference between being honest and being stupid.*

times say dumb things about themselves. For example, if you flunked out of college or were fired from a job, there is no reason why you should include this information on your resume. Stay with the facts relating to your strengths. If the employer wants to know about why you didn't complete college or why you left a particular employer, he or she will ask you during the interview. At that time, you can explain the circumstances surrounding such ostensibly negative experiences which hopefully have turned into positives—you learned and grew in the process. There's a difference between being honest and being stupid. Avoid the latter throughout your job search.

MYTH #30: **You should avoid writing a combination resume. Chronological and functional resumes work best.**

REALITY: The chronological resume is the most popular form of resume. However, it also is one of the least effective resumes. Emphasizing the chronology of one's work history, this resume often works against a candidate's best interests. If you have a strong record of accomplishments, regardless of particular work settings, the combination or hybrid resume will best showcase your skills and accomplishments. Rich in accomplishment statements that directly relate to an objective, these resumes can present a powerful picture of performance to employers. Always avoid the traditional chronological resume that emphasizes dates first. If you do not have a clear chronological pattern of accomplishments or if you are changing jobs or careers, you may want to select the functional format. But keep in mind that the functional resume is the weakest form. It may raise more questions than it answers. Indeed, many employers may feel you are hiding something in your background when you present a functional resume.

MYTH #31: **Electronic resumes are primarily designed to be e-mailed.**

REALITY: Electronic resumes should be designed for optical scanners—few graphic elements and rich in keywords. These resumes can be either mailed or e-mailed. An e-mailed resume may or may not be scanned. You should always check with an employer to learn if your resume will be scanned into a resume database. If it will be scanned, you need to send by mail or e-mail an electronic version of your resume.

MYTH #32: **Most resumes can be e-mailed.**

REALITY: Any text document can be e-mailed but the question is how will it look when transmitted? Conventional resumes do not e-mail well.

When transmitted, they lose their graphic elements such as emphasizing techniques and layout. Only resumes designed to be e-mailed can be properly e-mailed. When developing an e-mail version of your resume, you must pay particular attention to characters per inch (fewer than 65) and graphic elements (limit yourself to all caps and asterisks). Resumes transmitted via e-mail as attachments for a particular word processing program should retain all their basic design elements. However, most employers do not want to receive resumes as attachments. After all, they must open the file in the same word processing program you use, which may or may not be compatible with their program, and your file could potentially include a computer virus. It's best to create an e-mail version of your resume, which also may be scanned into a resume database, that follows the rules of e-mail resumes. Expect to send this resume in the body of your e-mail message which will essentially function as a cover letter.

> *Most employers do not want to receive e-mailed resumes as attachments.*

MYTH #33: **It's a good idea to create a video or multimedia resume for today's job market.**

REALITY: We're not great fans of video or multimedia resumes, and for good reason. When you introduce video elements into a resume, you change the whole nature of job search communication. You begin incorporating aspects of a job interview—verbal and nonverbal communication—that may be best left to the interview stage. Like a photo on a resume, you don't know how the viewers will respond when they view you in this medium. You lose control when you present yourself in a video or multimedia format. However, there are situations where these resumes may be appropriate, especially if you are applying for a position in sales, film, theater, modeling, or video and multimedia production. Our advice: know your audience before venturing into the video and multimedia resume business. These can be costly productions that may actually work against your best interests.

MYTH #34: **Once you've drafted your resume, you should go directly into production.**

REALITY: After completing an initial draft, you should conduct two types of evaluations—internal and external. You conduct an *internal evaluation* by comparing various aspects of your resume to a checklist of evaluation points. The *external evaluation* is done by others, preferably individuals who are in hiring positions, who give you thoughtful feedback on the quality of your resume. Each evaluation should indicate what changes need to be made before you complete the final copy.

MYTH #35:   **It's okay to handwrite notes on a resume in lieu of sending a cover letter.**

REALITY: Handwriting notes on a resume in lieu of a cover letter is tacky. It says a lot about your level of professionalism—low. Resumes should always be accompanied by cover letters that are typed and produced in a professional manner.

MYTH #36:   **The purpose of your resume is to give an employer as much information as possible on your background so he or she can best make a hiring decision.**

REALITY: The purpose of a resume is to get the job interview. The job interview may lead to a hiring decision. Be careful what information you include on the resume. Only include what is necessary in order to get invited to the interview. Many resume writers include too much information or they include inappropriate information. Always remember that your resume is your calling card for requesting an interview.

MYTH #37:   **When examining your resume, employers look for positive reasons to call you for an interview.**

REALITY: Remember, however well packaged you are with an attractive resume and a fine telephone voice, you are still a stranger—an untested quantity—to most employers. You're joining the employer's "family" by way of a hiring process. Therefore, employers look for all kinds of reasons to *eliminate* you from joining the family. Indeed, the job search is often analogous to football—the coach looks for reasons to eliminate you from the team. In the case of your resume, these reasons can be anything from the lack of required experience and skills to misspelled words, grammatical errors, and an unprofessional presentation. Employers look at you with critical eyes. Not only does the employer ask *"Why should I hire you,"* he or she also asks *"Why shouldn't I hire you? What problems can I expect from you? Are you more trouble than you are worth—or more worth than you are trouble?"* Always be prepared to deal with *objections* to hiring you. On your resume, these objections may be obvious (time gaps, lack of education, limited experience) or subtle (obnoxious tone, critical of previous employer, self-centered objective).

PRODUCTION

MYTH #38: **It's best to produce your resume using one of the standard software packages designed for resume writing.**

REALITY: It's not necessary to go to this expense. Most standard word processing and desktop publishing programs allow you to produce attractive resumes. In fact, many of the software programs produce canned resumes; they force you into predesigned categories and templates that may not be appropriate for you. If you want to reflect the "unique you" in your resume design and content, you may want to create your resume without the assistance of such "quick and easy" packages.

MYTH #39: **It's best to have your resume professionally typeset and printed.**

REALITY: It's no longer necessary to go to such an expense. Most word processors, letter quality printers, and copy machines are capable of producing top quality copy. In addition, this technology allows you to custom-design your resume and run as many or few copies as you desire.

MYTH #40: **Employers are most attracted to resumes printed in black ink and on off-white paper.**

REALITY: The color of the ink and paper really doesn't make much difference as long as you stay with dark inks and light colored papers. Since your resume may be scanned, it's best to stay with black ink on white paper. Other color inks and papers may be difficult to scan.

MYTH #41: **Avoid using colored papers.**

REALITY: While we prefer white or off-white papers, other colors may be appropriate for different types of jobs. For example, if you are applying for a job in advertising, art, or printing, you might want to go with a paper that is most appropriate for these fields.

MYTH #42: **Always print your resume on a good quality bond paper.**

REALITY: For a conventional resume, you can achieve a very professional look by using a good quality bond paper—20 lb. or heavier—with a nice texture. However, an electronic resume that will be scanned should be produced on regular paper without texture.

MYTH #43: **Always print your resume on 8½" x 11" paper.**

REALITY: While this is the normal size for most resumes, some resume writers report success with smaller resumes—7" x 10". An unusual sized conventional resume does get attention for being unique. If your resume will be scanned, stay with the 8½" x 11" size.

MYTH #44: **Print your two-page resume front to back on a single sheet of paper so that the second page doesn't get separated.**

REALITY: Never do this. Each page of your resume should be printed on one side of a page. Use a continuation page notation (Page 2 of 2) along with your name to identify additional pages. Resumes printed on two sides cannot be scanned with ease and may be even overlooked by the human reader.

MYTH #45: **You should always staple a multi-page resume.**

REALITY: Don't staple your resume. The employer will staple the pages together if necessary. Since your resume is likely to be scanned, any staples will have to be removed prior to scanning. Just make sure you label a second page as page 2 of your resume in case it gets separated from the first page.

MYTH #46: **Print at least 100 copies of your resume.**

REALITY: Assuming you have word processed your resume and printed it on a laser printer, make as many copies as you need. You may need as few as five copies or as many as 1,000. Commercial copy rates tend to go down in increments of 100, 500, and 1000 copies.

MYTH #47: **Put an e-mail version of your resume in a separate file so you can send it as an attachment.**

REALITY: You'll want to put the e-mail resume in a separate file but do not send it as an attachment unless asked to do so. In fact, most employers do not want to receive a resume as an attachment. If you automatically do so, chances are they will not open the file and read it. Always prepare an e-mail version of your resume so it can be dropped into the body of your e-mail message.

DISTRIBUTION

MYTH #48: **Try to send your resume to as many employers as possible.**

REALITY: You will get better results if you target your resume on a select group of employers that you have researched and know they are looking for someone with your qualifications. If you broadcast your resume to hundreds of employers, chances are you'll get very few responses. You may feel you are making progress because you are sending out many resumes, but you are likely to be disappointed with the results. If you decide to engage in resume broadcasting, expect few results. On the other hand, you may land one or two interviews that lead to a job offer. While we're not discounting this resume distribution method altogether, we do want you to have realistic expectations of what is likely to happen if you engage in an expensive resume broadcast campaign—high costs and low returns.

MYTH #49: **It's a good idea to employ the services of a resume broadcast firm to send your resume to hundreds of employers.**

REALITY: This direct-mail, dumb luck approach is a controversial resume distribution method that can be a waste of time and money. We have no way of judging the effectiveness of the method other than that it seems suspect. Firms that advertise resume broadcasting schemes make what appear to be exaggerated claims of effectiveness. If you decide to go this route, make sure you check out previous clients who have used such services. Use a firm that has developed a very targeted approach—they send resumes to employers and headhunters who either request such resumes or are known to be in a hiring mode.

MYTH #50: **The best way to get your resume in the hands of employers is to respond to classified ads, post your resume on the Internet, and get your resume into electronic resume databases.**

REALITY: The best way to get your resume in the hands of employers is through networking and referral interviewing—the Haldane approach. These job search methods result in targeting particular employers who are most interested in your qualifications. Responding to classified ads, using the Internet, and entering your resume in electronic resume databases are crap shoots. You may be competing with hundreds of others for low- and mid-level positions. When you network and conduct referral interviews, you limit the competition as well as target mid- to high-level positions. In other words, if you want less competition for high quality jobs, you should develop an active networking campaign that puts your resume in the right hands.

MYTH #51: **It's a waste of time sending your resume to headhunters; they are only interested in working with employers.**

REALITY: While headhunters work for employers, they are always looking for qualified individuals they can market to their clients. They must constantly replenish their pool of qualified candidates. In fact, headhunters are some of the most active users of commercial Internet employment sites. They use the Internet to find individuals that meet the qualifying criteria of their clients. If you put your resume in the resume databases of their Internet sites, you may be contacted by a headhunter rather than by an employer. Indeed, one of the best ways of contacting headhunters is to put your electronic resume online. Since headhunters search resume databases by keywords, make sure your resume is rich in keywords. If you have the skills and experience headhunters need, make sure your distribution activities include headhunters. For a listing of major headhunters, review the latest edition of *The Directory of Executive Recruiters* (Kennedy Information).

MYTH #52: **Informational or referral interviews are a waste of time.**

REALITY: Informational or referral interviews are the most important element of an active networking campaign. If conducted according to Haldane principles, referral interviews result in uncovering jobs and connecting with the right people who have the power to hire. The problem with most informational interviews is that they are conducted for the wrong purposes and with the wrong people. When done in conjunction with an active networking campaign, referral interviews yield some of the best job search results. Your resume plays an important role in the referral interview. In addition to setting the agenda for discussion, the person with whom you conduct the referral interview will most likely read and respond to your resume, including giving you useful feedback for revising your resume.

MYTH #53: **Use attention-getting special delivery methods, such as FedEx and Express Mail, when mailing your resume.**

REALITY: This may be one of those unnecessary expenses and over-hyped "dress for success" elements attached to delivery methods. Chances are your correspondence will arrive in the mail room where it will be sorted or separated from its envelope by a low level employee before it's delivered to the intended recipient. A powerful cover letter accompanying your resume will be more effective than the size and color of the envelope or the particular delivery methods. Our companion volume, *Haldane's Best Cover Letters For Professionals*, addresses such distribution issues.

MYTH #54: **Handwrite the address on the mailing label or envelope.**

REALITY: This is the old car salesman and real estate and insurance agent trick taught in thousands of seminars each year to "personalize" a relationship with potential clients. It's overused and potentially can backfire on job seekers—indicates you're trying to manipulate the recipient with a "personal" communication approach. Indeed, letters with handwritten addresses scream "unprofessional." Remember, you're not selling cars, real estate, or insurance, and you're not writing to your best friend. You're entering a professional business relationship in which you should put your best professional foot forward. This is business correspondence in which you demonstrate your best professional effort. Always type addresses as well as your correspondence. Handwritten approaches are best left to other types of businesses that feel a need to interact with the recipient on a very personal basis.

MYTH #55: **Avoid faxing or e-mailing your resume; it's always best to mail your resume.**

REALITY: Since more and more employers request that you fax or e-mail your resume, be prepared to do so. Given the popularity of these distribution methods, many of the traditional "dress for success" elements associated with resumes—paper color and texture, graphics, emphasizing techniques, layout, and type style—become less relevant than the content of your resume language. You should pay particular attention to the choice of **language**, especially the increasing role of "keywords" associated with electronic resumes. Whether action verbs or nouns, all resumes should be rich in keywords and phrases that clearly communicate your qualifications to employers. If you initially fax or e-mail your resume, it's a good idea to put an original copy with a cover letter in the mail as a follow-up.

> *Only fax or e-mail your resume if requested to do so.*

MYTH #56: **Employers prefer faxed and e-mailed resumes to mailed resumes.**

REALITY: You should only fax or e-mail your resume if requested to do so. If you are sending an unsolicited resume, send it by mail. Faxes and e-mail are considered privileged communication channels that should only be used upon invitation. If you send an unsolicited resume by fax or e-mail, you may be viewed as undesirable for having violated an employer's privacy.

MYTH #57: **It's best to affix a postage stamp to your envelope rather than use a meter strip for postage.**

REALITY: It really doesn't make any difference. Like the handwritten address, efforts to personalize the envelope are largely a waste of time. In reality, the audience for your personalized envelope will probably be the mailroom clerk! However, it could be viewed negatively if it appears you are using your employer's postage meter for your personal mail.

MYTH #58: **You should only give your resume to people who are interested in your qualifications.**

REALITY: Don't hide your resume from others who might be able to give you good advice and referrals. Let people in your network know you are looking for a job and give them a copy of your resume. Chances are many of these people might know someone who would be interested in your qualifications. If you don't give them a copy of your resume, they may not know what you're looking for nor can they speak intelligently about your accomplishments. Our notion of broadcasting a resume is to get your resume in as many hands as possible within your network rather than throw it to the wind by sending it to hundreds of strangers who do not know you.

FOLLOW-UP

MYTH #59: **If you e-mail or fax your resume, no follow-up is necessary.**

REALITY: You should follow-up an e-mailed or faxed resume with a mailed copy of your resume that observes the rules of conventional resumes, including being printed on nice quality paper and accompanied by a cover letter indicating that you just faxed or e-mailed a copy of the resume. This follow-up will remind the individual of your qualifications as well as put you in a more professional light. Also, follow-up according to Myth #62.

MYTH #60: **If an employer is interested in your qualifications, you'll be contacted for an interview.**

REALITY: Nothing is automatic in the world of employment. Things happen because people take certain actions that benefit them. When faced with lots of good resumes, employers often have difficulty deciding whom to interview. If your timing is right, your follow-up telephone call may result in moving your resume from a "maybe" pile to a "yes" pile. However, if your resume is already in the "no" pile, chances are your follow-up call will not resuscitate it beyond the "maybe" pile. It's best to move on to other more promising employers.

MYTH #61: **Employers don't like to be pestered with follow-up calls. They are too busy to respond to your special request.**

REALITY: It depends on the employer. Some employers feel strongly about follow-up calls by indicating in their job announcements "no calls please." Others don't mind the follow-up call. After all, two important things happen for the employer when you initiate the follow-up call: you indicate a certain level of interest and enthusiasm for the position, and you volunteer to be screened over the phone. In other words, your follow-up call helps them make an initial screening decision on your candidacy.

MYTH #62: **It's best to follow-up within seven days by mailing, faxing, or e-mailing a second copy of your resume and letter.**

REALITY: This is not a smart follow-up method. Avoid becoming a repetitious pest. Individuals who send multiple copies of their resumes are remembered as being redundant individuals—an action that puts them in the "no" pile faster than if they had not followed-up at all. We prefer making a follow-up telephone call within seven days to inquire about the status of a resume. As a transition, you should indicate in your cover letter that you will give the recipient a call at that time *"to answer any questions you may have about my candidacy."* This statement puts the employer on notice that you will be calling at a specific time. Chances are he or she will look at your resume and letter in greater depth in preparation for your call. Best of all, this follow-up action enables you to invite yourself to a telephone screening interview which is one step from being called for a face-to-face job interview. If you fail to make a follow-up telephone call, you will miss the opportunity for this interview.

MYTH #63: **If I can't get through to the employer by telephone, it's best to write a follow-up letter.**

REALITY: If you persist, you will get through or at least receive a response from someone who will check on the status of your application. In today's complicated communication world, you will probably have to leave a voice message. That's okay; in fact, it may be better than actually getting through to the person because you are about to demonstrate your tenacity to this potential employer. Whatever you do at this stage, you must be pleasantly persistent. Call every day for at least seven days, and each time leave a nice message indicating who you are and the purpose of your call: *"Hi, this is Mary Edner. I'm just following up on the letter and resume I sent to you on May 3rd. My number is 333-2222. I look forward to speaking with you soon."* That's all you need to say, and you need to say it in a very upbeat and enthusiastic manner. Do not indicate any disappointment or anger on your part for not having your earlier phone calls returned. Chances are the person will call you back after the fifth phone call. After five calls most individuals begin feeling guilty for not returning your call. Before returning your call, the individual will most likely examine your resume and letter and make a preliminary decision on your status in anticipation of you raising this question. The person also may have an assistant call you to let you know the status of your application. Your follow-up call may result in a job interview.

MYTH #64: **If you're not selected to interview with the employer, forget them and go on to other employers.**

REALITY: If you've invested your time and effort in getting a resume and letter to the employer but the outcome is a rejection, don't just forget this employer. Send a nice thank-you letter indicating your appreciation for their taking time and effort to consider your candidacy. Express your continuing interest in the company and request that you be considered for another position that might best relate to your qualifications. Surprisingly, many people have gotten jobs based on this type of follow-up thank-you letter to a rejection! Because this type of letter is so rarely received by employers from the losers, it can have a very positive impact: you're remembered and reassessed as a very thoughtful person who might still fit into the organization.

42 RESUME MISTAKES YOU MUST NOT MAKE

Will your resume be "dead upon arrival" or will it see the light of day with a potential employer? If myths were not enough, here are some of the major mistakes job seekers make in writing, producing, distributing, and following-up their resume before seeking the services of Bernard Haldane Associates. Most of these mistakes will kill your chances of getting an interview since your resume effectively is "dead upon arrival":

Resume Writing Mistakes

1. Not written with the reader's interests or needs in mind—experience appears irrelevant to the job in question.

2. Inappropriate length—too long or too short.

3. Poor appearance—heavy text, crowded pages.

4. Typos and spelling and grammatical errors.

5. Mentions low GPA scores.

6. Unclear and unsupported career objective.

7. Includes a first name that conveys a negative impression.

8. Long and wordy phrases, sentences, and paragraphs.

9. Very amateurish with lots of canned resume language.

10. Appears boastful, arrogant, or suspect.

11. Missing important categories, including experience and skills.

12. Difficult to interpret because of poor organization.

13. Unexplained time gaps in work history.

14. Fails to include accomplishments or evidence of future performance.

15. Body of resume does not support objective.

16. No objective or objective is unclear.

17. Seems over-qualified or under-qualified for the position.

18. Includes a photo, and it's not particularly flattering.

19. Includes inappropriate personal information, such as height, weight, age, marital status, and religious affiliation.

20. Includes negative comments about previous employers.

21. Lacks sufficient contact information (telephone or fax number) or appears somewhat anonymous (uses a P.O. Box for an address).

22. Constantly refers to "I" and appears self-centered—fails to clearly communicate what he or she will likely do *for the employer*.

23. Includes "red flag" information such as being fired or incarcerated, confessing health or performance problems, or stating salary figures, including salary requirements that may be too high or too low.

Resume Production Mistakes

24. Poorly typed and reproduced—hard to read.

25. Printed on both sides of paper.

26. Printed on poor quality paper or on extremely thin or thick paper.

27. Includes handwritten changes (crosses out "single" and writes in "married"!).

28. Soiled with coffee stains, hand prints, or ink marks.

Resume Distribution Mistakes

29. Sent to the wrong person or department.

30. Mailed to "To Whom It May Concern" or "Dear Sir."

31. Faxed or e-mailed to "To Whom It May Concern."

32. Enclosed in a tiny envelope that requires the resume to be unfolded and flattened several times.

33. Arrives without a stamp—the employer gets to pay "overdue" postage!

34. Envelope double-sealed with tape and is indestructible—nearly impossible to open by conventional means!

35. Back of envelope includes a handwritten note indicating something is missing on the enclosed resume, such as a telephone number or address.

36. Accompanied by extraneous or inappropriate enclosures which were not requested, such as copies of self-serving letters of recommendation, transcripts, or samples of work.

37. Arrives too late for consideration.

38. Comes without a cover letter.

39. Cover letter merely repeats what's on the resume—does not command attention nor move the reader to action.

Resume Follow-Up Mistakes

40. Follow-up call made *before* the resume and letter arrives.

41. Follow-up call is too aggressive or the candidate appears too "hungry" for the position—communicates that this candidate is very needy or may be more trouble than he or she is worth.

42. Leaves an angry message after a few phone messages are not returned.

If you follow the advice and examples in the remainder of this book, you should avoid many of the myths and errors outlined in this chapter. You'll present a first-class image to employers who will invite you to job interviews because they believe you may be the perfect "fit" for their company.

$$\boxed{5}$$

SELECT THE RIGHT RESUME
FOR YOU

One of the first resume writing decisions you need to make concerns the type of resume you should write and distribute. Only a few years ago this decision was relatively simple: write a chronological, functional, or combination/hybrid resume. These are known as the three major types of conventional or formatted resumes. However, with the advent of optical character recognition (OCR) systems, or optical scanners, and the Internet in the job search, today the choices include several types of conventional and electronic resumes.

TWO AUDIENCES: HUMANS AND COMPUTERS

You now need to consider two types of resume readers: humans and computers. If you only write a conventional resume, your resume may not be computer-friendly and thus you may be passed over for consideration. Such a resume will be unprepared for optical scanners that are widely used by major employers, employment agencies, search firms, headhunters, and employment Web sites for managing (storing, retrieving, screening) resume databases by keywords.

You also must be prepared to e-mail your resume to an employer. Indeed, more and more employers, including those who recruit executive-level talent, require candidates to send them an e-mail version of their resume which may or may not be scanned into a resume database. The very act of properly e-mailing your resume also distinguishes you from other candidates who may appear less than computer and Internet competent—important skills in today's workplace. These new types of resumes differ in both form and content from conventional resumes.

RESUME ALTERNATIVES

We recommend writing two types of resumes—conventional and electronic—because of the different resume audiences you are likely to encounter. You will probably need a conventional or paper resume since ultimately your mailed or faxed resume will be read by a human being. You'll also want to take such a resume with you to a job interview. But you also should write an electronic version of the same resume to ensure that your resume is both machine readable and capable of being properly e-mailed as a plain text document. If you fail to send the appropriate resume to an employer who uses a computerized resume management system or requests an e-mail resume, you will be at a disadvantage in today's job market. It's best to assume that you will need to send an electronic version of your resume since more and more employers, headhunters, and online employment sites require electronic resumes. Indeed, within the next few years, we expect most employers will require electronic resumes. But don't expect conventional resumes to disappear. They will continue to play a significant role in the job search, especially during the interview, but to a much lesser extent than today. They will primarily be used by small businesses and for executive level positions that are not overwhelmed with hundreds of resumes requiring automated resume management systems.

The major differences between conventional and electronic resumes are the use of language, formatting techniques, graphic elements, and paper quality and color. Since conventional resumes are primarily read by people, they are designed to impress human readers. As such, they are usually rich in action verbs and include several "dress for success" elements: varied formatting and layout techniques (two columns, use of white space, attractive type styles), graphic design (emphasizing techniques, such as bold, italics, boxes, and bullets, headers, reverses) and printed on good quality bond paper of varying colors. A well constructed conventional resume should both read and look great to the human eye as well as feel good to the human touch. While the reader of a conventional resume will primarily concentrate on the content of the resume—especially on how you present your experience and accomplishments—the reader can't help but be influenced by the overall professional quality of the presentation as exemplified in the choice of visual elements. Since a scannable electronic resume is designed to be machine readable, it must adhere to the more limiting rules of electronic resumes: the use of nouns (keywords) rather than action verbs; few emphasizing techniques other than all caps and asterisks; and limited margins. The reader of an electronic resume primarily focuses on skills and qualifications.

The differences between an e-mail electronic resume and conventional and scannable electronic resumes are primarily in the format and layout. E-mail resumes must be designed in plain text file format (ASCII) so they can be electronically transmitted. If you take a conventional resume that has been composed and saved in a word processing file and try to e-mail it, the result will most likely be an unreadable resume. Formatting and graphic elements will disappear, letters may change, and margins will shift. Even if readable, your e-mail resume will not be a pretty sight! The choice of language in an e-mail resume will vary depending on whether or not it will be electronically scanned or entered directly into a resume database that uses search and retrieval software. If you know an employer will not be scanning your e-mail resume, go ahead and e-mail a conventional version of your resume.

A third type of electronic resume is the Web resume. Also known as an HTML resume, it can be developed and accessed on the Internet in different forms. The most ambitious resumes are multimedia creations complete with sound, video, and links to work samples. Such resumes also can function as conventional resumes as well as scannable and plain text resumes.

The following chart summarizes the major differences amongst the various types of resumes.

Type of Resume	Readers		Language		Format/Layout	
	Humans	Machines	Verbs	Nouns	Open	Closed
Conventional (paper)						
Chronological	X		X	X	X	
Functional	X		X	X	X	
Combination/Hybrid	X		X	X	X	
Electronic (digital)						
Scannable		X		X		X
E-mail	X	X	X	X		X
Web (HTML)	X	X	X	X	X	X

Conventional resumes allow you to be most creative with language, format, and layout. Electronic scannable and e-mail resumes tend to follow very strict rules relating to language, format, and layout. These are not particularly creative resumes for capturing the attention of human readers. They tend to be especially strong on core competencies. Crafted in the language of keywords, these resumes place primary emphasis on skills and accomplishments. As such, electronic scannable resumes tend to be very employer-oriented and nondiscriminatory.

CONVENTIONAL RESUMES

As we outlined in Chapter 2, employers expect to receive one of three types of conventional resumes: chronological, combinational, or functional. Each type has its particular strengths and weaknesses, depending on how you wish to communicate your qualifications and strengths to employers. While some people may tell you there are no rules to writing a resume, in reality, most conventional resumes should adhere to these 40 general rules:

Conventional Resume Writing "Do's"

1. **Do** start by creating a database centered around key categories based on the worksheets at the end of Chapter 8.

2. **Do** include sufficient contact information (name, address, phone and fax numbers, e-mail address) at the very top of the first page.

3. **Do** include your name and page number at the top left of the second page.

4. **Do** pay particular attention to the quality of your resume language— crisp, expressive, and direct—and its relevance to the employer and the industry.

5. **Do** keep sentences and paragraphs short, succinct, and to the point.

6. **Do** develop an employer-oriented objective and relate all other categories to this objective.

7. **Do** include a powerful "Summary of Qualifications" or "Professional Profile" immediately after the objective.

8. **Do** describe your core competencies (your major skills and accomplishments) in the language of action verbs and key nouns.

9. **Do** put the most important information first.

10. **Do** keep the length of the resume to within two pages—one-page if you have limited work experience.

11. **Do** incorporate design elements and formatting techniques that will make your resume visually appealing—such as ample white space, graphics, and special fonts—as well as easy to read.

12. **Do** use emphasizing techniques, such as bullets, boxes, italics, bold, caps, and underlining, but be careful not to overdo it to distraction.

13. **Do** select a standard proportionate font such as Helvetica or Times.

14. **Do** use a 10 to 12 point font for the text of the resume; headings may look best at 14 point and in bold.

15. **Do** plan to include a powerful cover letter with the resume that emphasizes why the reader should consider your candidacy.

16. **Do** check for correct spelling, grammar, and punctuation.

17. **Do** make sure each section is error free by evaluating your resume step-by-step.

18. **Do** include information that you'll enjoy talking about in the job interview. Avoid anything you must later defend.

19. **Do** embellish but always be honest and truthful.

20. **Do** communicate your energy and enthusiasm—that you really love what you do.

Conventional Resume Writing "Don'ts"

1. **Don't** forget the needs of your audience when writing each section of your resume. Make your resume employer-centered rather than self-centered.

2. **Don't** include extraneous information, such as your age, height, weight, religion, marital status, family members, or a photo.

3. **Don't** write an amateurish or "gimmicky" resume.

4. **Don't** create a cramped, cluttered, or disorganized looking resume.

5. **Don't** select a format that is inappropriate for your level of experience.

6. **Don't** start writing the resume before you have conducted a thorough self assessment of what you do well and enjoy doing.

7. **Don't** cut corners by creatively plagiarizing others' resumes or hiring someone to write your resume from scratch; do the initial work yourself, including a first draft.

8. **Don't** include numerous design elements that may make your resume too busy and thus irritating to the reader.

9. **Don't** use negative language or criticize a former employer.

10. **Don't** refer to yourself as "I".

11. **Don't** provide extensive details on jobs that are more than 10 years old.

12. **Don't** write a different resume for each job or employer.

13. **Don't** accentuate obvious time gaps.

14. **Don't** use a P.O. Box number for your address.

15. **Don't** use a typeface that is hard to read.

16. **Don't** include salary information or requirements.

17. **Don't** include references.

18. **Don't** be dishonest about your education and experience.

19. **Don't** develop an unrealistic objective that appears unrelated to your stated skills, accomplishments, and education.

20. **Don't** turn your resume into an obituary by focusing solely on your past—remember, employers want to hire your future!

The **chronological resume** is the most widely used and least revealing resume when written in the traditional manner. It typically emphasizes employment dates, employers, and duties and responsibilities. For many people, this resume reflects poorly on their strengths. By highlighting employment dates, employers, and duties and responsibilities, these resumes say little or nothing about goals and accomplishments. Employers are left to interpret what exactly the individual may be able to do for them. For individuals with little work experience, or for those who have changed careers, these resumes accentuate the lack of direct work experience. Indeed, employers can immediately tell whether or not you have a pattern of work experience relevant to their needs.

At the same time, the chronological resume can work well if the job seeker (1) has many years of work experience and (2) the work experience is directly related to the position in question. Furthermore, if written in the language of accomplishments, rather than duties and responsibilities, these can be powerful resumes. If you do not have a lengthy record of progressive work experience, or if your work experience is not directly relevant to the position in question (for example, you're changing careers or trying to move into a different career field), this type of resume will work against your best interests. Unfortunately, most job seekers do not know there are other types of resumes that can much better showcase their qualifications to employers. Indeed, by choosing one of these other resume formats, the job seeker can more clearly relate his qualifications to the specific needs of the employer.

> *Chronological resumes that highlight employment dates, employers, and duties and responsibilities say little or nothing about goals and accomplishments.*

The structure of a first-class chronological resume follows a very similar pattern. These resumes usually are divided into five distinct sections. These are almost always mandatory for a chronological resume:

1. **Contact information:** Appears at the very top and includes name, address, telephone and/or fax number, and e-mail address.

2. **Objective:** Usually a 2-3 line employer-oriented statement of what you want to do. It should relate to all other elements in the remainder of the resume.

3. **Summary of Qualifications:** Either a summary statement or a bulleted listing (4-5 items) highlighting your major skills and accomplishments. This is a powerful executive summary of what you are good at doing— your core competencies or central qualifications.

4. **Qualifications or Experience:** This is your summary of work history. It should be described in the functional language of skills and achievements rather than presented as formal duties and responsibilities. Arranged chronologically, with your most recent employment summarized first, each section includes your position, employer, and inclusive employment dates. Since you want to place the greatest emphasis on your skills and accomplishments, the least important element—inclusive employment dates—should be placed at the end of each section rather than at the beginning.

5. **Education and Training:** This section summarizes your formal education and training. University graduates should not include their high school diploma. You also should include any specialized training that supports your objective.

Other elements that may be included on a chronological resume are:

6. **Professional Memberships, Affiliations, or Activities:** List relevant professional memberships, affiliations, or activities that relate to your objective.

7. **Publications and Presentations:** List relevant publications or presentations that relate to your objective.

8. **Special Skills or Licenses:** Include any special skills or licenses that may further strengthen your objective.

9. **Personal Summary Statement:** Be very careful here. Not recommended unless you have a personal statement that really enhances, rather than distracts from, your objective.

Whatever you do, make sure you first assess whether or not your particular career objective and work experience are best presented in a chronological resume or are better summarized in a different resume format. Let's look at two other types of conventional resumes that may better meet your needs.

In many respects the **functional resume** is the logical opposite of the chronological resume. This type of resume primarily emphasizes a career objective and a series of related skills and accomplishments that reinforce the objective. It answers the one question many employers pose: What can you do for me? Organized by functional categories and rich in functional language (action verbs), these resumes present qualifications as sets of relevant skills and accomplishments with little or no reference to specific employers, jobs, or employment dates. Indeed, there is a curious lack of this standard historical information that readers are often left to wonder why this information is lacking. Is it because the person is trying to hide something—a history of job hopping, little full-time paid work experience, employment settings unrelated to the job in question? Or perhaps the individual is presenting lots of canned resume language.

Many employers become instantly suspicious of functional resumes—the writer may be trying to hide something.

Many employers become instantly suspicious of this type of resume because it does not satisfy their need to know about work history, especially specific employers, positions, and employment dates. These resumes are often highly generalized to the point of being meaningless for decision-making purposes. For example, stating that you *"supervised a team in achieving 100% of targeted goals"* could mean that you did anything from working with your child's soccer team to managing a group of 50 professionals who generated more than $25 million in revenue, which represented a 25 percent increase in a 12 month period. The absence of work experience on functional resumes is what often turns them into "red flag" resumes for employers—despite impressive resume language, there's something wrong with this individual. Should I waste my time trying to find out what's wrong or should I request more information on relevant work experience? On the other hand, these are great resumes for someone first entering the job market or making a major career change. Indeed, they hide the fact that you have little work experience directly relevant to the position in question.

The structure of a functional resume is similar to a chronological resume with one major exception: the "Qualifications and Experience" section does not include employers, positions, or inclusive employment dates. This section includes functional descriptions of skills and accomplishments related to the objective. It's rich in using action verbs to describe skills and accomplishments, such as:

organized	initiated	implemented	designed
supervised	advised	directed	managed

The **combination or hybrid resume** is the perfect choice for many job seekers, especially for those who have a solid record of accomplishment related to the skills required but whose work experience may not be a perfect fit. This is the resume of choice for career changers with extensive work experi-

> *The hybrid resume best showcases our clients' objectives, skills, and accomplishments.*

ence. It is the resume of choice for Haldane clients who have a strong record of accomplishments. We work with thousands of clients who have found this type of resume best showcases their objectives, skills, and accomplishments. The structure of this resume is similar to a chronological resume. However, the "Qualifications and Experience Section" is written similar to a functional resume. In addition, this type of resume includes a "Work Experience" section, located immediately after the "Qualifications and Experience" section, that briefly summarizes positions, employers, and inclusive employment dates.

ELECTRONIC RESUMES

You will most likely encounter two types of electronic resumes: scannable and e-mail. **Scannable resumes** are read by computers. Faced with managing numerous resumes, more and more employers now use Optical Character Recognition (OCR) software to store and retrieve resumes in automated resume databases. They take original copies of resumes and scan them into databases for future reference. These resumes are structured similarly to conventional resumes but with one major exception: instead of an objective, they include a "keyword summary" at the very beginning of the resume. This keyword summary is filled with nouns and short phrases that describe the individual's major skills and accomplishments. After the resume is scanned into the database, it is retrieved by keywords. You are qualified for a position if your resume matches many of the keywords required by the employer. Consequently, you should attempt to include as many keywords as possible in your keyword summary as well as in other sections of the resume. For example, if an employer is looking for someone with these keywords,

corporate planning, mergers and acquisitions, negotiations, Harvard MBA and most of these keywords appear on your resume, your resume will be selected from the database for further scrutiny and hopefully an invitation for a job interview. In addition to including numerous keywords, an electronic scannable resume should follow these basic rules:

Scannable Resume Writing "Do's"

- **Do** a 1-2 page scannable resume.
- **Do** use standard-sized 8½" x 11" paper.
- **Do** print on white paper and with black ink.
- **Do** left justify.
- **Do** place your name at the top of the page on its own line.
- **Do** use a standard address format below your name.
- **Do** keep the design simple.
- **Do** submit a laser-printed original.
- **Do** produce on 20 lb. paper (avoid heavier paper).
- **Do** use a standard type style (Helvetica, Futura, Optima, Universe, Times, Palatino, Courier) in 10 to 12 point size for the body of the resume; headers can be in 14 point and your name in 16 point.
- **Do** emphasize skills and accomplishments as keywords.
- **Do** use the jargon and acronyms specific to your occupational field.
- **Do** check for spelling, grammar, and punctuation errors.
- **Do**, if space permits, describe your interpersonal traits and positive MBTI (Myers-Briggs Type Indicator) buzz words.

Scannable Resume Writing "Don'ts"

- **Don't** use standard emphasizing techniques such as underlining and italics.
- **Don't** let letters touch; select a font with sufficient space between letters.
- **Don't** fold resume.
- **Don't** staple resume.
- **Don't** use columns.
- **Don't** include graphic elements such as boxes, shading, or reverses.
- **Don't** incorporate vertical or horizontal lines.
- **Don't** abbreviate except for common ones such as BA, MA, or PhD.

Bernard Haldane clients often use the following section headings and sequencing. This format provides the initial step when preparing a scannable resume that can then be used to enter an electronic applicant tracking system:

OBJECTIVE

QUALIFICATIONS

EDUCATION

ACHIEVEMENTS

EXPERIENCE

ACTIVITIES

AFFILIATIONS

SKILLS

Any or all of these section headings may be selected for preparing a scannable resume. Other titles may be used for each of the sections. The second section, QUALIFICATIONS, may be stated as follows:

QUALIFICATIONS AND CAPABILITIES

QUALIFICATIONS AND BACKGROUND

BACKGROUND SUMMARY

SUMMARY OF QUALIFICATIONS

The fourth section, ACHIEVEMENTS, may be variously stated as follows:

EXAMPLES OF EFFECTIVENESS

EXAMPLES OF EXPERTISE

COLLEGIATE ACHIEVEMENTS

SELECTED ACCOMPLISHMENTS

The fifth section, ACTIVITIES, and sixth section, AFFILIATIONS, might become:

ACTIVITIES AND HONORS

COLLEGE ACTIVITIES

ACTIVITIES AND AFFILIATIONS

AFFILIATIONS AND CERTIFICATIONS

The final section, SKILLS, should be reserved for those skills dealing with computers and languages:

LANGUAGE SKILLS

COMPUTER SKILLS

FOREIGN LANGUAGES

Most of the resume examples that appear in Chapters 10 and 11 are scannable.

An **e-mail resume**, also known as an Internet resume or plain text resume, is the ugly duckling resume. While initially opened as a word processing document and then saved as an ASCII or text only file, these resumes will not follow normal formatting rules associated with a standard word processing program. There's nothing fancy or pretty about a resume that gets transmitted via e-mail. This is strictly a functional resume—provides information on your qualifications to employers. An e-mail resume can be a conventional or scannable resume that has been converted to an e-mail format. The categories for your e-mail resume can remain the same as your scannable resume. Since many e-mail resumes get entered into resume databases, you are well advised to convert your scannable resume into an e-mail resume. The basic problem in doing so relates to format: word processing and e-mail formats are incompatible and thus require adherence to e-mail formatting rules. Your e-mail resume should follow these rules:

E-mail Resume Writing "Do's"

- **Do** initially compose your resume in a word processing document but be sure to set your margins so each line does not exceed 65 characters.
- **Do** use a fixed-width, rather than proportional, typeface such as Courier.
- **Do** use a hard return (hit Enter key) at the end of each line.
- **Do** save your word processed resume as a text only document. This procedure converts it to a plain text resume (ASCII document).
- **Do** use the subject line to identify and advertise yourself.
- **Do** include a keyword summary.
- **Do** limit yourself to four emphasizing techniques—all caps, asterisks (*), plus signs (+), and dashes (-). Use all caps for your name and headings.
- **Do** spell check.
- **Do** reopen your text resume and check for formatting problems. Use your space bar and Enter key to fix any formatting problems.
- **Do** evaluate your e-mail composition by sending it to yourself or a friend to check for formatting problems.

E-mail Resume Writing "Don'ts"

- **Don't** try to format the resume with margins and columns which create havoc for e-mail resumes. Set your left and right margins at 0 and 65 respectively.
- **Don't** use proportional typefaces such as Helvetica or Times.
- **Don't** incorporate standard emphasizing techniques. All caps work best.
- **Don't** use word wrap or automatic hyphen. Use a hard return at the end of each line.

- **Don't** use tabs. Indent, center, or create white space by using the space bar and Enter key.

- **Don't** send attachments. Your letter and resume should go together as a complete e-mail document.

Examples of e-mail resumes in ASCII format appear on pages 67 and 68. While not particularly appealing to the eye, they do transmit well by e-mail.

Given the numerous resume distribution and recruitment channels available in today's job market, how well you write and distribute your resume will be key to opening the doors of employers. If you write both a conventional and an electronic resume that follow the principles of Bernard Haldane Associates, you should be well on your way to landing job interviews with employers who see you as someone who can add value to their operations. Just make sure you are prepared to communicate your qualifications to both human and computer readers in today's new job market!

E-mail Resumes In ASCII

```
Terry A. Example
123 Cherry Lane
Lancaster PA 11223

OBJECTIVE:
A Web Designer and HTML Programmer position.

EMPLOYMENT HISTORY:
11/95 to present.
Ross Public Relations. Philadelphia PA.
HTML Programmer. HTML code for all Web Pages designed by Ross
Public Relations. Developed client Web Sites including flow
charts, Perl Scripts, and web-to-database applications.

5/95 to 11/95.
Ross Public Relations.
Graphic Designer: Created four color brochures; magazine ads; and
multimedia presentations. Product manager for client creative
projects. Database system developer for client archived files.
Network integration assistant within the art department.

9/94 to 5/95.
Ursinus College. Collegeville PA.
Assistant Graphic Designer: Helped develop advertising materials
including a Macromedia Director presentation. Designed flyers for
promotional events. Assisted in producing mechanicals.

5/93 to 9/94.
The Logeen Corporation. York PA.
Computer Operator: Entered client data into billing database.
Managed client files. Generated database reports in response to
account inquiries.

EDUCATION:
BA Communications. Ursinus College Collegeville PA 1995.
GPA: 3.45

SPECIAL SKILLS:
Computer:  C and C++
Language:  Fluent in French and English
```

JASON LARAMY 9079 Door Street, Annapolis, MD 22030 (410) 555-1212

OBJECTIVE: GENERAL MANAGER position encompassing golf/ proshop/facilities operations; full service food, beverage, and banquet services; personnel training and staff development programs; and capital improvement/expense forecasting and strategic planning for a prestigious member-owned country club.

BACKGROUND SUMMARY: Over 10 years experience developing expertise in: Training; Strategic Forecasting; Events Planning; Recruiting; Financial Management; Customer Service; Team Building; Membership Marketing; For Profit Operations; and Fine Dining/Banquet/Party Supervision.

ACHIEVEMENTS: Increased membership by instituting an Ambassador program; introduced fine dining, food and beverage quality standards; and established staff structuring.

Introduced a distinguished lecture program featuring President Gerald R. Ford, Henry Kissinger, David Stockman, Jean Kirkpatrick among others at the Loyola City Club to the delight of the Loyola Chamber of Commerce.

Effected cash flow turnaround, from a $30,000 loss to a profit of $110,000 after first 12 months, and improved revenues by over 9% each year thereafter for Club Association of America at the Chambersville City Club.

One of four individuals representing 60 clubs in the region to be nominated for Club Corporation of America's Manager of the Year, 1991.

Created a warm and inviting atmosphere among employees, members, and the Board/Trustees at every club by using a "hands-on" management style.

EXPERIENCE:
Maxidrive Golf Management, Centerville, VA
General Manager, Running Brook Country Club, Manassas, VA, 1995-1996.
Directed the activities of this former privately owned, thirty year old, 350 member club on behalf of a management consulting organization. Prepared the 1996-2000 strategic plan and capital expense forecast. Supervised golf/proshop, course facilities, dining/banquet/party ops.

Club Association of America (CAA), Scaggsville, MD.
Club Manager, Laurel City Club, Laurel, MD, 1993-1995.
Managed a prestigious 2,000 member downtown city club to ensure efficient and profitable operation. Actively participated in expanding the membership, improving cash flow, and establishing member equity. Did the financial and strategic planning.

Club Manager, Chambersville City Club, Chambersville, MD, 1987-1993.
Developed the club into a catalyst for business growth in downtown Nashville. As the sole employee of CCA, established standards for service to members while increasing revenues and profits. Established a Distinguished Lecture Series with banquet format.

Associate Club Manager, River Club, Durham, NC, 1985-1987.
Completed the associates training program earning CCA Rookie of the Year award.

EDUCATION:
BA, Communications, The University of Baltimore, Baltimore, MD, 1985.
Certified Club Management & Operations Trainer, CAA, Scaggsville, MD, 1994.

IDENTIFY THE UNIQUE YOU:
Assessing Your Skills and Abilities

The key to writing a winning resume is knowing your strengths—exactly what you do well and enjoy doing. Without this basic information about yourself, you may wander aimlessly in the job market, unable to clearly communicate to employers exactly what you can do and will do for them. You will eventually find a job, but it may not be a good "fit." This information is what makes up the "unique you." It tells employers what is so special about you in comparison to others. You identify this critical information on yourself by conducting a thorough assessment of your skills and abilities before writing your career objective on communicating your accomplishments to employers.

At Bernard Haldane Associates our clients do first things first—conduct a thorough assessment to identify their major strengths, formulate a clear career objective, and generate an appropriate language for communicating their qualifications to employers *before* writing resumes and letters, networking, and interviewing. While we use a variety of assessment techniques, including the popular Myers-Briggs Type Indicator for identifying preferred work activity and work environment, our trademark technique is **Success Factor Analysis**. Developed and refined by Bernard Haldane Associates over the past 50 years, this powerful assessment technique yields essential data for identifying strengths and developing a career objective.

While you can conduct Success Factor Analysis on your own if you have strong analytical skills, it is best conducted with the assistance of an experienced Career Advisor. In this chapter we outline the basic elements involved in Success Factor Analysis.

ASSESSMENT ALTERNATIVES

We strongly urge you to begin your job search and resume writing activities with a thorough assessment of your skills and abilities. This assessment will help give direction to your job search and help you better communicate your qualifications to employers. It will provide essential information for writing each section of your resume and for handling yourself well in job interviews. But how do you do this?

Career assessment is a big business that often raises more questions than it answers. Often viewed as "magic pills" for unlocking pathways to success, most assessment devices tend to be more art than science. They involve everything from professionally administered psychological tests to self-administered paper and pencil exercises. Three of the most widely used assessment devices are the professionally administered *Myers-Briggs Type Indicator, Strong Interest Inventory,* and the *Self-Directed Search (SDS).* Classifying individuals into basic typologies, most of these assessment devices are designed to uncover personality styles, career interests, and preferred work activities and environments. They tell you little about what you really do well and enjoy doing—the realities of work. Many of these assessment devices work especially well for individuals with little or no work experience (high school and college students) who wish to explore career alternatives that relate to their interests. As career directional devices, they give users some indication of what they might like to do in the world of work. They may or may not be useful for you, depending on your level of work experience. Indeed, many people who take these tests often experience the "ahah" effect—the tests confirm what they already know ("ahah") but give them little direction on what they should do next! In other words, these exercises are diagnostic rather than prescriptive.

Assuming you already have work experience, it will probably be more useful for you to conduct Success Factor Analysis. Indeed, this widely used career assessment technique is often more accurate in prescribing and predicting career success than more professionally administered assessment devices. The reason is simple: Success Factor Analysis is based upon a thorough analysis of what you do well and enjoy doing—your motivated skills and abilities—rather than upon what you feel you are interested in doing. In other words, it's based upon an analysis of work realities instead of work fantasies. Better still, individuals who have conducted Success Factor Analysis and developed a job search based upon this type of self assessment have gone on to successful jobs and careers. Bernard Haldane Associates, along with numerous career counselors who incorporate this technique in their practice, have thousands of cases of success.

Client Feedback

"I can honestly say that no organizational entity to date has provided me with so much useful, practical information as Bernard Haldane Associates. Haldane has helped me to understand the value of perceiving achievement versus perceiving simply 'what has not been done,' something I will value for my entire lifetime. . . Words cannot express my thanks for introducing me to the Haldane principles."

—M.R.

ACHIEVEMENTS

Underlying Success Factor Analysis is the notion that your best self—the person employers want to hire—can be identified from an analysis of your past strengths or achievements. While it is important to know your weaknesses and failures so you don't repeat them, it's more important to know what it is you really do well and enjoy doing so you can best communicate your strengths to employers. By focusing on your strengths, you identify what's right about you. You overcome any negative thinking about yourself as you articulate positive things about yourself. By analyzing your achievements and focusing on your positives, you should be able to identify your motivated skills and abilities that are largely responsible for your continuing successes. Success Factor Analysis will enable you to flush out your motivated skills and abilities in order to develop a powerful job and career objective.

DISCOVERING YOUR MOTIVATIONAL PATTERN

Success Factor Analysis is also based upon the observation that most people have a *recurring motivational pattern* which they take with them from one setting to another, regardless of whether or not they are in a work setting. In other words, most people repeat their behavior in familiar patterns that can be readily observed and analyzed. While you can easily identify your career interests, skills, and abilities as well as your work habits, understanding your *pattern of motivated skills and abilities* is most important for determining your future career success.

> ## Client Feedback
>
> *"I was skeptical as I began this program. Why did I have to list 10-15 achievements and what happened and how old I was at the time? I now know that every achievement from my childhood was one step closer to my goal in seeking a professional career."*
> —S.J.

By analyzing and synthesizing your *achievements*, you will get a better understanding of what constitutes your particular motivated skills and abilities. You'll be able to communicate this pattern to employers who are most interested in hiring your strengths and your future which, in effect, constitutes your pattern of motivated skills and abilities. It's this *pattern* that largely determines whether or not a particular job is a good "fit" for both you and the employer. And it's your pattern that influences to what degree you are happy doing what you do.

Once you understand your unique pattern, which is the basis for the "unique you," you should be able to make smart career decisions. You'll know which jobs to avoid and which jobs to seek out as most compatible with your motivated skills and abilities. You'll begin thinking positive about yourself as you focus on your strengths rather than accentuate your weaknesses in the workplace. Best of all, you should be able to write an outstanding resume that showcases the "unique you" as someone who has a strong pattern of motivated skills and abilities that should add value to the employer's operations. When you're invited to that job interview, you will be well prepared to communicate your strongest qualifications to the employer who is looking for someone with the right motivated skills and abilities to do the work. You should be an excellent "fit" for the job which should develop into a long-term career centered around motivated skills and abilities.

SUCCESS FACTOR ANALYSIS

Success Factor Analysis focuses on identifying, analyzing, and synthesizing or reformulating one's major achievements in the form of a job and career objective. An **achievement** is anything you did well, enjoyed doing, and felt a sense of satisfaction in doing. A **success factor** is any ability or skill that contributes to an achievement.

Success Factor Analysis involves a 10-step process culminating in the development of a job and career objective:

1. **Identify 10-15 of your major achievements.** Your achievements need not be solely work related nor adult experiences. Start with your childhood and think about achievements as occurring in all types of settings—school, leisure, religious, social, volunteer, military. Begin with 10-15 blank sheets of paper. At the top of each page, write one of your achievements. Remember, achievements occur throughout your life and in numerous work and non-work settings. They are very revealing of your motivations, especially voluntary behavior that takes place in non-work settings. *An achievement is anything you did well, enjoyed doing, and felt a sense of pride, satisfaction, or accomplishment in doing.* Start with examples of non-work experiences such as these:

   "Within the first six months of joining the Girl Scouts, I won the award for selling the most Girl Scout cookies in my group."

   "Even though I was short, I became the leading scorer on my high school basketball team."

   "At age 15, I organized a successful landscape business with three friends. The business helped finance my first two years of college."

   "I took over an unpopular college newspaper and within two years turned it into a well respected and nationally award-winning newspaper."

   "Finished my Bachelor's degree within 3 years while working part-time during my final two years."

   "Earned an 'A' in a speech class from one of the toughest professors on campus who also became my mentor."

   "Proposed a jogging path through our development which became a reality within a year and has now become a major center of activity for our community."

   "Designed and built a 30' sailboat which ran first in the annual Cape Albert races."

While not necessarily indicative of voluntary behavior, relevant work related achievements might include the following:

> *"Organized a new team of software developers who completed the company's new e-commerce project six weeks early and 20% below budget."*

> *"Developed an innovative marketing partnership with our leading competitor that resulted in expanding our customer base by 25% and increasing revenues by 35%."*

> *"Received the 'Employee of the Year' award for exceeding sales projections by 15%."*

> *"Implemented an innovative cost-containment program that cut medical costs by 25%."*

> *"Led successful downsizing of regional offices that resulted in a 20% reduction in workforce and a 30% increase in revenue."*

> *"Established the county's first substance abuse treatment center which became a successful model for more than 100 other counties nationwide."*

> *"Reorganized the corporate collections system which resulted in a 100% improvement in the collections process."*

2. **Prioritize your 10 most significant achievements,** the ones you believe were the most exciting and satisfying ones for you.

   1. _____

   2. _____

   3. _____

   4. _____

   5. _____

   6. _____

   7. _____

   8. _____

   9. _____

   10. _____

3. **Detail each of your top 10 achievements.** Go back to each piece of paper and begin writing about the details of each achievement. Write as much as possible on each achievement. Go for volume since you need to flush out as much information as possible for later analyzing and synthesizing each achievement. Each detailed description might run from 1 to 5 pages. Be sure to include answers to the following questions in your descriptions:

- How did you initially become involved?

- What exactly did you do?

- How did you do it?

- What was especially satisfying about it?

- What were the major outcomes or results for you and others?

For your convenience, make copies of the form on page 76 and complete a copy for each of your 10 achievements.

4. **Expand on each achievement with the help of others.** This is an optional step. You may want to enlist the assistance of a friend or your spouse at this stage. Give one or two people a copy of the form on page 77. Ask them to interview you about your achievements. They should ask you questions that might further reveal your major skills, abilities, and personal qualities. Ask them to question you about:

- The details of each achievement.

- Your part in the achievement.

- What exactly you did.

- How your actions affected others.

This exercise should help reinforce as well as validate the information you generated on yourself. The interviewers should compile a list of terms that represent your Success Factors for inclusion in the next step which involves analysis.

5. **Analyze your achievements by identifying as many Success Factors as possible for each achievement.** Examine what you have written for each achievement. Identify nouns, verbs, or phrases that best describe what actions you took that contributed to the achievement. For example, you might say:

Description of Achievement	Relevant Success Factor
I organized a . . .	Organization
Planned the . . .	Planning
Put together a . . .	Coordination
Spoke with the newspaper . . .	Public relations
Presented a proposal . . .	Communication

DETAILS OF MY ACHIEVEMENTS

ACHIEVEMENT # _____ : _____

_____

_____

1. How did I initially become involved? _____

   _____

   _____

   _____

   _____

2. What did I do? _____

   _____

   _____

   _____

   _____

3. How did I do it? _____

   _____

   _____

   _____

   _____

4. What was especially satisfying about doing it? _____

   _____

   _____

   _____

   _____

5. What were the major results or outcomes? _____

   _____

   _____

   _____

RECURRING SKILLS AND ABILITIES INTERVIEW

Interviewee _____ Interviewer _____

INSTRUCTIONS: For each achievement, identify the **skills and abilities** demonstrated by the achiever. To get more details on each experience, ask **what** was involved with the achievement and **how** the individual made the achievement happen. Avoid "why" questions which tend to mislead. Ask for examples or illustrations.

Achievement # _____

Achievement # _____

Achievement # _____

Recurring Skills and Abilities:

Developed a software program . . .	C++
Designed a Web page that . . .	JavaScript
Figured out how to . .	Problem solving
Met with a group to . . .	Persuasion
Went ahead and started . . .	Initiative and decision making

Many Success Factors identified from an analysis of your non-work achievements will probably relate to standard work skills; many relate to organization and management skills as well as project-related skills:

managing	analyzing	meeting deadlines
organizing	team building	negotiating
supervising	problem solving	creating
planning	trouble shooting	designing
communicating	persuading	developing strategies
decision making	selling	coordinating

Other Success Factors may be more qualitative in nature—sets of personal characteristics readily sought by employers but which are difficult to quantify in the language of results or outcomes:

perceptive	honesty	dedication
accurate	integrity	ingenuity
sensitive	perseverance	energetic
discrete	drive	reliable
adept	initiative	savvy
diplomatic	commitment	versatile

6. **Consolidate all of your Success Factors into one master list.** Pull together all Success Factors identified from an analysis of your achievements and list them on a separate piece of paper.

7. **Organize your Success Factors into Success Factor Groups consisting of related skills and abilities.** Here you begin to move from analysis to synthesis. If you are good at both analysis and synthesis, this grouping process should be relatively easy. If not, find someone who has strong analytical and synthesis skills to help you work through this critical step in the assessment process. On a separate piece of paper, begin the process of grouping related Success Factors into Success Factor Groups. If, for example, you have a random list of 25 Success Factors, you may be able to create seven Success Factor Groups consisting of three Success Factors each:

Group 1:   Organizing
            Managing
            Supervising

Group 2:   Selling
             Persuading
             Public Speaking

Group 3:   Creating
             Designing
             Initiating

Group 4:   Teaching
             Team building
             Communicating

Group 5:   Planning
             Analyzing
             Coordinating

Group 6:   Problem solving
             Trouble shooting
             Negotiating

Group 7:   Perseverance
             Drive
             Initiative

> ### Client Feedback
>
> *"I vividly recall our first meetings in March 1998. I came to you bitter and demoralized after several frustrating months of a fruitless job search. The feedback you provided was right on target; learning to know myself and my marketable skills helped me to regain my self-confidence and ability to once again successfully rejoin the work force."*
>
> —P.S.

8. **Identify your Key Success Factors.** While this exercise so far has helped you generate a rich skills vocabulary based on an analysis of your achievements, you need to go one step further in synthesizing the similar skills you've thus far organized into groups. For example, if you combine Group 3 (creating, designing, initiating) with Group 6 (problem solving, trouble shooting, negotiating), your Key Success Factor might be "Design Consultant." Group 2 (selling, persuading, public speaking) combined with Group 7 (perseverance, drive, initiative) might become "Public Relations."

9. **Prioritize your Key Success Factors.** Specify which Key Success Factors you would like to include in your career and rank them accordingly. If, as outlined in the example above, you feel a career in "Public Relations" would be better for you than one in "Design Consulting," then develop an objective centered on Public Relations as well as incorporate examples of achievements relating to demonstrated public relations skills throughout your resume.

10. **Reality-test the conclusions of your Success Factor Analysis.** Check to see if indeed your analyses and conclusions accurately reflect the "unique you." You can do this three different ways. First, place each of your Key Success Factors on a separate piece of paper. Give specific examples of

achievements that support each of your Key Success Factors. If, for example, Public Relations is a Key Success Factor, give concrete examples of what you did relating to public relations. Focus on what a future employer should know about your public relations skills and experience. Second, ask a friend or your spouse to evaluate your strengths in relation to your Key Success Factors. Give them a copy of the "Strength Evaluation" form on page 81 and ask them to be as honest as possible in evaluating your strengths. Third, you may want to take a standard psychological or aptitude test to see how the information gained from these tests relates to your Success Factor Analysis. If the information is contradictory, you are well advised to do a more in-depth analysis of your skills and abilities. Chances are these tests will confirm and reinforce what you learned from our Success Factor Analysis.

Now you should be ready for the first step in writing your resume—developing a powerful objective that should appear immediately following the contact information on your resume. In the next chapter, we pull together the information in this chapter to create this powerful objective for writing your resume and directing your job search.

STRENGTH EVALUATION

TO: _____

FROM: _____

I am going through a career assessment process and thought you would be an appropriate person to ask for assistance. Would you please candidly respond to the questions below? Your comments will be given to me by the individual designated below; s/he will not reveal your name. Your comments will be used for advising purposes only. Thank you.

What are my strengths?

What weak areas might I need to improve?

In your opinion, what do I need in a job or career to make me satisfied?

Please return to: _____

FORMULATE YOUR JOB OBJECTIVE

R esume writers have long debated whether or not it's necessary to include an objective on a resume. Those who oppose it do so for several reasons: an objective limits your flexibility to seek out different positions; it takes up important space; it's self-serving; it's often trite; or it's usually unrealistic, distracting, or meaningless to the reader.

Those who propose including an objective on a resume do so because they feel an objective communicates to employers what you want to do. It brings organization and coherence to a resume and emphasizes the "fit" between the candidate and the position. As such, an objective says you are a focused individual.

THE CASE FOR OBJECTIVES

Haldane job search methods stress the importance of objectives. But for us an objective must have substance and provide direction. Indeed, we can't imagine someone conducting a job search—or even running a business which is exactly what you are, a product that must be marketed—without a clear idea of what they want to do. Furthermore, we strongly recommend including an objective on both conventional and electronic resumes. In fact, the whole purpose of our Success Factor Analysis in Chapter 6 is to provide a firm foundation for developing a powerful objective that will guide your job search laser-like into a job that's fit for you. Without a clear and purposeful objective, your job search may be difficult to organize and keep on target. You will most likely go off into many different directions. In the end, you'll find a job but chances are it will not be a job "fit" for you.

> *Your objective may be the most difficult 25 to 50 words you will ever craft for your job search.*

Objectives developed by Bernard Haldane's clients are not your run-of-the-mill objectives. If properly formulated, they may be the most difficult 25 to 50 words you will ever craft for your job search. It may take hours, if not days, to come up with the perfect objective statement that truly reflects what you want to do. Indeed, much of the criticism aimed at objectives in general actually focuses on poorly developed and stated objectives—not Haldane objectives. Our objectives have real meaning that go far beyond a simple wishful self-centered statement of what you think you would like to do to enhance your income or advance your career. As outlined in Chapter 6, our objectives are based on a thorough assessment of your skills and abilities as identified from an analysis of your many work and non-work accomplishments. Our clients develop a realistic objective that reflects their pattern of motivated skills and abilities. Best of all, these thoughtfully crafted objectives appeal to employers because they speak their language of future performance.

TYPES OF OBJECTIVES

So what exactly does a Haldane objective look like? How does it differ from other types of objectives? And how can you develop your own such objective?

The most common objective appearing on resumes is what the critics rightfully observe as a relatively meaningless and trite objective. It's usually a single self-serving sentence that identifies a particular position the individual aspires toward:

OBJECTIVE: A management consulting position.

CEO of a major manufacturing firm.

A computer programming position that leads to career advancement.

Not that there is anything inherently wrong with such weak objectives. It's just that they say little or nothing that would enhance a resume; they tend to be self-serving—communicate what the individual wants (a position and career advancement) rather than what the individual is prepared to give the employer (performance). One would assume you are sending a resume in reference to the position identified in such an objective. Our advice: if you can't say anything more meaningful than restating the position for which you are applying and setting a self-serving tone for your resume, skip the objective altogether. It may handicap you more than you realize. Employers may view you as a self-centered individual who really doesn't know what he or she wants to do. The critics are right: this

Client Feedback
"The goal setting experience is one that I consider crucial. It creates a criteria upon which to judge a career opportunity, to create a match. Goal setting reminds me as I make a career decision, that I am not just 'getting a job'—I'm 'getting a life.' Yes, it's that important! Haldane taught me that!"
—G.O.

type of objective takes up valuable resume space that can be more productively used for presenting your skills and abilities.

A meaningful objective—one that primarily focuses attention on skills and accomplishments relevant to future performance—can have a significant impact on your job search. Oriented toward the needs of employers, such an objective tells employers exactly what you want to do. Take, for example, these objectives which were developed by three of Haldane's successful clients:

Objective #1

To provide a consultative service that facilitates managing on-going business analysis, oversee project teams, and develop improvement plans, utilizing proven ability to:

- Resolve problems efficiently and design/manage change
- Communicate effectively at all levels and assemble Natural Work Groups
- Plan and manage business projects, handling negotiations and implementation

Objective #2

To provide a consulting service that enables attorneys and business owners to focus on real issues and problems while developing approaches that achieve necessary objectives, utilizing a proven ability to:

- Communicate effectively at all organizational levels
- Develop strategies based on critical analysis
- Plan and manage business projects

Objective #3

Customer Service Management position using proven skills of organizing, planning, record keeping and succeeding in a fast paced, growth oriented company where customer satisfaction is a top priority.

As you can quickly see, these are not the typical trite or self-centered objectives that appear on most resumes. These are thoughtful, employer-oriented objectives that address the whole issue of job and career "fit"—how the candidate's skills relate to the employer's needs. Individuals behind these resume objectives present themselves as skilled and experienced professionals who solve problems and add value to the employer's operations. Haldane clients who included these objectives on their resumes did so after they completed their Success Factor Analysis. They knew exactly what they did well and enjoyed doing. Furthermore, they had a clear idea of the type of job they wanted and the kind of employer and company they wished to work for. Focusing on their skills in relation to the needs of the employer, they developed employer-centered objectives that stressed their *core competencies*. Most

---

Client Feedback

"If I had never found a new position, this career counseling program would still be one of the best things I have ever done. It has put me in touch with myself, my wife, and my family. I know who I am, what I want, and where I want to go from here."

—R.R.

important of all, as we will see when we examine the resume examples in Chapters 10 and 11, the remaining sections of these individuals' resumes provide *supports* for their objective.

STATING OBJECTIVES AS SKILLS AND OUTCOMES

Objectives can be presented in many different ways. However, the most effective objectives stress both **skills and outcomes** relevant to the employer. Take, for example, the third objective above. It follows a basic pattern. This objective:

- stresses the individual's experience, skills, and core competencies

- identifies possible outcomes for the employer

> ### Client Feedback
>
> *"I think the most important thing I learned from our sessions is that I enjoy being a civil servant, whether it's military or civilian. Although I thought I did, I now realize I have no desire to work in the private sector. So for focusing me, I thank you."*
>
> —R.B.

Unlike the typical self-centered objective that appears on most resumes, our objectives are employer-centered. They speak the language of both the candidate and the employer. As such, they present a potential perfect fit for both parties involved.

In developing your own employer-centered objective, begin by stating your skills and outcomes in this basic format:

I would like a job where I can use my ability to (skills and core competencies) that will result in (outcomes) for the employer.

In our previous example for a Customer Service Management position, this initial statement might read as follows:

I would like a job where my ability to organize, plan, and keep records will result in greater customer satisfaction for the employer.

The final statement that appears as the resume "Objective" could read as follows:

Customer Service Management position using proven skills of organizing, planning, record keeping and succeeding in a fast paced, growth oriented company where customer satisfaction is a top priority.

If you completed your own Success Factor Analysis in Chapter 6, you should be well prepared to state your own Objective using this basic skills and outcome format. Review the data on yourself and begin drafting and redrafting your Objective until it clearly represents exactly what you want to do. Once you develop your Objective using this format, you should be well prepared to write each remaining section of your resume. The resumes in Chapters 10 and 11 provide excellent examples of how to write each of these additional sections.

8

COMPLETE EACH
RESUME SECTION

Most combination or hybrid resumes follow a similar structure involving six basic categories: Contact Information, Objective, Qualifications, Achievements, Experience, and Education. As outlined in the example on page 87, most of these sections flow logically from your Objective. Let's examine each section in preparation for writing your own resume and for better understanding our examples in Chapters 10 and 11. In so doing, you'll create a targeted database for drafting each section of your resume.

DEVELOP A FIRST DRAFT

You should approach the resume writing task as consisting of two drafts and a final refined version. In the first draft, go for volume. Create your database from which you will make your strongest "case." Don't worry about the final format; it will come together after you've made refinements. Concentrate on making factual statements (just the facts) that describe what you have done rather than statements of what you believe you may be able to do (your opinions). Keep in mind that you may need to explain the facts with examples of what you have done. Focus on including information that helps the reader best understand your Objective and your Qualifications for carrying out that Objective.

CONTACT INFORMATION

The very first item appearing on your resume should be your Contact Information. This consists of your name, address, and contact numbers. Follow these general rules in completing this section:

- **Name:** Your name should be in large type (14 to 16 point) and bold. Use your full professional name. Avoid using only your initials for your first and

RESUME EXAMPLE

John Doe
777 Elm Street
Anywhere, U.S.A. 00000
(513) 999-9999

OBJECTIVE:

~~~~~~.

QUALIFICATIONS:

~~~~~~

~~~~~~ .

ACHIEVEMENTS:

~~~~~~.

~~~~~~.

~~~~~~.

~~~~~~.

EXPERIENCE:
Title.Company.

~~~~~~

~~~~~~~ .Date

Title.Company.

~~~~~~

~~~~~~~ .Date

EDUCATION:
B.A.Major.College.

middle name (F. T. Wells) or including a nickname (James "Jimsy" Martin). Many professionals prefer using their first name and middle initial (Fran T. Wells) whereas others only use their first and last name (Fran Wells). The more you embellish your name, the more psychological distance you may create between you and the employer. For example, which of the following names appeals more to you: F. T. Wells, Fran Teresa Wells, Fran T. Wells, or Fran Wells? Avoid creating greater distance between you and the reader by selecting an appropriate name format.

- **Addresses:** Provide a complete address, including zip code, that enables someone to contact you by mail. It's best to use your home address as well as a street number. P.O. Box numbers may send the wrong messages—you have something to hide or you are at a temporary and thus unstable address. If you have an e-mail address, be sure to include it immediately after your telephone and fax numbers. If you don't have an e-mail address, consider getting one as soon as possible. In today's work world, individuals without an e-mail address may appear to be from a previous generation of workers who have yet to make the transition to today's modern high tech world.

- **Contact numbers:** Include telephone, pager, and fax numbers that will enable someone to contact you during both the day and evening. We don't recommend including a current work number if confidentiality is important to you. If you decide to include a work number, indicate it as such:

> 344/731-2984 (home)
> 344/731-3122 (work)

Highly mobile individuals should consider using a pager, enlisting a telephone answering service, or using a telephone answering machine.

As for choosing a format, you can choose from several alternatives. For examples of what looks best, please see our examples in Chapters 10 and 11.

OBJECTIVE

Your Objective should immediately follow your Contact Information. It's the first written element to orient the reader to your unique qualifications. Designed to immediately grab the reader's attention, it should stress your core competencies and expected outcomes for the employer. It should project the image of someone who has a "take charge" attitude that is both positive and appealing. Follow the guidelines we outlined in Chapter 7 for developing this key resume element.

QUALIFICATIONS

The Qualifications section should be a very brief summary of your qualifications as they relate to your Objective. Brief, clear, and easy to scan, this summary should be presented in narrative form or in single words or terms. The language here can relate to your experience, education and training, or specific functions required by the Objective. Much of this language will come from the results of your Success Factor Analysis in Chapter 6. When developing this section, put yourself in the shoes of the employer who will be reading your resume or interviewing you for a job that relates to your Objective. What are the key elements the reader is looking for in a candidate? If an interviewer refers to your resume and asks, *"I see you want to do (your Objective). What makes you think you are capable?"* how would you respond with the fewest, most stimulating words? In our example of Objective #3 on page 84, the following Qualifications statement immediately follows the Objective:

OBJECTIVE

Customer Service Management position using proven skills of organizing, planning, record keeping and succeeding in a fast paced, growth oriented company where customer satisfaction is a top priority.

QUALIFICATIONS AND BACKGROUND

Over 9 years of progressive responsibility and expertise in:

- Team Building
- Record Keeping
- Organizing Meetings
- Planning

- Purchasing Raw Materials
- Inventory Management
- Scheduling Production
- Forecasting

In another example, a Haldane client reinforces an Objective with a strong summary statement of major related qualifications:

OBJECTIVE

To serve in a leadership role in a medium-size business or large division and enable an organization to improve its performance, develop positive direction and realize its potential by building relationships with employees and customers.

QUALIFICATIONS

A visionary leader with significant achievements in **multi-national, multi-facility** environments. A proven record in **leading rapid growth, improving returns** and **enhancing profitability** through an intense customer focus. Served 10 years in senior management positions directing service and manufacturing operations, engineering, business development, sales, product support activities. Demonstrated qualities and strengths include:

- Stimulating Business Growth
- Results Oriented
- Intense Customer Focused

- High Standards
- Strategic Planning
- Leading Positive Change

- Maximizing Performance
- Team Development
- Improving ROI

ACHIEVEMENTS

The Achievement section presents your strongest *supports* for your Objective. It gives evidence of past capabilities that should continue into your next job. Drawing on the examples you identified in your analysis of Key Success Factors in Chapter 6, this section proves to the reader that your Objective is realistic. Be sure to write your Achievements as succinctly as possible. Focus on what you did (action) and the outcome (result). You must include the *result*. Use verbs that describe the achievement in the past tense ("ed") rather than as present participles ("ing"). You should include revealing examples of real achievements—not formal duties and responsibilities assigned to your position or outlined in a job description. The fact that you were "responsible for" a particular function says nothing about how well you carried out your assigned responsibility. The focus here is on communicating as loudly and clearly as possible that you are a performer; present the evidence that you have performed exceptionally well in previous jobs.

Your Achievements provide evidence that you have a realistic Objective because you have a track record of relevant Accomplishments. You present <u>results</u> as well as use <u>statistics</u> to succinctly make your points and to provide supports.

When stating your Achievements, use words and phrases, especially strong adjectives, that directly relate to your Objective. Use statistics whenever possible to support your claims. Be brief but give enough information so the reader will be sufficiently motivated to call you for a job interview. During the interview, you can go into greater depth in explaining your various Achievements.

Using our last example above—the individual whose Objective was to serve in a leadership role—the first five of more than 13 supporting Achievements he listed on his resume included the following:

ACHIEVEMENTS

Doubled sales in three years for a division that was projected to be flat.

Increased return on investment from an above average 20 percent range to more than 50 percent, the highest in Bridgestone Aerospace, for four straight years. Doubled business volume in three years with only 40 percent increase in direct labor and 20 percent increase in net capital employed.

Reduced service cycle time of customer-owned assemblies by 82 percent, saving customers over $20 million in inventory.

Developed and consistently communicated an expected "Customer First" culture that enabled the entire organization to be one of the best performing in all BA for four straight years.

Reduced backlog by 50 percent by implementing 42 like-product business teams in 11 facilities, with 1,100 employees, that overhaul/repair 50,000 different aircraft components.

Such Achievements provide evidence that this person has a realistic Objective because he has a track record of relevant Accomplishments. He presents *results* as well as uses *statistics* to succinctly make his points and to provide supports. For many employers, this individual is a very desirable candidate who should be called for a job interview. During the job interview, the candidate provides more information on these and other Achievements of interest to the employer.

EXPERIENCE

The Experience section outlines your employment history. The worksheets at the end of this chapter will help you generate this data. Here you should be providing additional supports for your Objective, Qualifications, and Achievements. List in reverse chronological order (your most recent or most relevant position) your job title, employer/company, a brief description of the major functions or duties of your job, and inclusive employment dates (years only). If a particular job title does not accurately reflect your actual responsibilities, convert this job title to a functional title. You may need a career professional to help you make these conversions. When describing your previous jobs, be sure to emphasize those duties that directly relate to your current Objective. If your inclusive employment dates tend to raise negative questions, such as why you only stayed with your last two employers for 12 months each, consider including a positive yet truthful statement that would neutralize this potential red flag:

Left for a more challenging career opportunity

Expanding on the example above of the individual seeking a leadership role, he wrote his Experience section as follows:

EXPERIENCE

Bridgestone Aerospace, St. Louis, Missouri

Vice President Operations, **Component Services Division.** Directed operations of 11 aircraft component repair and overhaul facilities in a $175 million-plus division. Products include landing gears, wheels, brakes, instruments, avionics, flight controls surfaces, thrust reversers, cockpit seats, electrical assemblies, hydraulics assemblies, and mechanical assemblies. Managed Customer Service, Material Planning, Inventory Control, Engineering, Manufacturing Engineering, Human Resources, Quality, and Production. 1997 - Present.

General Manager, **Wheel and Brake Services Division.** Led a $50 million-plus autonomous business servicing the world-wide wheel, tire, and brake maintenance needs of operators of commercial, cargo, and military aircraft. Accountable for profit-loss, setting strategic direction, return on investment, day-to-day operations, sales, program management, and developing a productive work environment. 1994 - 1997

Airline Sales Manager, **Commercial Wheel and Brake Division.** Directed the worldwide sales force of the $150 million-plus commercial wheel and brake division in a highly competitive environment. 1992 - 1993

Product Support Manager, **Commercial Wheel and Brake Division.** Responsible for maintaining worldwide customer satisfaction with the division's products. Accountable for leadership of Technical Services Engineering, Field Service Representatives, Customer Service Representatives, Technical Publications, and Advertising/Customer Relations. 1990 - 1991

Manager, **Management Information Systems.** Led data processing team in the development and maintenance of manufacturing and financial business systems. 1988 - 1989

Bridgestone Aerospace Corporation, Springfield, Missouri

Section Manager, **Information Resource Management.** 1987 - 1988
Program Manager/Business Development Representative. 1984 - 1986
Engineering/Engineering Computer Systems. 1979 - 1984

3M - Minneapolis, Minnesota

Systems Analyst. 1978

Notice how the discussion of duties for each position reinforces his Objective, Qualifications, and Achievements. While this individual has over 20 years of work experience, he only elaborates on the past 10 years of experience which is most relevant to his Objective and to his next employer's concerns about his current pattern of performance.

EDUCATION

The positioning of the Education category depends on how relevant your education is to your Objective. If it is directly relevant, include it closer to the Objective, directly following the Qualifications section. However, if your educational background is less directly relevant, include it toward the end.

This section should include your highest degree first. Add any non-academic education, training, or certification if it is relevant to your Objective. Our client in the above example included the following brief notation in his Education section:

EDUCATION

MBA; Management, St. Louis University
BS; Computer Science, University of Missouri

While his academic education certainly contributed to his skills and accomplishments, in this case it will not be viewed by an employer as a key qualification. It indicates he is a college graduate who completed an advanced degree relevant to his occupational field. This information will probably not affect his candidacy one way or the other, except if the interviewer attended one of the universities and thus feels an instant bond to a fellow alumnus!

OTHER SUPPORTING DATA

You also may want to include memberships, awards, certifications, technical expertise, publications, presentations, and patents, but do so only if they support your Objective. Be careful about putting personal information on your resume, such as your age, marital status, health, and children, since these are not bonafide qualification criteria. Such information can distract the reader from the major thrust of your resume. Worst of all, some personal information may raise more questions about you than you want the reader to answer on his or her own. Never include salary information or references on your resume. In lieu of references, you may want to include quotes from previous employers or clients that support your Objective.

Never include salary information or references on your resume. In lieu of references, include quotes from previous employers or clients that support your Objective.

Always try to include positive information that supports your Objective. Avoid any information that could be interpreted as negative. If all else fails, follow this principle: *When in doubt, leave it out!*

EVALUATE, REVISE, AND FINALIZE

Once you've completed the initial draft of your resume, go back over it and evaluate it according to the following criteria:

INSTRUCTIONS: Evaluate the first draft of your resume by responding to each of the following statements. Circle the appropriate number to the right that most accurately reflects the quality of your resume and note what corrective actions need to be taken next:

SCALE: 1 = strongly disagree   3 = maybe, not certain 5 = strongly agree
    2 = disagree   4 = agree

Action Needed

1. Put most important information first.   1 2 3 4 5 _____

2. Eliminates all extraneous information.   1 2 3 4 5 _____

3. Includes complete contact information.   1 2 3 4 5 _____

4. Objective based on Success Factor Analysis.   1 2 3 4 5 _____

5. Objective includes skills and outcomes.   1 2 3 4 5 _____

6. Objective is employer-oriented.   1 2 3 4 5 _____

7. Qualifications section supports Objective.   1 2 3 4 5 _____

8. Achievement section indicates Objective is realistic.   1 2 3 4 5 _____

9. Achievement section focuses on results.   1 2 3 4 5 _____

10. Achievement section includes statistics of accomplishments.   1 2 3 4 5 _____

11. Experience section includes duties supportive of the Objective.   1 2 3 4 5 _____

12. Language throughout resume is positive, up-beat, and energetic.   1 2 3 4 5 _____

13. Uses action verbs and the active voice.   1 2 3 4 5 _____

14. Handles any obvious time gaps or problems with Experience in a positive manner.   1 2 3 4 5 _____

15. Uses crisp, succinct, expressive, and direct language throughout the resume.   1 2 3 4 5 _____

16. Checks for any spelling, grammar, or punctuation errors.   1 2 3 4 5 _____

Once you've completed this evaluation and taken corrective actions, it's time to move into the final stage. Here you need to make decisions concerning format, design, and layout. For example, should you select a one- or two-page format? The general rule of thumb is that individuals with fewer than 10 years of work experience should select a one-page resume. If more than 10 years of experience, use a two-page resume. However, this is not a hard and fast rule. In some cases, as we will see in Chapter 11, you may want to go to a four-page portfolio-style resume.

When deciding on design and layout, make sure you know whether you should be designing a conventional or electronic resume. If your resume will be screened by a person rather than a machine, try to direct the reader's eye to the most important information first. Remember, most conventional resumes get quickly scanned by individuals rather than read word for word. Keep the design and layout simple. Use spacing, capital letters, underlining, italics, bold, and bullets to emphasize the most important information. However, do not overdo such emphasizing techniques and thereby create a busy looking resume that may turn off the reader. In the end, your resume should be eye catching and easy to read.

As with the written content of your resume, evaluate its design and layout according to the following criteria:

Action Needed

1. One- to two-pages in length.   1 2 3 4 5 _____

2. Resume has an inviting, uncluttered
   look.   1 2 3 4 5 _____

3. Uses sufficient white space to be easily
   scanned by the human eye.   1 2 3 4 5 _____

4. Incorporates a standard type style and
   size.   1 2 3 4 5 _____

5. Uses highlighting and emphasizing
   techniques to improve readability.   1 2 3 4 5 _____

6. Contact information attractively for-
   matted to introduce resume.   1 2 3 4 5 _____

7. Achieves an overall positive visual
   impression.   1 2 3 4 5 _____

8. Looks very professional.   1 2 3 4 5 _____

Once you've evaluated, revised, and finalized both the form and content of your resume, you're ready to produce, distribute, and follow it up. In the end, your resume is only as good as the quality of your distribution and follow-up plans.

DATA WORKSHEETS

Use the following worksheets to compile information on your background. While most of this information will not appear on your resume, some of it will be incorporated in the Experience, Education, and Other sections. You will probably need to make multiple copies of the first worksheet on Employment Experience. Your goal here should be to generate as much detailed information on your background as possible. Even though you will not include all of this information on your resume, you will at least have a complete and systematic record of your background which you may need to refer to later when preparing for your job interview or when you complete a company's required paperwork for applicants and new employees.

Employment Experience Worksheet

1. Name of employer: _____

2. Address: _____

   _____

3. Inclusive dates of employment: From _____ to_____
   month/year   month/year

4. Type of organization: _____

5. Size of organization/approximate number of employees: _____

6. Approximate annual sales volume or annual budget: _____

7. Position held: _____

8. Earnings per month/year: _____

9. Responsibilities/duties: _____

   _____

   _____

   _____

10. Achievements or significant contributions:_____

    _____

    _____

11. Demonstrated skills and abilities:_____

    _____

    _____

12. Reason(s) for leaving: _____

    _____

Military Experience Worksheet

1. **Service:** _____

2. **Rank:** _____

3. **Inclusive dates:** From _____ to _____.
   month/year   month/year

4. **Responsibilities/duties:** _____

   _____

   _____

   _____

   _____

5. **Significant contributions/achievements:** _____

   _____

   _____

   _____

   _____

   _____

6. **Demonstrated skills and abilities:** _____

   _____

   _____

   _____

   _____

   _____

7. **Reserve status:** _____

Community/Civic/
Volunteer Experience

1. **Name and address of organization/group:** _____

_____

_____

_____

2. **Inclusive dates:** From _____ to _____.
        month/year   month/year

3. **Offices held/nature of involvement:** _____

_____

_____

_____

4. **Significant contributions/achievements/projects:** _____

_____

_____

_____

_____

5. **Demonstrated skills and abilities:** _____

_____

_____

_____

_____

EDUCATIONAL DATA

1. Institution: _____

2. Address: _____

_____

3. Inclusive dates: From _____ to _____.
   month/year   month/year

4. **Degree or years completed:** _____

5. **Major:** _____ **Minor(s):** _____

6. **Education highlights:** _____

_____

_____

7. **Student activities:** _____

_____

_____

8. **Demonstrated abilities and skills:** _____

_____

_____

9. **Significant contributions/achievements:** _____

_____

_____

_____

_____

10. **Special training courses:** _____

_____

11. **G.P.A.:** _____ (on _____ index)
    point

ADDITIONAL INFORMATION

1. **Professional memberships and status:**

   a. _____

   b. _____

   c. _____

   d. _____

2. **Licenses/certifications:**

   a. _____

   b. _____

   c. _____

3. **Expected salary range:** $ _____ to $ _____ (but do not include this on your resume)

4. **Acceptable amount of on-the-job travel:** _____ days per month.

5. **Areas of acceptable relocation:**

   a. _____   c. _____

   b. _____   d. _____

6. **Date of availability:** _____

7. **Contacting present employer:** _____

   a. Is he or she aware of your prospective job change? _____

   b. May he or she be contacted at this time? _____

8. **References:** (name, address, telephone number—not to appear on resume)

   a. _____

   b. _____

c. _____

d. _____

9. Foreign languages and degree of competency:

a. _____

b. _____

10. Interests and activities: hobbies, avocations, pursuits

a. _____

b. _____

c. _____

d. _____

Circle letter of ones which support your Objective.

11. Foreign travel:

Country	Purpose	Dates
a. _____	_____	_____
b. _____	_____	_____
c. _____	_____	_____

12. Special awards/recognition:

a. _____	_____	_____
b. _____	_____	_____
c. _____	_____	_____

13. Special abilities/skills/talents/accomplishments:

a. _____

b. _____

c. _____

9

PRODUCE, DISTRIBUTE, AND FOLLOW-UP

Now that you've crafted a first-class resume that represents the unique you, what do you plan to do with it? How will you produce it? Whom should you send it to? How will you send it? What can you do to ensure it gets read and responded to? Are there certain things you can do related to your resume to increase your chances of getting called for a job interview?

Be sure you produce, distribute, and follow-up your resume with the same attention to quality and detail that led you to writing your resume in the first place. Your resume should look and feel first-class. It should end up in the right hands—people who will call you for a job interview. At this stage, you need to develop marketing strategies that will ensure that your resume gets referred, read, and responded to. Without a sound marketing strategy centered on getting your resume in the right hands, your job search is likely to flounder.

PRODUCING A FIRST-CLASS RESUME

Most resumes today are word processed using a standard word processing program such as Word or WordPerfect or a desktop publishing program such as PageMaker, QuarkXpress, or Ventura. These programs allow you a great deal of flexibility in selecting type fonts, manipulating graphic elements, and creating attractive layouts and designs. We prefer the flexibility of these programs to using an off-the-shelf resume software program that forces you into using predetermined fill-in-the-blank templates. Most such programs produce attractive looking resumes, but their categories and content leave much to be desired. You can do just as well, indeed better, by using a standard word processing or desktop publishing program.

Assuming you are using a computer to produce your resume, be sure to use a letter quality printer with a dpi (dots per inch) of at least 300; 600 to 1200dpi is preferred, especially if you are producing an original copy from which to make multiple copies.

The choice of paper can vary depending on your audience. In general, go with a conservative color and texture. A white, off white, light tan, or light gray bond paper—20 to 60 lbs. with 100 percent cotton fiber ("rag content")—with some texture works best. Certain combinations of these colors, such as a gray paper framed with a half-inch white border, also work well. Avoid very heavy or very light weight papers. Make sure the paper you use for your cover letter and envelope match with the resume paper.

JOB VACANCIES AND THE JOB MARKET

Before you begin marketing yourself to potential employers, you need to decide how you will approach the job market. This so-called job market tends to be highly decentralized and unpredictable; it's characterized by multiple entry points. Communication within this market is often incomplete and difficult to manage. Most job seekers enter this market to look for job vacancies. When they see an interesting job, they usually respond with a resume and cover letter. And then they wait for a response. Overall, participating in this job market is a relatively passive activity for most job seekers—just read, respond, and wait.

Proactive, entrepreneurial job seekers approach the job market differently. They view the job market as a highly fluid and unpredictable arena within which new and exciting opportunities arise for those who take action. While they participate in the standard read, respond, and wait ritual, they do much more. They use their resume to open the doors of employers who may or may not publicize job vacancies by developing an active networking campaign involving the use of referral interviews. Rather than respond to a perceived reality, they create their own reality.

An effective job search is one that is highly proactive. It creates its own opportunities rather than responds passively to publicized job vacancies.

Most jobs are more or less advertised through a variety of sources. The most highly publicized job vacancies are those that are advertised in both the print and electronic media: ads found in the classified sections of newspapers or posted on Internet home pages and online employment sites. Most such ads instruct candidates to submit either a paper or electronic resume along with a cover letter as an initial application for a position.

Less publicized sources for job vacancies include employment firms, headhunters, trade publications, specialized job newsletters, bulletin boards, job banks, job hotlines, and job fairs. Most of these sources seek resumes and letters as part of either a formal application process or as a requirement for being entered into a resume database.

The least publicized sources for job vacancies are found through word-of-mouth and interpersonal networking. Jobs found through these sources tend to be less competitive and they pay more. Proactive job seekers develop an active networking campaign to market themselves for these types of jobs.

An effective job search is one that is highly proactive. It creates its own opportunities rather than responds passively to publicized job vacancies. It does so through both print and electronic media.

MAILING, FAXING, AND E-MAILING YOUR RESUME

Most job seekers use a single distribution method—mail their resume in response to classified ads. Many people do find jobs by using this time-honored distribution method. At the same time, there are many other effective distribution methods you should incorporate in your job search arsenal.

Mailing, faxing, and e-mailing your resume in response to classified ads is the traditional read, respond, and wait approach. Each day thousands of individuals do this in response to printed classified ads in newspapers, magazines, and newsletters and to electronic job postings on the Internet. The major differences between print and electronic ads are the following:

- **The electronic ads on the Internet tend to be more informative**—many run 2-3 pages and include information on the community and company culture—since they are not constrained by the short "column inch thinking" of print ads.

- **Most electronic ads are easier to sort** because they appear on Web sites with search engines that allow job seekers to specify desirable job criteria: location, salary range, keywords.

- **Electronic ads tend to be more abundant than print ads.** Since electronic ads are less expensive and reach a much broader geographic audience than print ads, both employers and headhunters increasingly use the Internet to post job vacancies and search online resume databases for qualified candidates.

- **Electronic ads tend to separate the digital "haves" from the digital "have nots"** when it comes to locating specific skills. The Internet tends to draw more highly skilled and qualified candidates than print ads. Employers increasingly discover the best qualified candidates tend to use the Internet to locate employers. Being Internet savvy, these candidates know how to use computers, access information quickly, and communicate electronically. They tend to be younger, better educated, and their skills more up-to-date than their older and more experienced counterparts who primarily rely on the print media for job vacancy information.

When you respond to a classified ad by mail, fax, or e-mail, make sure your resume is accompanied by a cover letter. The most effective responses tend to come from candidates who develop a cover letter that clearly shows a close "fit" between the skills specified in the ad and the skills possessed by the candidate. Pioneered by Bernard Haldane Associates, this type of cover letter is known as the "T" letter. It sends a powerful message—*"I'm your perfect fit"*—by matching and highlighting the employer's required skills with the candidate's demonstrated skills. An example of such a classic cover letter, used in various forms by Haldane clients, appears on page 106. For more information on these and other types of letters, see our companion volume, ***Haldane's Best Cover Letters For Professionals.***

As for the mechanics of distribution, when mailing or e-mailing your resume, it's best to follow these basic rules:

1. **Address your mail, fax, or e-mail to a specific person, if possible.** Knowing who handles your resume is especially important when doing a follow-up. If you cannot get a name, address your mail or e-mail to the organizational unit or position specified in the ad. Many organizations prefer not giving a name for fear of being inundated by pushy job applicants who aggressively follow-up by telephone. However, a low-key telephone approach can often result in revealing a name: *"Hi, this is Mandi Forbes. I'm in the process of sending my resume to your company. To whom should I address my letter?"*

2. **Always include an attention-grabbing cover letter with your resume.** A resume without a cover letter is incomplete, thoughtless, and unprofessional.

3. **Mail your resume and letter flat using a 9" x 12" envelope.** It's okay to use a matching #10 business envelope. However, folded resumes are more difficult to handle, especially when electronically scanned.

> ### Client Feedback
>
> *"I will have to say that I reaped three major items from the Haldane process: 1) resume format; 2) the "T" letter; and 3) constant advice. The most striking aspect of the resume format was the "task" and "results" structure of the business accomplishments. As for the "T" letter, I enjoyed how it helped me pull out the most important aspects of the position from the job ad. In addition, I also received many great comments about my cover letters from both friends and prospective employers. Lastly, knowing that someone is there to provide "unbiased" advice and support is always reassuring."*
>
> —R.W.

4. **Fax or e-mail your resume only if requested to do so.** When asked to do so, make sure you include a cover sheet with your faxed resume and letter. Create an attention-grabbing announcement line so your e-mailed resume and letter does not get lost in a sea of other e-mail messages.

5. **Never enclose letters of recommendation, transcripts, samples of work, or other information unless requested to do so.** They distract from your central message and they may leave a bad impression on the reader. Remember, the purpose of your resume is to get an interview. If you include extraneous materials with your resume, you may kill your chances of getting called for the interview. If an employer wants letters of recommendation,

5555 Sharon Drive
Glen Burnie, MD 21061

April 10, 1999

National Business Employment Weekly
c/o The Wall Street Journal
1701 Page Mill Road
Palo Alto, CA 94304

Dear Advertiser:

In response to your advertisement dated February 8, 1999, in the National Business Employment Weekly, for "Vice President of Manufacturing," please consider the following:

Your Requirements	My Qualifications
Set and make happen aggressive monthly shipping plan.	Over 8 years aggressive direct sales program/production management experience; PLANNED, SCHEDULED, COORDINATED, EXPEDITED 100+ electronic defense contracts, meeting monthly fab, test, Q.C., shipping schedules to include stateside/offshore subcontracting.
Bring continuous stream of new products from engineering release to production inventory ready to ship.	Over 8 years of aggressive COORDINATED/INTEGRATED engineering configuration manufacturing new/prototype and existing designs from release to production—stock—delivery in multi-project environment.
Plan and implement a cost reduction program that has major influence on the company's performance.	IMPLEMENTED/MONITORED earned value system; recovered $1M loss; INITIATED economies-of-scale production; increased 2% loss to 10% profit for business segment.
Maintain the company's reputation for providing quality products.	INTEGRATED/MONITORED engineering, manufacturing, quality activities; CONDUCTED CCB reviews; won follow-on contracts.

Enclosed is my resume for your consideration.

Sincerely,

Alexander Smith

Alexander Smith

Enclosure

transcripts, or samples of your work, he or she will probably request them after your first interview.

6. **Type rather than handwrite the mailing label.** Remember, at this stage you want to demonstrate your best professional effort rather than try to personalize a relationship with a stranger.

7. **If time is of the essence, send your resume and letter by priority mail or special next-day delivery services,** such as FedEx, UPS, Airborne, or DHL. In most cases, it's okay to send your materials by first-class postage. Remember, it's the content of your resume and letter (your skills and demonstrated accomplishments) rather than the delivery method or "dress for success" delivery elements that most impresses employers. Using expensive next-day delivery services may send the wrong message—you're not very cost conscious!

BROADCASTING YOUR RESUME

Broadcasting your resume to numerous potential employers is another conventional resume distribution method. Conducted in a traditional manner, this is a direct-mail approach to employers that produces few results. Like most direct-mail operations, the returns from broadcast distribution depend on the quality of your mailing list and follow-up activities. If, for example, you have a mailing list of key CEO's who are looking for someone with your particular skills and abilities, chances are you will get a good response. However, chances are no such mailing list exists, and if you compiled one yourself, you would want to do a targeted mailing linked to an aggressive telephone follow-up campaign rather than a broadcast mailing.

At Bernard Haldane Associates, we use a more targeted form of the broadcast method which we call the **Proactive Profile**. Working with a Career Advisor, the client develops a brief profile of approximately 100 words which highlights nine distinct elements: job title, industry, level of position, experience, education, geographic location, geographic preference, exceptional skills, and contact information. While some individuals use their own name and address, others wish to maintain confidentiality by using a Client # directed to our organization. The following three clients, for example, presented these profiles:

HUMAN RESOURCES MANAGER: 15 years experience in the food manufacturing and retail grocery industries, in both union and non-union environments. Expertise in the areas of employee relations, compensation, benefits, and training. Developed and implemented a comprehensive training/cross training program that helped: reduce turnover 35%, enhance morale, and increase line productivity 41%. Seeking opportunity in the South or Midwest that will provide an appropriate challenge to a Human Resource Professional who has managed a staff of 10 professionals. Currently employed in Chicago, IL. Confidential Job Search. Call (333) 333-3333 to contact.

PROJECT/OPERATIONS MANAGER: 15 years experience in manufacturing and retail management, including leadership roles in 2 business start-ups. Have proven success in improving profitability (increased sales 20% for 18 consecutive months in a $13MM operation), and controlling costs (reduced material costs 15% saving $300K for an $8MM manufacturing function). Additional successes in vendor sourcing (analyzed 40 vendors and procured necessary resources to eliminate major bottleneck within 4 weeks), and contract/procurement (secured an average of 15 major contracts for 5 years valued up to $250K), hiring/training for a variety of positions (managed complete start-up of 74 seat restaurant operation, hiring/training 50 employees within 6 months). Earned Bachelor of Business Administration with dual emphasis in Marketing and Business Management from Kent State University. Currently employed in Central California, and open to relocation. To contact call John Smith (777) 123-4567.

SALES MANAGEMENT EXECUTIVE: 15+ years of successful sales management experience which includes managing a North American direct sales force, distributors, international sales, and strategic accounts. Served most recently as Vice President, Sales for a major manufacturer of medical equipment/disposables in the Midwest. Here, grew revenues from $22MM to $58.7MM; increased market share in all categories (up to 66%); and improved company earnings 67%. Has extensive experience with Fortune 500 companies with a strong consumer products background. Currently seeking an opportunity in the Southeast or Southwest with expansion minded company in need of strong sales management to get them to the next level. B.A. Harvard University. Confidential search. Contact Client #511613 (881) 631-1111.

Another approach to the broadcast method is to dispense with the resume altogether and instead send a one- to two-page broadcast letter. Some executive-level candidates report success with this method. This approach letter is the functional equivalent to our Proactive Profile—it announces one's job interests and availability, stresses key skills and accomplishments, and provides contact information for further discussion. This broadcast letter is often more effective than a broadcast resume because it makes a very different statement than a resume. A broadcast resume indicates you want to apply for a position, if one's available. A broadcast letter indicates you may be available for discussions; if interested, please contact me for more information, including a copy of my resume. The letter provides more flexibility than a resume in indicating where you are coming from and where you hope to go in the near future; it can be a very powerful personal statement of interest and intent.

NETWORKING AND REFERRAL INTERVIEWS

One of the best marketing methods involves networking and referral interviews. Over the years our clients have discovered one of the most interesting facts of job search life: the easiest way to get a job is to never ask for a job; instead, ask for information, advice, and referrals from those who have the power to hire. In the end, a job will come calling for you through your extensive networking and referral interview activities. Our clients develop these skills which effectively open the doors of many employers who would not normally advertise job vacancies. Using a combination of telephone calls, letter writing, and face-to-face meetings, the job seeker makes numerous contacts with individuals—many of whom are friends, colleagues, contacts of contacts, and ultimately key decision-makers—who offer information, advice, and referrals. If you constantly expand your network of job contacts by focusing on information, advice, and referrals, you will build a personalized word-of-mouth network that should result in landing job interviews. In so doing, you will uncover jobs that never get advertised or you may create a situation in which a job is literally developed around your unique skills and abilities.

The key to making this approach work is the *referral interview*, a particular type of interview initiated by the job seeker in the pursuit of job information, advice, and referrals. As detailed in our companion volume—***Haldane's Best Answers to Tough Interview Questions***—the referral interview is one of the most powerful approaches to marketing yourself. By conducting referral interviews, you learn a great deal about the current state of the job market; uncover jobs and employers who might not normally advertise a position or whom you might overlook in your job search; and acquire useful information on how to better sharpen your job search. It's this last point that is most relevant to your resume. One of the most important benefits of networking and referral interviews is the ability to conduct an *external evaluation* of your resume. Unlike the *internal evaluation* outlined in Chapter 8, where you evaluated each section of your resume in reference to specific writing criteria, an external evaluation involves getting feedback from potential employers in the job market. When you conduct a referral interview, you do so with the idea of

> *The referral interview is one of the most powerful approaches to marketing yourself.*

getting useful information, advice, and referrals. At the same time, you want to use this opportunity to get feedback on your resume so you can improve its contents. Getting feedback on your resume usually occurs at the very end of the referral interview—just before you close. Ask the person you are interviewing if he or she could take a moment to look at your resume. The dialogue might go something like this:

> I really appreciate the time you've taken to discuss my career interests. From our discussion, I've learned a great deal about some of the major problems and new directions in this field. I would like to ask two additional favors. First, I've put together a preliminary resume and was hoping to get some feedback on how I can best improve it. Do you feel this resume is appropriate for the jobs we discussed? Are there certain things you would recommend that I include or exclude? Second, would you know people in these types of jobs who would be willing—like yourself—to provide me with additional information?

This closing statement at the referral interview does two important things:

1. It gets your resume read, reviewed, and revised by someone who is close to the type of job you're interested in pursuing. This is the ultimate external resume evaluation. Indeed, the only evaluation that really counts is the one made by the employer. And someone you interview as part of your networking is the closest you will probably get to the employer who invites you to a job interview.

2. It expands your network in the direction of individuals who might be interested in your resume. These individuals are most likely potential employers who, in turn, will give you useful feedback on your resume.

In a final statement, after being referred to others, ask to be **remembered** with your resume:

> I would appreciate it if you could keep me in mind if you hear of anyone who might be interested in my background and skills. Please keep this copy of my resume for reference.

If you indeed revise your resume based upon this person's comments, be sure to send him or her a copy of your revised resume with a nice thank-you letter. Express your appreciation for meeting with you and the resume advice. Remind the individual to keep you in mind should he or she hear of anyone interested in your background.

Be careful when initially approaching a network contact with a copy of your resume. Try to be subtle. If not, you may send the wrong message and scare them away. Indeed, they may feel you are using them to get a job—rather than merely asking for information, advice, and referrals. Most people love to give advice, but they are reluctant to take responsibility for your career fate. Ask me for information, advice, and referrals, but don't ask me to give you a job! When you give a contact a copy of your resume before providing them with a context, you put them in an uncomfortable position: your not-so-subtle message is that you want them to find you a job. Many people abuse the referral interview by being deceptive in their intent. Never, ever use the referral interview to exploit someone. Your goal is to get useful information, advice, and referrals that could lead to an unadvertised job. Ideally, you would like your interview to end with a comment such as this:

> From what you've told me about yourself and from looking at your resume, I think Jerry Stanford at A.L. Manufacturing might be interested in your background. If you don't mind, I'll give Jerry a call and send him a copy of your resume. He's a good person to keep in touch with. I think you may have many things in common.

When you elicit such a response at the end of your referral interview, you know you're on the right track to career success. Everything you've done, from conducting your Success Factor Analysis in Chapter 6 to drafting your resume in Chapter 8, now comes together in a very targeted marketing campaign that puts you in the right place at the right time for the right jobs. By networking and properly conducting information interviews with your powerful resume, you should land a job that is truly "fit"—for both you and your employer!

ELECTRONIC INITIATIVES

As we noted earlier, today's job seekers need to embrace the Internet. During the past five years, much of the traditional paper and telephone job search has moved online as more and more employers post vacancies on Web sites and search resume databases for qualified candidates. The Internet also has become the best friend of headhunters who regularly use the Internet to locate qualified candidates to present to their clients. The electronic resume—one that is capable of being e-mailed, scanned, and retrieved by keywords—is the key to conducting an online job search. As more and more employers, headhunters, and job seekers use the Internet, much of the job market will encompass the Internet. Indeed, nearly 70 percent of all employers now incorporate the Internet into their recruitment efforts. If you're not using the Internet in your job search, you may be missing out on some important employment opportunities. Within the next few years, we expect most employers will regularly use the Internet to recruit for many types of positions. They will do so because Internet recruiting is much more cost effective and efficient than traditional classified ads, employment firms, and headhunters.

> *Nearly 70 percent of all employers now incorporate the Internet into their recruitment efforts. If you're not using the Internet in your job search, you may be missing out on some important opportunities.*

Using the Internet in your job search primarily involves four activities: acquiring job market information, researching specific employers, responding to job listings, and posting resumes to bulletin boards and commercial employment sites. You should spend some of your job search time—perhaps as much as 15 percent—engaged in these online job search activities. Let's briefly look at each.

1. **Acquire job market information:** You can learn a lot about the job market by spending a few hours "surfing the net." Using a variety of search engines, such a Yahoo, AltaVista, HotBot, and Lycos, you can visit numerous sites that yield useful information on jobs in your particular occupational field, salary ranges, benefits, professional associations, communities, relocation, and job search skills.

2. **Research specific employers:** Most employers have their own home pages that include all types of information useful to job seekers. Many include current job openings, resume databases, profiles of employees, examples of projects, information on company culture, and even tips on how to land a job with their organization. Take, for example, the Web site for one of the world's leading consulting firms, the Boston Consulting Group: *www.bcg.com*. It's a job hunter's paradise. As you research employers on the Internet, you may want to respond to their job listings by e-mailing them your resume.

3. **Respond to job listings:** More than 3,000 commercial online employment sites include job listings which are similar to classified ads found in newspapers and trade publications. In most cases, employers pay fees, which run from $150 to $300 a month, to post job vacancies on these sites. Most sites are free to job seekers who can search hundreds of job listings. They typically respond to a vacancy announcement by e-mailing their resume and letter. Using the Internet

in this manner is a high tech version of responding to printed classified ads. One of the largest sites with classified ads, which also is supported by over 30 major newspapers, is CareerPath: *www.careerpath.com*

4. **Post resume to online resume databases:** Most commercial online employment sites include an online resume database that allows job seekers to post their resume. In most cases, employers pay user fees to access these databases; they search by keywords for qualified candidates. This is the new passive side of the job search: just enter your resume in a database and your resume works for you 24 hours a day. If you're lucky, you may be contacted by an employer or headhunter who discovers your resume based upon their unique keyword search.

Embracing the Internet essentially means you incorporate the Internet in your job search. You use the Internet to conduct research, you monitor job vacancies, and you enter your resume in as many resume databases as possible. It's this latter activity that constitutes a relative new dimension to resume distribution—entering your resume into online databases.

> *Our Career Strategy 2000 system helps our clients extend the Haldane job search methods to the Internet.*

Haldane clients have access to our newly developed proprietary Career Strategy 2000 system which includes numerous Internet job search components. For example, users can research major companies through the Dun and Bradstreet Million Dollar database; examine numerous salary surveys; submit resumes to major Web sites; simultaneously search the top 30 Web sites for job listings; and broadcast resumes to thousands of employers. The unique search capabilities and numerous databases available through the Career Strategy 2000 system enable our clients to research and target specific employers as well as expand their job search to hundreds of thousands of additional employers. Comprehensive and integrated, the Career Strategy 2000 system saves our clients a great deal of time and money in using the Internet in their job search. Indeed, the system allows our clients to quickly embrace the Internet!

If you are not a Haldane client and thus do not have access to the Career Strategy 2000 system, your Internet job search will be more laborious. We strongly encourage you to get your resume in as many online resume databases as possible. While some of these databases may be operated by your professional association, others are popular online commercial employment services that should be part of your regular online job search.

The Internet also can be very seductive. Embrace it, but don't spend too much time playing the online read, respond, and wait game that has been traditionally associated with a job search focused on print classified ads. Much of what appears on the Internet for job seekers is merely an electronic version of classified ads. Complete with search engines, resume databases, and banner ads, these sites are designed to attract the advertising dollars and user fees of employers. From the perspective of employers who regularly use these Internet sites, online recruiting works; it's cheap and effective. Many employers claim they recruit better quality candidates online than off-line.

But for the job seeker, using the Internet may give you a false sense of making progress in the job market. Introverted individuals may spend a disproportionate amount of time on the Internet because of its impersonal nature. We know many people are using the Internet in their job search, but it's still unclear how many of these same people actually find jobs via the Internet. Our proactive, targeted methods centered around networking and referral interviews continue to work well for our clients. These methods result in getting your resume into the hands of employers who are interested in hiring your skills. Our Career Strategy 2000 system helps our clients extend the Haldane job search methods to the Internet.

In today's highly competitive job market, you are well advised to conduct both an online and off-line job search. Embrace the Internet, but don't let it embrace you and thereby neglect many of the time-honored resume distribution approaches that continue to work for our clients. In the end, you should find the Internet to be one of many exciting tools for conducting an effective job search.

For more information on how to use the Internet in your job search, including electronic resumes, see the following books:

CareerXroads 2000, Gerry Crispin and Mark Mehler (Kendall Park, NJ: MMC Group, 2000)

Cyberspace Resume Kit, Fred E. Jandt and Mary Nemnick (Indianapolis, IN: JIST Works, 1999)

The Guide to Internet Job Searching, Margaret Riley, Frances Roehm, and Steve Oserman (Lincolnwood, IL: NTC Publishing, 1998)

Heart & Soul Internet Job Search, Chuck and Donna Peerce Cochran (Palo Alto, CA: Davies-Black Publishing, 1999)

How to Get Your Dream Job Using the Web, Shannon Karl and Arthur Karl (Scottsdale, AZ: Coriolis Group Books, 1997)

Internet Resumes, Peter D. Weddle (Manassas Park, VA: Impact Publications, 1998)

Job Hunting on the Internet, Richard Nelson Bolles (Berkeley, CA: 10 Speed Press, 1999)

Job Searching Online For Dummies, Pam Dixon (Foster City, CA: IDG Books, 1998)

Resumes in Cyberspace, Pat Criscito (Hauppauge, NY: Barrons, 1997)

Resumes For Dummies, Joyce Lain Kennedy (Foster City, CA: IDG Books, 1998)

FOLLOW-UP, FOLLOW-UP, FOLLOW-UP

One of the major weaknesses in most job searches is the failure to follow-up. Most job seekers send their resumes to prospective employers and then wait to be called for a job interview. Few take initiative to ensure their resume gets read and responded to. Indeed, many job seekers believe it's incumbent upon the employer to respond to their resume and letter. If they don't hear from the employer, they assume they were rejected for consideration. Some even believe it's discourteous for an employer not to acknowledge receipt of their resume. If you believe such nonsense, you are a good candidate for an attitude adjustment!

> *Employers are busy people who respond to the people who count the most—qualified candidates who should be called for a job interview.*

Employers are busy people who do not have the time nor money to respond to every solicited and unsolicited resume. They respond to the people who count the most—qualified candidates who should be called for a job interview. Some use automated resume management systems to acknowledge receipt of resumes by sending "personalized" form letters to individuals who send them solicited or unsolicited resumes:

Thank you for sending your resume. We hope to make a decision shortly.

or

Thank you for sending your resume. While we do not have a position available at present, we will keep your resume on file for future reference.

While such courtesy statements may make you feel good, they tell you nothing about the actual decision-making process which may have already resulted in discarding your resume.

If you send a resume and then wait to be called, your chances of getting an interview will most likely not be good. Indeed, waiting is not a good job search strategy. You must take initiative in contacting employers if you want to improve your chances of getting a job interview based upon your resume and letter.

Consider the typical resume screening process of employers. You advertise a position and within one week receive 100 resumes. While many of the resumes are obvious rejections, because the candidates' skills and experience appear unrelated to your position, many others are possibilities. Your initial task is to sort these 100 resumes into three categories: no, maybe, yes. Your ultimate goal is to identify three to five "yes" resumes and then call each candidate for an initial telephone screening interview. Many employers sort resumes by quickly scanning them—perhaps spending 10 to 30 seconds reading each—while other employers let electronic scanners do the sorting and screening. Resumes rich with the right combination of skills, accomplishments, and keywords will grab the attention of either the human eye or electronic scanner. These are the resumes that will to be responded to with a telephone screening interview. Based on your telephone conversation, you then select the three top candidates for a formal face-to-face interview.

So what can you do to ensure that your resume moves into the "yes" pile? If your resume initially falls into the "no" pile, chances are you'll have difficulty getting it moved into the "maybe" and then "yes" pile. But if your resume starts in the "maybe" pile, you may be able to move it to the "yes" pile through certain follow-up techniques that affect the discretion of resume screeners.

As a job seeker, you need to regularly follow-up your job search communications with telephone calls, faxes, e-mail, and letters. Start with the assumption that most employers will not contact you unless you first contact them. If you want to affect the status of your resume, it's incumbent upon you to take certain follow-up actions.

So what can and should you do to follow-up your resume in order to increase your chances of getting a job interview? We recommend doing the following:

1. **Follow-up your resume within seven working days of mailing, faxing, or e-mailing it with a telephone call.** Assuming you have a name and telephone number of the recipient, call and ask if they have received it and ask when you might expect to hear from them about the position. In some cases, this follow-up telephone call may result in an initial screening interview. In other cases, you may be politely told *"we should be making a decision shortly."* This follow-up call can help move your resume from the "maybe" pile to the "yes" pile. Be sure to include a follow-up statement in your cover letter to prepare the recipient for your call:

   > I'll call your office on the morning of June 15 to answer any questions you may have and to see if we might be able to schedule a meeting at a mutually convenient time.

   This follow-up statement may result in giving your resume added attention—instead of being given the quick 10-30 second scan it actually gets read for more than one minute—as the employer prepares for your expected telephone call.

2. **If you are unable to get through after seven telephone attempts, follow-up with a fax or e-mail.** In many cases you will not be able to get through to the resume recipient with a telephone call because of voice mail and human gatekeepers. When you call and leave a message, be sure to be very professional, enthusiastic, and upbeat. Under no circumstances should you indicate your frustration or irritation at not having your phone call returned. Be pleasantly persistent. Indeed, many individuals will not return their call unless they receive five or more messages. Feeling guilty for not returning their calls, they then bend over backwards to be accommodating. If this happens to you, chances are the individual will make a special attempt to read your resume and letter before returning your call. However, after seven unanswered calls, it's time to give up on this telephone strategy; you've probably made a pest of yourself, although the person also may feel too guilty to call you! At this point, do a fax or e-mail follow-up. Remind the recipient that you sent a resume and letter on a certain date and you are interested in speaking with him or her about how your interests and skills best meet their needs. This type of follow-up indicates interest, initiative, persistence, and tenacity—qualities sought by many of today's

employers. Your ostensibly failed follow-up efforts may be rewarded with an invitation to a job interview.

3. **Follow-up a faxed or e-mailed resume with an original copy of your resume and cover letter.** While it is not necessary to do this, because employers already have your resume and letter on file and many are inundated with paper, it doesn't hurt to send a copy of your original resume and letter as a follow-up. In addition to reminding the employer of your interest in the position, you will be communicating your best professional effort with a resume and letter that both look and feel professional. Within a few days, make your follow-up telephone call.

4. **Be sure to follow-up all networking contacts and individuals who granted you a referral interview with a thank-you letter.** Two of your major goals in networking and conducting referral interviews are to be *remembered and referred* to others. One of the best ways to get remembered and referred is to send a nice thank-you letter in which you express your genuine appreciation for the individual's time and advice. This is a thoughtful thing to do, something most job seekers fail to incorporate in their job search. Indeed, thoughtful people tend to be liked and helped by others.

The whole purpose of your follow-up efforts is to put an interesting and enthusiastic human being behind your resume and letter. Like the referral interview, you are attempting to increase your chances of getting an interview. If you just sit around and wait for employers to call you, rather than take follow-up actions as outlined here, don't expect your resume to go very far. Having spent so much time writing, producing, and distributing the perfect resume, you owe it to yourself to present your best professional effort in getting the job interview. Employers need to hear from you before they invite you to the face-to-face interview.

Whatever you do, always remember the purpose of your resume—to get a job interview. Getting someone to take action that leads to the job interview often means you must follow-up, follow-up, and follow-up. Persistence and tenacity, when done in a professional and enthusiastic manner, often pays off with big dividends. For in the end, it's the job interview that determines whether or not you get that job!

10

HALDANE RESUME
TRANSFORMATIONS

Many Haldane clients come to us with a prepared resume. It may be a resume they wrote themselves or one produced by a professional resume writer. In most cases, a Career Advisor works with the client to create a new resume that clearly reflects Haldane's career management principles. This often means completely re-working or "transforming" the client's resume after conducting a complete assessment involving Success Factor Analysis, which identifies the individual's strengths and accomplishments. Many of our clients also take the Myers-Briggs Type Indicator to identify their preferences for working environment and working style.

The following "before and after" resume examples are drawn from the files of Haldane clients. In each case, the first resume arrived with the client. After the client had an opportunity to complete assessment exercises and become oriented into the Haldane system, a new or "after" resume was developed with the assistance of a Haldane Career Advisor. In some cases, the transformations are quite dramatic. In other cases, the changes are more subtle. However, in all cases, the "new look" is one that is consistent with Haldane's principles of career management. The transformed resumes are very focused around an *objective*; they stress the individual's *accomplishments*. As such, they speak the language of employers.

The examples in this chapter should give you a clear picture of what goes into creating a first-class Haldane resume. These powerful resumes get job interviews. In some cases, the resume transformations also helped transform our client's life. Now focused on their strengths and accomplishments, these clients went on to get interviews and job offers that led to continuing career success.

All names, addresses, and employers have been changed to protect the confidentiality of our clients. Any resemblance to real persons or organizations is purely coincidental.

117

BEFORE

Barry Thomas
181 Queens Street
Albany, New York 11111
(555) 555-5555

****

EDUCATION: New York State University. Buffalo, New York.
B.S. Economics. June, 1990.
Emphasis: Finance.

EXPERIENCE:

11/92-Present   TILTON MANUFACTURING, Albany, New York. (555) 555-5555.
Management Quality Assurance:

Set daily production goals.	Ensure performance standards.
Performance appraisals.	Compile reports.
Train/supervise staff.	Train Staff.
Compile reports.	Assist member services as needed.
Control costs. Safety Committee.	

8/92-9/92   WILLIAMS RENT-TO-OWN, Buffalo, New York. (444) 444-4444.
Retail:
Open and close store.
Cashier.
Compile reports.
Customer service.

11/91-7/92   BARRETT TEMPORARY SERVICES, Albany, New York. (333) 333-3333.
and   **Production:**
10/92-11/92   Sanitation.
Manage production rooms.
Train/supervise staff.
Line production.

8/91-10/91   VOLUME DISCOUNTERS, Albany, New York. (111) 111-1111.
Store Manager Trainee:
Train/supervise staff.
Performance appraisals.
Compile reports.
Control costs.
Cashier.
Customer service.

REFERENCES: Available upon request.

****

AFTER

BARRY THOMAS

181 Queens Street
Albany, New York 11111   **(555) 555-5555**

OBJECTIVE

An entry level position in human resource administration involving skills in communication, project management and training.

QUALIFICATIONS

Ten years of progressively increasing responsibility and expertise in:

- Managing   • Supervising   • Communicating   • Negotiating
  - Conceptualizing   • Motivating   • Evaluating

ACHIEVEMENTS

Streamlined a production department for manufacturing company. Reorganized; established and implemented new procedures. *Results:* Erased a production deficit and produced a surplus in two months.

Conceptualized a new process for a sawmill. Ascertained the problem; perceived the solution; researched the feasibility; presented findings to management. *Results:* Dramatic improvement in effectiveness and time efficiency.

Negotiated own schedule for a manufacturing company. Perceived the need; orchestrated the schedule; monitored the results. *Results:* Increased productivity; reduced employee turnover.

Motivated Boy Scouts to attain requirements. Coached; counseled; educated them. *Results:* Scouts generally achieved requirements ahead of schedule.

PROFESSIONAL EXPERIENCE

Tilton Manufacturing
Quality Assurance Lead Person   1992-1996
Analyzed and inspected production units to verify conformance to specifications; diagnosed technical problems; oral and written communication; compiled production reports; trained and supervised employees in work methods and procedures; initiated action on safety committee.

Department Supervisor   1994
Supervised and coordinated activities of employees; trained employees in work methods and procedures; troubleshot; planned production operations; developed operational procedures; initiated personnel actions; compiled, sorted and retrieved production data using computer.

Barrett Temporary Services
Production   1991-1992
Supervised and coordinated activities of employees; trained employees in work methods and procedures; compiled production reports.

Great Investor's Inc.
Registered Representative   1990
Identified, solicited, and interviewed clients; provided information and advice, initiated action on developing and implementing financial plans.

Thomas
Page Two

Zebra Lumber   1987-1990
Assistant Supervisor
Supervised and coordinated activities of employees; trained employees in work methods
and procedures; troubleshot; served on safety committee.

EDUCATION

B.S., Economics   New York State University   Buffalo, NY

AFFILIATIONS

Toastmasters International

GARY L. CALHOUN

BEFORE

1250 Vancouver Ave, #123
Victoria, UT 88888-8888

Home Phone: 555-555-1212
E-mail: gary@anywhere.net

SUMMARY

I bring quantitative and analytical skills, an excellent education (PhD, MBA, CFP), business knowledge and extensive IS experience to my next position. I can program and design databases, manage a website, write, instruct, supervise salespeople and technical personnel, and make platform presentations. I can apply quantitative data-base marketing techniques (segmentation, Lifetime Customer Value, modeling etc.). And I have particularly strong and recent experience doing that in the financial services industry. I understand management's perspective because I have been both sales manager and marketing manager. I have worked in teams, conducted business overseas and participated in three start-ups. I particularly enjoy solving complex business problems in ambiguous settings.

MARKETING/DATABASE MARKETING

8/96 -present

Senior Consultant, **Data Matrix Technologies**
Project leader of three-person team to troubleshoot and redirect database marketing effort of women's clothing direct marketer in Germany. Designed, using *FrontPage 97* and provided content for 1:1 Marketing website on DataMatrix*'s* intranet. Developed database and 1:1 marketing strategies for DataMatrix ventures into the insurance industry. Performed market research, using Internet sources for banking, insurance, telephone and utility industries. Presented 1-hour slide lecture, summarizing database and 1:1 marketing opportunities and pitfalls at company-wide seminar. Marketing analyst for Project applying database and 1:1 Marketing strategies to an electrical utility's efforts to penetrate the corporate and residential retail energy market.

6/94-8/96

Consultant, Hyleton & Company, Inc.
Completely redesigned their consulting firm's database marketing program for the financial services industry. Applied SAS tools (Base SAS, proc SQL, and SAS/Assist) on a *Sun* SPARCstation to import our clients' data and restructure it into a relational format. Scrubbed, parsed and corrected the names and addresses, using a 900-line program I wrote in the SAS data step language. Householded the records, and overlaid individual-specific demographics imported from *InfoBase* (Acxiom). Using techniques that I developed specifically for the mutual fund, banking and insurance industries, I perfected formulas for Lifetime Customer Value, then applied proprietary segmentation strategies and account growth and attrition models to identify and prioritize those sales and customer service programs likely to be most effective.

8/93-5/94

Manager of Sales Administration, **Big Money Investor Services**
As inside support for the field sales staff, recognized that the DBMS the Sales Department was using was inadequate, identified a distributed, relational database called *Commence* and adapted it to the department's needs. So successful were my efforts that the use of *Commence* spread to other departments.

11/91-12/92	*Director of Marketing, **Bronson, Hardig & Morris***

Identified, contacted and followed up on potential clients among moderate-size Manhattan businesses for this 20-professional CPA firm, utilizing a computerized method I developed of identifying, importing electronically from *D&B*, contacting, and following up on sales leads.

4/78-4/81	*Marketing Manager, **Magma Steel Corporation***

Prepared sales and marketing plans for this US subsidiary of a French multinational steel firm, designed and implemented a computerized sales reporting system, developed econometrics forecasts and set up a competition for and selected an advertising agency. Supervised a staff of 3 outside and 4 inside salespersons; sales increased 22% during my tenure.

SALES

11/81-11/87	*Sales Engineer, **Chadwick Associates, Inc.***

In my spare time, I developed a spreadsheet/database program that reduced the time needed by the clerical staff to calculate salespersons' monthly commissions from days to hours while also providing management with more meaningful reports. My primary responsibility was sales of metalworking services, however and within 4 years, I had tripled sales in my territory to $4.55 million, taking the territory from worst to best in the firm.

1982-1983	*Certified Instructor, **Rockefeller Sales Course***

After being top student, taught the course to three successive classes in my spare time.

FINANCIAL SERVICES

12/92-7/93	*Investment Advisor, **Secure Insurance Services***
4/90-12/90	*Financial Planner, **The Peterson Group***
6/89-4/90	*Insurance Agent/Registered Representative, **Smithson Financial Group***
8/88-5/89	*Insurance Agent, **American Insurance Company***

Sold individual and group life and health insurance, fixed and variable annuities, limited partnerships and mutual funds for all four firms.

1989-1990	*Instructor, **Financial Management Seminar***

Taught at *Riverdale Junior College* in Riverdale to successively larger classes.

PROFESSIONAL

- **MBA**, The University of Virginia
- **BS**, **MS** and **Ph.D**. in Metallurgy, Boston Institute of Technology
- Certified Financial Planner (**CPF**).
- Attended first semester of New York University Computer Technology & applications program, Relational Database option.
- Able to speak, read and write German fluently.
- Proficient in SAS, MS Front Page, and MS Office 97, including Access 7.0.

GARY L. CALHOUN

AFTER

9834 152nd Avenue
Victoria, UT 88888

Tel: (555) 555-1212
E-mail: gary@anywhere.net

BUSINESS PROCESS ARCHITECT

Decision Support. . . Activity-Based Management. . . Demographics. . . Data Warehousing
Balanced Scorecard. . . Business Process Mapping. . . Customer Relationship Management

Preoccupied with turning <u>outside</u> data into information, information into knowledge.

STRATEGY

According to Peter Drucker (Forbes, August 24, 1998), "collecting and analyzing <u>outside</u> information is the next frontier in information systems for top management." Analyzing and restructuring business processes with an eye on applying such <u>outside</u> information as customer demographics to calculation of Lifetime Customer Value for past five years. Over that span, I have changed the way insurers, mutual funds, and utilities look at their customers and the effectiveness of the sales, customer service and marketing processes that serve them*.

EXAMPLES

In the course of creating a database marketing program for a Wall Street consultant, perfected Lifetime Customer Value parameters for firms in the insurance, banking and mutual fund industries. RESULT: A quantitative approach to planning, executing and evaluating their respective marketing campaigns.

For a soon-to-be deregulated electrical utility, developed a technique for segmenting the customer database in terms of business and individual demographics. RESULT: Utility had a basis for comparing customer segments in terms of the value each brought to the bottom line.

Reorganized product data from legacy system silos belonging to a large southern life insurance company into a customer-centric data warehouse. Identified and corrected data inconsistencies and omissions, restructured data into a relational database architecture, calculated Lifetime Customer Value and ran statistical analyses. RESULT: An analysis which Gary Desalt, co-inventor of *Multi-part Marketing* liked so much, he plans to use it in his next book.

EDUCATION/ADVANCED TRAINING

Ph.D. in Metallurgy	*Boston Institute of Technology*	Boston, MA
M.B.A. in R&D Management	*University of Virginia*	Charlottesville, VA
Computer Applications classes	*New York University*	New York, NY

* MANAGEMENT BOOKS THAT INFLUENCED ME	• WORKING KNOWLEDGE • THE ONE-TO-ONE FUTURE • CUSTOMER INTIMACY	• THE LOYALTY EFFECT • BUILT TO LAST • COST & EFFECT	• STRATEGIC DATABASE MARKETING • COMPETING FOR THE FUTURE

EXPERIENCE

Sequence Computer Systems, Inc.   *(Salt Lake City, UT)*   1998
<u>Product Marketing Manager, Worldwide Decision Support Marketing</u>. Responsible for "vertical" industry marketing plans, integrating company's computer hardware, partner software and professional services. Gave 90-minute illustrated talk on One-to-One Marketing as part of call center training for sales force in the UK. Oversaw production of multimedia CD-ROM on customer relationship management.

DataMatrix Technologies, Inc.   *(Park City, UT)*   1997
<u>Senior Consultant</u>. Led and participated in consulting projects to implement database marketing at a retailer, an electrical utility and an insurance company. Designed and provided content for company's One-to-One Marketing intranet site. Performed market research on banking, insurance and electrical utility industries, using Internet resources. Presented one-hour slide lecture on the opportunities and pitfalls of database marketing.

Hyleton & Company, Inc.   *(Jersey City, NJ)*   1994-96
<u>Consultant</u>. Designed *NylRoad*, this consulting firm's database marketing program for the financial services industry. Applied SAS tools (*Base SAS, proc SQL, and SAS/Assist*) on a Unix workstation to import our clients' data and restructure it into a relational format. Scrubbed, parsed and corrected the names and addresses, using a 900-line program I wrote in the SAS data step language. Householded the records and overlaid individual-specific demographic information imported from *Acxiom*. Perfected formulas for Lifetime Customer Value, then applied proprietary segmentation strategies and account growth and attrition models to identify and prioritize those sales and customer service programs likely to be most effective.

Big Money Investor Services, Inc.   *(Jersey City, NJ)*   1993
<u>Manager of Sales Administration</u>. Maintained database of customers and prospects on a distributed, relational database, called *Commence*, which I adapted to the Sales Department's needs, then overlaid commercially available data *(Sheshunoff)* on banking industry prospects. Prepared proposals, contracts, follow-up letters. Participated in design of sales materials.

Bronson, Hardig & Morris   *(Jersey City, NJ)*   1992
<u>Marketing Manager</u>. Organized and maintained database of prospective customers for this 30-person accounting firm, using sales automation software. Contacted prospects for sales presentations by firm's principals.

American Life, New Jersey Mutual, State Mutual   *(Jersey City, NJ)*   1992
Financial Insurance Services   *(Essex County, NJ)*   1989-91
<u>Insurance Agent/Investment Advisor/Certified Financial Planner</u>. Sold life/health insurance, annuities and mutual funds to individuals and small businesses. Used sales automation software *(Act!)* to facilitate efforts.

Magna-Empire, Inc.   *(Garden City, NJ)*   1988
<u>Sales & Purchasing Manager</u>. For this 125-person manufacturer of jet engine components, coordinated sales activities of two field representatives and purchase of over $3 million in Mil-spec parts.

Chadwick Associates   *(Brooklyn, NY)*   1982-87
<u>Sales Engineer</u>. Sold metalworking services for this manufacturer's representative, mostly to aerospace firms on Long Island.

Hy-Core, Inc.   *(Queens, NY)*   1981
<u>Sales & Marketing Manager</u>. Created a business plan for this foundry start-up, covering production, pricing, projected sales and marketing. Identified and then surveyed national market; rank-ordered and contacted prospects. Identified tooling costs as major barrier to sale; reduced those costs by 60% through CAD/CAM.

Magma Steel Corporation   *(Queens, NY)*   1978-81
<u>Marketing Manager</u>. Prepared marketing plan, designed and implemented computerized sales reporting system, developed econometrics forecasts, set up and ran competition between 8 advertising agencies and worked with successful agency to draw up and implement an advertising plan. <u>Sales Manager</u>, Bar Department. Supervised eight employees, including three field salespersons; sales rose 22% during my tenure. <u>Sales Manager</u>. Foundry Department. Represented five foundries of *Magma SA* in the U.S., identifying and calling on US customers in the nuclear, hydroelectric and pump industries.

GARY D. PETERSON

1531 Plymouth Way
Vancouver, Washington 98685
(360) 555-1212

BEFORE

EDUCATION

University of Nevada, 1976; Bachelor of Science in Business Administration, emphasis in Accounting

West State University. Entered MBA program September 1992. Aspiration currently on hold.

Hundreds of hours of specialized training in areas such as Management and Supervision, How to Work with People, Equal Employment Opportunity, Interviewing, Dealing with Unions, Leadership, Managing for Results, Leading a Diverse Workforce, Team Building. Attend University Research Administration Association (URAA) annual meetings and training sessions.

SPECIAL ACHIEVEMENT

Successfully completed CPA exam.

EXPERIENCE

August 1984-Present
Manager, Sponsored Projects Administration - Washington Health Science University
Responsible for the cash management and financial administration of $101 million, ($17 million when hired), which is 650 projects, (137 when hired), of grants and contracts from outside public and private sponsors; prepare external and internal reports; interpret various rules, regulations and guidelines applicable to each reward.

Responsible for 12 individuals, including 1 Manager. Despite tremendous growth, coupled with rapid changes which are inherent in this type of operation, have successfully kept staff morale to the point of that my average employee has been with me 8+ years.

The University has only incurred a cumulative $34.00 audit disallowance during my tenure. Identified $1,600,000 of annual indirect cost billings that had been overlooked. Oversee office budget. Member of multiple committees. Brought PC's into office and oversaw conversion. Assisted in the conversion from the State's General Ledger to an internal system (Oracle), and in the conversion from a State agency to a Public Corporation.

May 1983 - August 1984
President and Owner - Peterson Family Enterprises.
Developed and manufactured games and novelty items. Product development, engineering, manufacturing, art work, advertising, marketing and sales.

April 1979 - May 1983
Chief Accountant - Vancouver Wire and Iron Works/Central Products.
General ledger through financial statements, investment analysis, banking and cash management, leases and contracts, shareholder reports, fleet manager, insurance administration, credit and collections, review all payable vouchers, Profit Sharing Committee Chairman. Participated with all levels of management, including written and oral presentations.

GARY D. PETERSON   Page 2

EXPERIENCE (CONTINUED)

March 1976 - April 1979

<u>Accountant I & Auditor II</u> - State of Washington

Hired as an Accountant I for the Washington Department of Fish and Wildlife. Promoted to Auditor 2 with the Washington Department of Transportation, Fuels Tax Division. As an accountant, was responsible for the general journal, financial statements, budgets and internal auditing. Implemented/coordinated statewide financial reporting for the department, filed federal grant reimbursement forms. At the Fuels Tax Division, audited records of licensed motor fuel dealers, prepared audit reports, extensive travel, worked in client offices.

PROFESSIONAL ASSOCIATION

University Research Administration Association (URAA).

COMPUTER EXPERTISE

Extensive experience on PC's: Excel, Quattro Pro, paradox, WordPerfect, Oracle General Ledger system, Banner Payroll System, Netscape, Dos, Windows 3.1 and Windows 95. Hardware trouble shooting, repair and replacement.

HONORS AND ACTIVITIES

Earned four scholarships to assist with tuition. Dean's List. Worked full-time while a student.

PERSONAL

Married 1972; six children ages 8 through 18. Enjoy sports, working with hands, and competing in pure strategy board games.

GARY D. PETERSON

1531 Plymouth Way
Vancouver, Washington 98685

(360) 555-1212
garyp@anywhere.net

OBJECTIVE

A challenging financial management position in a progressive firm utilizing proven skills in team building, organizing and problem solving to assist a growing organization enhance its customer service and reputation while maximizing revenues and protecting assets.

QUALIFICATION AND BACKGROUND

- Managing
- Training
- Simplifying Procedures

- Communicating
- Grant Accounting
- Researching

- Coaching
- Listening
- Computers

ACHIEVEMENTS

Managed the administration of $100 million annually of grants and contracts, which assured timely and accurate reporting as well as compliance with appropriate regulatory requirements.

Established communication lines with M.D.'s, Ph.D.'s and staff which resulted in a 13 year, $34 audit disallowance while administering $772 million in projects (figures are cumulative).

Identified shortfall in indirect cost recovery policy, which resulted in a $1.6 million annual increase in indirect cost revenue.

Developed methods of leadership to build a cohesive team which resulted in a unique capability to absorb a 500% increase in workload with a 200% increase in staffing levels.

Evaluated the diverse needs of customers and staff which resulted in a significant reduction in client complaints while maintaining a long-term devoted staff.

Interpreted and **negotiated** conflicting rules and regulations with supervisor and staff, identified innovative solutions.

Promoted new concept which protected the organization from potential lawsuits concerning classified employees traveling on their own time.

Successfully completed the national CPA exam.

PROFESSIONAL EXPERIENCE

Manager, Sponsored Projects Administration

Washington Health Sciences University   1984 - Present

Managed the financial administration of $101 million annually ($17 million when hired) of grants and contracts from outside public and private sponsors; supervised 12 individuals, including one manager in multiple support services; controlled office budget; negotiated with principal investigators as necessary; developed departmental plans, set goals and deadlines; dismissed employees; formulated internal personnel policy; identified hostile researchers/sponsors and defused the situation; coordinated the members of multiple departments on various projects; interpreted rules and regulations applicable to each award; converted office to PCS; participated in the conversion of an internal accounting system (Oracle); contributed to the transformation from a State Agency to a Public Corporation.

General Manager

Peterson Family Enterprises   1983-1984

Developed and manufactured games and novelty items, product development, engineering, manufacturing, artwork, advertising, marketing, sales.

Chief Accountant

Vancouver Wire and Iron Works/Central Products   1979-1983

Oversaw the general ledger through financial statements; coordinated investment analysis; presided over banking and cash management; negotiated leases and contracts; prepared shareholder reports; managed the automotive fleet; administered insurance requirements; supervised credit collections; Chairman of the Profit Sharing committee.

Accountant I and Auditor II

State of Washington   1976-1979

Hired as an Accountant I for the Washington Department of Fish and Wildlife. Promoted to Auditor II with the Washington Department of Transportation, Fuels Tax Division. As an accountant, managed the general journal through financial statements; analyzed budgets; implemented/coordinated statewide financial reporting; internal auditor for the department. At the Fuels Tax Division, audited records of licensed motor fuel dealers; prepared audit reports; worked independently in client offices.

EDUCATION/ADVANCED TRAINING

(M.B.A.)	West State University	Portland, OR	(2000)
B.S. - Business	University of Nevada	Reno, NV	1976

AFFILIATIONS

University Research Administration Association (URAA)

Martha Ralston Miller
1234 Sunset Way, San Francisco, CA 91111
555-555-1212

BEFORE

EXPERIENCE	**The Charleton Grains Company, Foodservice Division, Chicago, IL**
June, 1990- September, 1997	*Assistant Marketing Manager*. April 1996 - September, 1997

- Developed and executed Foodservice operator and distributor marketing plans, programs, and promotional events for the Western Zone.
- Developed in-house creative production, market research, and direct mail capabilities and managed outside production of POS literature, premiums, and promotional items.
- Analyzed and quantified trends and opportunities to support marketing plan development, financially rationalized field programs, performed pricing and mix analysis, and assisted in the development of the marketing portion of the annual financial plan for the Foodservice Division. Created a new process for managing and tracking marketing development funds.

Financial/Planning Analyst: June, 1990 - March, 1996
- Responsible for the development of the annual financial plan for the Western Zone including sales forecasting and product mix and margin analysis. Participated in negotiation of final plan accountabilities with Eastern Zone and Food Service Division management.
- Developed standards and quarterly business review processes for the Western Zone and tracked performance versus plan in order to identify key issues and trends in support of management and logistics decision making.
- Monitored and tracked cost management savings and developed reporting and audit-trail processes to support internal financial and legal audit.
- Provided ad hoc cost/benefit financial analysis to Division management, Product Managers, Regional Sales Managers, and Field Marketing Managers.

Ad Hoc Project Management. 1992-1997.
- **Operator Chain Management Project:** conceptualized and developed a new process for managing chain account business which won Team Charleton and Charleton Golden Oat awards for outstanding achievement and developed the information technology that is its foundation. Led the team that implemented the new process nationwide in 1994.
- **Customer Payment/Pricing Project:** project leader for a team assigned to develop a new process for managing and controlling customer payments associated with chain account programs including financial rationalization of program rebates and pricing to Division plan margin targets.
- **Work Process Improvement and Database Development:** Developed new work processes and related custom software applications with user interfaces to : manage budgeting and tracking of market development funds; audit and control distributor spending; customize operator call reporting using a third-party database; manage a new distributor marketing fund allocation process; and automate monthly financial reporting for the field. These applications are all now used nation-wide by Field Sales, Marketing, and Finance.
- **Training and Development:** Developed computer skills training curriculum and materials and conducted training sessions in computer literacy, Windows, Excel, Word, e-mail, and Charleton mainframe programs for field laptop computer recipients.

September, 1983 - July, 1989	**Marston Communications, West Coast office, Palo Alto, California.**

Show Operations Manager: Exposition Division, 1988 - 1989. Managed the marketing, promotion and operations functions for 10 annual trade and consumer shows. Accountable for P&L performance of the portfolio.

Director of Human Resources, West Coast, 1985 - 1988. Managed all HR/Personnel activities including recruiting, training and development, employee relations, compensation, etc. Supervised the Administrative Services function and was accountable for all budget activities related to staffing, training, purchasing, and operations.

Administrative Services Manager, 1983 -1985. Managed personnel and office services activities including office equipment purchasing and maintenance, mailroom, liaison with building management, communications services, and in-house fulfillment activities. Accountable for developing and managing the departmental budget.

April - August, 1983

American Radio Service, Washington, D.C.

Consultant: Directed marketing and research activities for an adult education project involving a consortium of colleges and universities and public radio stations including the co-writing of a $2,000,000 grant proposal to the Broadcasting Corporation of America.

September, 1980-December, 1982

Sunnydale University, Sunnydale. Full-time student, Bachelor's Degree program.

August 1976 - June 1980

Bernadino Community College, Bernadino Valley, California.

Telecourse Development Associate: Coordinated projects related to development of college-level television courses for credit including curriculum research, course evaluation, writing funding proposals, and planning related national meetings.

EDUCATION

June, 1994

MBA, Marketing Emphasis. *University of the Nation, San Jose, California.* Graduated With Distinction.

August, 1989-May, 1990

Juris Doctor. *Western University, College of Law, Santa Barbara, California.* Completed first year courses: Contracts, Torts, Property, Civil Procedure, and Legal Writing.

April, 1988

BBA, Human Resources Emphasis. *University of the Nation, San Jose, California.* Graduated Magna Cum Laude.

TECHNICAL SKILLS:

- Advanced project management and work process re-engineering skills including team leadership, critical path analysis, process mapping, stakeholder consensus building, and management presentation.
- Advanced information management expertise, particularly decision support systems and relational database design and application.
- Advanced user of Microsoft Access, Excel, PowerPoint, Word, and Project and various custom mainframe applications used by Miller.
- Skilled user of e-mail and Internet services.

MARTHA MILLER

AFTER

1234 Sunset Way
San Francisco, CA 91111

(555) 555-1212
email: martham@anywhere.net

OBJECTIVE

An organizational development position for a company that is changing functions and processes to meet competitive challenges in its marketplace.

QUALIFICATIONS

More than fourteen years experience creating and developing job functions and processes to improve organizational performance and profit. Demonstrated proficiency in project leadership, change management and process implementation.

RELATED SKILLS

- Broad business function knowledge
- Team building and leadership
- Training and staff development
- Project management

- Human resources management
- Process innovation and improvement
- Performance measurement
- Program development and implementation

TECHNICAL SKILLS

Advanced user of Microsoft spreadsheet, project, word processing, presentation and Internet software. Advanced database design and development skills with MS Access.

KEY ACCOMPLISHMENTS

Charleton Grains Company
- **Created** and **developed** new sales, marketing and finance job functions and related processes and technology resulting in improved analysis, performance tracking and strategic decision making.
- **Proposed** and **led** a series of projects to re-engineer the processes for managing and controlling customer-related sales and marketing programs. The cumulative impact from improved strategic management and elimination of program abuses and poor financial controls was $1 million annually.
- **Designed** and **managed** training programs for the implementation phase of a re-engineering projects resulting in successful national roll-out of the new processes and technology.

Marston Communications
- **Developed** a full-service human resources organization that reduced turnover, improved performance planning and development of internal human resources and reduced legal exposure resulting from poor employment practices.
- **Restructured** and **streamlined** the administrative services function supporting two company divisions that reduced the cost of administrative overhead by 25%.
- **Restaffed** and **restructured** the show operations function after a mass resignation and led the new team in the production of ten trade and consumer shows, which were produced on time and within budget.

EXPERIENCE

Project Manager	The Charleton Grains Company	1992 - 1997
Assistant Marketing Manager	The Charleton Grains Company	1996 - 1997
Financial/Planning Analyst	The Charleton Grains Company	1990 - 1995
Director for Show Services	Marston Communications	1988 - 1989
Director of Human Resources	Marston Communications	1985 - 1988
Administrative Services Manager	Marston Communications	1983 - 1985

EDUCATION

MBA - Marketing Emphasis	University of the Nation	San Jose, CA
BA - Human Resource Emphasis	University of the Nation	San Jose, CA
Juris Doctor	Western University College of Law	Santa Barbara, CA

BEFORE

STEVEN R. JACKSON, JD, MBA
3140 SW Door Road
Salt Lake City, UT 93359
405-555-1212

SUMMARY STATEMENT

I have a combination of legal and financial experience including ten years in law as a transaction negotiator and business attorney, four years in finance as a business appraisal expert, and three years as a mediator and arbitrator.

FINANCIAL EXPERIENCE

- **BUSINESS APPRAISAL** - Four years of experience appraising closely-held corporations and intangible assets for companies with equity ranging from $100,000 to $50,000,000.

  - Appraisals performed in variety of industries including: professional practices, retail clothing, trucking, automobile parts retailing, equipment leasing, garbage collection, manufacturing, steel and rubber industries, hard rock minerals, oil & gas, natural resources.

  - Expert witness testimony offered before the Utah Department of Revenue and civil divorce courts concerning business valuation issues.

- **DAMAGE ASSESSMENTS** - Financial analysis and research for damage assessment of the Universal Tanker Express oil spill, including the development of database using 10,000 inter-related pieces of information and financial calculations to evaluate $300 million in claimed damages.

- **BUDGETING/FINANCIAL ANALYSIS** - Developed annual operating budgets and five year plans for companies earning $10-$20 million per year. Designed, modeled, and administered a corporate overhead cost allocation program for Fortune 500 company, resulting in better profitability analysis and restructuring of job functions to the subsidiary level.

LEGAL EXPERIENCE

- **NEGOTIATION** - Ten years of experience in contract negotiation for a Fortune 500 corporation.

  - Drafted and negotiated over $500 million in financing facilities with 20 major financial institutions like New York Mutual, American Data Exchange, Flocassa, & Carmichael, Inc. The arrangements allowed the company to avoid approximately $2 million in interest expense.

  - Negotiated hundreds of business transactions in a wide variety of areas including more than $20 million in engineering and construction contracts, $5 million in office leasing, $10 million in real estate transactions, $10 million in joint venture agreements, $750,000 in loan workouts, and a variety of equipment leases, joint operating agreements, and royalties.

  - Successfully negotiated a variety of major contract disputes which directly resulted in more than $4 million improved profit.

STEVEN R. JACKSON
3140 SW Door Road
Salt Lake City, UT 93359
405-555-1212

- **LEGAL ADMINISTRATION**

  - Designed and implemented a company wide contract system covering the acquisition of more than $50 million of goods and services annually from 500 contractors in four states. The system included computerized monitoring of contractual data and performance. Indemnity shifting provisions allowed the company to avoid about $5 million in damages.

  - Worked with Risk Management Department to review insurance coverage in due diligence review of $500 million acquisition candidates. Managed program to enforce insurance coverage provided by outside contractors.

  - Managed the liquidation and buy-out of five publicly held and financially distressed limited partnerships. Program was accomplished without incurring any legal consequences from the 600 limited partners, reduced overhead by over 5,000 hours per year, and cleared title to properties.

  - Designed internal procedure and computerized system to manage 30-40 active lawsuits, directed outside counsel, and acted as an intermediary to Risk Management department.

- **MEDIATION & ARBITRATION -** Three years of experience mediating and arbitrating disputes on a variety of matters including debt collection, breach of contract, warranty, real estate transactions, business transactions, and consumer law. Conducted more than 140 mediations and 35 arbitrations.

EDUCATION

- **MASTERS OF BUSINESS ADMINISTRATION**
  - University of California
  - California Executive MBA

- **JURIS DOCTORATE**
  - University of Oregon School of Law
  - Top 20% of Class

- **BACHELORS OF SCIENCE IN FINANCE**
  - University of Utah
  - Top 10% of Class

ORGANIZATIONS

- California Bar Association, Membership number 3142
- Cyranda Bar Association - Alternative Dispute Resolution Committee
- California Mediation Association

STEVEN R. JACKSON

3140 S.W. Door Road
Salt Lake City, UT 93359   **(405) 555-1212**

OBJECTIVE

A member of a strategic planning team using proven skills in legal and financial analysis, organization and negotiation to solve complex business problems for a values-driven organization.

QUALIFICATIONS AND BACKGROUND

Eighteen years of progressively increasing responsibility and expertise in:

Appraising Businesses	Negotiating	Planning
Problem solving	Organizing	Analysis

ACHIEVEMENTS

Organized a calculation of damages caused by the Universal Tanker Express for the North America Pipeline Liability Fund which resulted in awards of $40 million on over $450 million in claims.

Negotiated $500 million of trading lines for a commodities producer which protected them from market fluctuations and saved $2 million in interest.

Planned and **implemented** a standardized contract system for a Fortune 500 company resulting in the purchase of over $50 million in goods and services annually.

Conceptualized and **negotiated** a buy-out program to eliminate the legal liability created by 500 individual minority working interest holders for an oil and gas company which saved about $1 million in reduced administrative time and potential litigation costs.

Analyzed the financial impact of a buy out provision in the sales contract of plastics manufacturer for the attorneys representing the seller. The $5.4 million value of the provision brought the estimated total sales price to $32.5 million.

Appraised a steel manufacturing facility for property tax hearing; the taxpayer received a refund of $1.8 million in past property taxes.

JACKSON   **Page Two**

PROFESSIONAL EXPERIENCE

Self-Employed
Business Valuation   1991 - Present
Research and appraisal of businesses and business interest; expert testimony; project management; report writing; marketing; client consultation. Clients include the North America Pipeline Liability Fund, Sugar Sweet Corporation, Panzer Steel, Superseek, California Steel Corporation, Sweet Roll-Ups.

Contract Compliance Administrator
STENI Oil & Gas, Inc.   1990 - 1991
Managed company contracts; reviewed and negotiated sales, transportation, construction, land purchases and sales, joint operating agreements and other contracts; supervised insurance documentation; conducted due diligence reviews; monitored outside litigation.

Director of Legal Services
STENI Minerals Company   1986 - 1990
Reviewed and negotiated company contracts prior to execution; coordinated with outside counsel on conflicts and litigation; managed relationships with gold brokers/dealers, royalty holders, joint venture partners; performed other projects as assigned.

EDUCATION

Juris Doctorate   University of Oregon
Master of Business Administration   University of California
Bachelor of Science - Finance   University of Utah

AFFILIATIONS

California State Bar Association
Cyranda Bar Association
Alternative Dispute Resolution Committee

Sandra Flowers

631 Eastern St.   phone: (718) 555-7777
Portsmouth, NY 56321   Email: sflowers@anywhere.net

CAREER OBJECTIVE

After two years of post-doctoral research, (studying antimicrobial proteins at surfaces), I am now looking for a research and development position in the food industry.

DEGREES

B.S.   Zoology, New York State University
B.S.   Medical Technology, New York Health Sciences University
Ph.D. Food Science and Technology, New York State University

PREVIOUS EMPLOYMENT

Peace Corps, Med. Tech	Bermuda	1985 - 1987
Medical Technologist	Astoria, NY	1987 - 1989
Medical Technologists	Albany, NY	1989 - 1990
Graduate Research Asst.,	Albany, NY	1991 - 1994
Post-Doc Research Assoc.,	Albany, NY	1998 - 1997

PROFESSIONAL MEMBERSHIPS

Institute of Nutrition Technologists (INT)
Association of Enology and Viticulture (AEV)

SCHOLARSHIPS / AWARDS:

AEV Scholarship, 1991/1992
Brontaid Company Outstanding Graduate Student Scholarship, 1991/1992
The Honor Society of Phi Kappa Rho, 1992
Beta Sigma Honor Society of Agriculture, 1992
INT Certificate of Merit, 1992/1993
New York Sports Lottery Scholarship, 1993/1994
Registry of Distinguished Students, New York State University, 1995

PUBLICATIONS

Flowers, S.F., B.T. Miller, and M.A. Sandler. 1992. Applications of baceriocins in controlling bacterial spoilage and malolactic fermentation of beer. Proceedings 3rd Intl. Symp. Innovations in Brewing Technology. Deutscher Beirbauverband, Neustrasse 6, D-5300 Mainz. May 25-27. Frankfurt. P. 102-109.

Flowers, S.F., J. Peters, and M.A. Sandler. 1995. Suppression of *Listeria monocytogenes* colonization following adsorption of nisin onto silica surfaces. Appl. Natural Microbiol. 61: 992-997.

Flowers, S.F., J. Peters, and M.A. Sandler. 1995. Influences on the antimicrobacterial activity of surface-adsorbed nisin. J. Ind. Microbacter., 15: 227-233.

Flowers, S.F., J. Peters, and M. Sandler. 1996. The adhesion and detachment of bacteria and spores on food contact surfaces. Food Bacterial Trends Technol. 7: 152-157.

Flowers, S.F., M. Likinara, J. Peters, and M. Sandler. 1996. Nisin adsorption, exchange, and antimicrobacterial activity at interfaces. In Proceedings of the 3rd AFECH Conference on Food Engineering, G. Narsimhan and S. Lombardo (eds.), Cornell University, New York, pages 16-19.

Flowers, S.F., M.A. Sandler, and J. Peters. Antimicrobacterial barriers to microbial adhesion. F. Seut Sci. In Press.

Flowers, S.F., Q. Chu, and J. Peters. Activity losses among T3 lysozyme variants after adsorption to silica nanoparticles. Biomed. Biotech. In Press.

SANDRA FLOWERS

AFTER

631 Eastern Street
Portsmouth, NY 56321

(718) 555-7777
email: sflowers@anywhere.net

OBJECTIVE

A challenging leadership opportunity in research using my demonstrated skills in analytical problem solving, investigating and writing to contribute to an organization's success.

QUALIFICATIONS

Seven years of progressively increasing responsibility and expertise in:

- Conducting Research
- Writing Manuscripts

- Solving Problems
- Group Presentations

- Managing Laboratories
- Supervising Technicians

ACHIEVEMENTS

Researched and **prepared** seven original manuscripts for publication.
Evaluated and **edited** grant proposals, manuscripts and dissertations.
Maintained and **upgraded** lab computers (Macintosh, Windows and DOS platforms).
Skilled with numerous word processing, spreadsheet and graphics programs.

EXPERIENCE

Post Doctoral Research Associate

New York State University   *Albany, NY*   *1995 - 1997*

Conducted research, interpreted data and prepared manuscripts for publication. Managed active laboratory, supervised seven personnel and presented seminars.

Graduate Research Assistant

New York State University   *Albany, NY*   *1991 - 1994*

Conducted research, interpreted data, edited dissertations, presented seminars and prepared manuscripts. Maintained computers and laboratory equipment.

Medical Technologist

Good Samaritan Hospital   *Albany, NY*   *1989 - 1990*

Worked alone (night shift) in a busy hospital laboratory. Analyzed emergency specimens and handled all laboratory duties, including equipment maintenance and quality control.

EDUCATION

Ph.D.	Food Science and Technology	New York State University	Albany, NY
B.S.	Medical Technology	New York Health Sciences University	Astoria, NY
B.S.	Zoology	New York State University	Albany, NY

PROFESSIONAL MEMBERSHIPS

Institute of Nutrition Technologists (INT)
American Society of Nature and Viticulture (ANEV)

BEFORE

Charles G. Phillips
1852 Chutney Road   *(937) 555-1212*
Beaver, PA 56432   *(937) 555-1234*

Background: 41 year old retired Air Force officer.
               Married and have one son, Spencer (13).
               Active in the Beaver community, Boy Scouts of America, and
               St. Peter's Orthodox Church

Objective: A middle level or senior level management position in a security
               related field within the Beaver, Pittsburgh, or Philadelphia area.

Experience: Seventeen years of experience in a multifaceted security environment
               with increasing responsibility and documented success in the United
               States Air Force.

Education: West Virginia University   Wheeling, WV
               Forensic Studies   1978

               Central State University   Baldwin AFB, PA
               Masters in Administration   1998

WORK EXPERIENCE:

June 1993 – June 1995	Chief, B-2 Security Management Division
July 1992 – June 1993	System Security Engineering Manager
June 1990 – July 1992	Director, Space Systems Security Engineering Management
January 1988 – June 1990	System Security Engineer and Acquisition Plans Manager
October 1985 – January 1988	Chief of Security Police
February 1984 – October 1985	Squadron Section Commander
June 1983 – February 1984	Security Staff Officer
October 1982 – June 1983	Director, Security Police Operations
January 1979 – October 1982	Shift Supervisor

Charles G. Phillips

1852 Chutney Road, Beaver, PA 56432 • (937) 555-1212

OBJECTIVE   Operations Management

Lead a team of operations support professionals to develop and implement strategic plans, improve process flows, and enhance revenues – utilizing proven abilities to:

- Work with diverse groups of people to assess individual strengths, listen closely to innovative recommendations, and encourage open team communications.
- Identify problem areas, seek out expert advice, develop alternative solutions, follow-up implementation efforts and deliver results above expectations.

QUALIFICATIONS

- Team Building
- Process Improvement
- Project Management
- Policy/Procedures Development

- Consulting Expertise
- Strategic Planning
- Problem Solving/Innovation
- Interpersonal Communications

SELECTED ACHIEVEMENTS

Created new security discipline applied to an engineering process. Reviewed physical, personnel, electronic, industrial, and computer issues related to manufacturing. The process became an effective model, which was emulated throughout the Department of Defense.

Developed policy and planned a major public relations effort to manage crowds of 700,000. Coordinated with local, state, and government officials for 200 additional personnel and equipment to support this three day event. Widespread public approval was a key success factor and the event came off without incident.

Reorganized security office responsible for 300 people, five manufacturing plants, and over $900 million in equipment. Identified staffing shortfalls, developed new mission statement, and created implementation plan. This model system saved $25 million over a two year period.

Organized junior high athletic competition involving 12 schools, 75 student athletes, 20 parents, and city facilities. Developed implementation schedule, established deadlines, and ensured each event was properly staffed. Program was a tremendous boost for the school's public image, and the athletic department raised additional revenues.

Managed five individuals responsible for 120 employees, and $2 billion of resources. Initiated incentive programs which improved morale, and increased productivity. Instilled a high degree of professionalism which led to winning a quarterly achievement award ten times in four years.

Charles G. Phillips   Page 2

EXPERIENCE

Director, Security Management Division, BAFB, Baldwin, Pennsylvania 1993 – 1995

Manager, System Security Engineering, BAFB, Baldwin, Pennsylvania 1992 – 1993

Director, Space Systems Security Engineering Management, **Lenning AFB,** Chilton, KY 1990 – 1992

System Security Engineer and Acquisition Plans Manager, **Lenning AFB,** Chilton, KY 1988 – 1990

Chief of Security Police, **Main AB,** Germany 1985 – 1988

EDUCATION

MS *Administration*, Central State University, BAFB, Baldwin, Pennsylvania 1998

BA *Forensic Studies*, West Virginia University, Wheeling, West Virginia 1978

Pierre Devereaux
2105 Grant Street
Oak Park, IL
(618) 555-1212

BEFORE

OBJECTIVE: A career with an architectural firm where my broad experience in drafting and design can be utilized.

EDUCATION: **PARIS ARCHITECTURAL COLLEGE**
1972-1978   Paris, France
Six years professional degree program. BA in Architecture

1993   **AMERICAN DESIGN CENTER, INC.**
Chicago, Illinois
Computer Aided Design Arid Drafting, using AutoCAD, Release 12

EXPERIENCE: **ROGER LLOYD ASSOCIATES**
1995   Architectural Light & Design, 105 Park St. West
Beverly, CA 90124
Position: Architect
Duties included production and supervision of architectural drawings from design concept through design production and supervision of construction. Selected projects:
   Luxury Sunset Apartments, Los Angeles, CA
   Tiffany & Co, Beverly Hills, CA
   Smithly's Auction, Beverly Hills, CA
   Oasis Night Club, Beverly Hills, CA

1992-1994   **HENDERSON & CHAN ARCHITECTS, P.C.**
5341 Broadway, Beverly Hills, CA 90210
Position: Architect
Selected projects:
Winston residence in San Diego, CA
   Lebanese Congregation Synagogue, Los Angeles, CA
   Apartment Building, Prince Ave, Beverly Hills, CA
   Four Apartment Buildings, Palace Beach, Plato, CA

1985-1991   **STATE HEALTH PLANNING COMMISSION**
Paris. Project Architect of a Hospital of 600 beds in Romania and several Sanatoriums

1978-1985   **PARIS PLANNING COMMISSION**
Designer for Olympic Equestrian Sports Base in Paris two residential complexes of 16 and 25 stories respectively each containing 1,000 units, two recreational hotels in Chardonne near Paris, and a film and concert hall of 2,500 seats in Ardentes

REFERENCES   Available upon request

Pierre Devereaux   B.A. (Architecture)

2105 Grant Street, Oak Park, IL

`AFTER`

<u>**OBJECTIVE**</u>: **ARCHITECTURE—INTERIOR, EXTERIOR**

To Support or Manage Projects by providing creative input and contributing proven abilities to:

- **Exceed Organization Objectives and Deadlines** by managing special projects, coordinating teams, managing multiple operations, and developing innovative ideas and strategies.
- **Improve Programs, Procedures and Reporting Formats** through highly effective planning and organizational skills, and developing and coordinating highly organized systems and procedures.
- **Clearly Define Customer Needs** by developing informational resources, perceptively evaluating input, creating visualizations and concepts, and decisively responding to critical situations.

<u>**QUALIFICATIONS**</u>:

An **Innovative, Competent, Professional,** known for his ability to be focused on the details of a project to realize the vision, with skills encompassing:

• Creation / Innovation	• Learning Quickly / Adaptable	• Problem Solving Troubleshooting
• Project Management	• Supervising / Motivating	• Self Direction
• Organizing/Coordinating	• Investigate / Analyze / Implement	• Handling Critical Unexpected

<u>**ACHIEVEMENTS**</u>:

DESIGNED EXTRAORDINARY PRESENTATIONS using "Old Fashioned Techniques" such as watercolors, acrylic and built models and also incorporated "New Techniques" utilizing various computer applications.

BECAME THE YOUNGEST REGISTERED ARCHITECT at **age 25,** in the Society of French Architects (an organization of **5,000**) after completing **8** projects.

SUPERVISED CREW OF **25** at **age 28,** as project manager in charge of **multiple** projects. Coordinated crew actions including: contact the client, design concept, design production, and supervision of construction.

"BEAT ALL ODDS" by being accepted to college at age **16** as a result of having **perfect grades** in high school, and getting **straight A's on** a 6 part college admission test taking over 1 month to complete.

STARTED WORKING WITHIN **2** WEEKS after arriving in the United States with a full service architectural **firm** specializing in the areas of residential and commercial.

EXCEEDED MINIMUM REQUIREMENTS while in college by entering over **20** local and international shows and competitions, always placing, including **5** first places.

STARTED OWN FULL SERVICE FIRM IN FRANCE at age **33,** employing up to **40** people with billings in excess of **$.5MM;** paying employees more than the normal rate due to high quality projects.

<u>**PROFESSIONAL EXPERIENCE:**</u>

Exemplary and Honored Background in both a **Commercial** and **Residential Environment,** gained in successful positions as: <u>**Architect, Project Architect**</u> (meet with customers, contractors, supervise construction); design; drawing/illustrating; interior design. Firms include: King, Corbis, & Schaeffer Inc., (Segal, Utah); Roger Lloyd Associates (California),Henderson & Chan Architects (California); State Planning Commission (Paris); Paris Planning Commission (Paris); Self Employed (Paris, California, Illinois)

Additional Training: American Design Center (Auto CAD); California Real Estate Institute (California Real Estate License)

Pierre Devereaux   **B.A. (Architecture)**

SELECTED PROJECTS ADDENDUM

- Christ Lutheran Church, Chicago, IL
- National Bank/Renovation, Chicago, IL
- Oak Co., Board of Mental Retardation, ECFC, Park Heights, IL
- United Methodist Church, Oak Park, IL
- River Park High School, River Park, IL
- Luxury Sunset Apartments, Los Angeles, CA
- Tiffany & Company, Beverly Hills, CA
- Smithly's Auction, Beverly Hills, CA
- Oasis Night Club, Beverly Hills, CA
- Lebanese Congregation Synagogue, Los Angeles, CA
- Winston Residence, San Diego, CA
- Four Apartment Buildings, Palace Beach, Beverly Hills, CA
- Many Small Restaurants, Beverly Hills, CA
- 600 Bed Hospital, Paris
- Several Sanatoriums, Paris
- Designer for Olympic Equestrian Sports Base in Paris
- Two residential complexes of 16 and 25 stories respectively, each containing 1,000 units, Paris
- Two Recreational Hotels, Paris
- Film and Concert Hall, 2,500 Seats, Ardentes

SKILLS ADDENDUM

- Residential
- Commercial
- Customer Service
- Meeting with Clients
- Interior Design
- Exterior Design
- Construction Supervision
- Landscape
- Metric and English
- Project Management
- Illustrating / Drawing & Rendering
- Working & Shop Drawings

- AutoCad
- Oil
- Pencil
- Ink
- Tempera
- Acrylic
- Plans
- Elevations
- Sections
- Details
- Models

11

HALDANE'S BEST RESUMES

The following resume examples come from the files of Haldane's clients. They represent clients who have already completed several steps in their Haldane career management program. These clients have already transformed their original resumes or created a new resume. Each resume follows the many Haldane principles outlined in this book.

While many of our clients have strong management and sales backgrounds, others represent a variety of different occupational fields. We've selected resumes that represent the diverse occupational backgrounds and experience levels of our clients. Most of our clients have several years of professional experience and seek executive-level positions in their respective occupational fields.

As you examine the resumes in this chapter, please do so from the perspective of the employer. Ask yourself questions employers might ask about a candidate. For example, does this resume clearly communicate what the individual wants to do? Does it give you a strong sense of what the person has accomplished in the past and might most likely accomplish for you in the future? Does it motivate you to want to invite the individual for a job interview and ask questions relating to the resume?

Our resume formats vary depending on the client and the particular Career Advisor. All share one thing in common—a clear focus on goals and accomplishments. Haldane's best resumes speak the language of employers who seek individuals who can add value to their operations. Whatever you do, make sure your resume speaks this language loudly and clearly!

Several of the following resumes are produced in a smaller type size than we recommend. The type size has been intentionally decreased to fit the margins of this book, while still producing a realistic layout for the resumes.

As with the preceding chapter, all names, addresses, and employers have been changed to protect the confidentiality of our clients. Any resemblance to real persons or organizations is purely coincidental.

THOMAS JAMESON   M.S. (Personnel/Counseling), B.A. (Psychology)

222 Park Street, Charlottesville, VA 22191   **(540) 555-1212**

<u>**OBJECTIVE:**</u>   **CAREER MANAGEMENT/JOB SEARCH CONSULTING**

To Counsel/Advise Clients and Manage Career Development Processes and Programs at a growth oriented organization by contributing proven ability to:

* **Maximize Employee Potential/Effectiveness** by Establishing Strong Rapport/Trust, Perceptively Identifying and Analyzing Talent and Recommending Sound Career Decisions.

* **Provide Strong Team Support** by continually Encouraging Positive Attitudes, Openly Communicating/ Interacting and Developing Training/Motivational Programs.

* **Teach/Motivate/Empower Clients** in need of Recareering by Developing Career Marketing Strategies in Identifying and Targeting Markets and Focusing on Employer Needs and Wants.

<u>**QUALIFICATIONS:**</u>   A personable, energetic and multi-dimensional professional with career development and marketing skills offering over 25 years experience encompassing:

* Strategic Career Marketing
* Teaching/Training/Motivating
* Career/Occupational Advising

* Effective Interviewing Techniques
* Planning/Organizing/Implementing
* Written/Verbal Communication

* Consulting/Facilitating/Empowering
* Strong Interpersonal Rapport
* Learning Quickly/Adapting

<u>**ACHIEVEMENTS:**</u>

COUNSELED DIVERSIFIED STUDENT/ADULT LEARNERS over **18** years by identifying and resolving college preparation and career choice issues, **meeting** annual **placement needs** for **600+** graduates from **25** occupational/ transfer programs.

RECOGNIZED AS **"BEST IN THE NATION"** FOR 2 CONSECUTIVE YEARS among **175** career advisors by exhibiting **overall** performance in **leadership** and supervision of strategic marketing/career search campaigns for **75** new clients within **24** months in new position.

EXPANDED EXISTING PLACEMENT PROGRAM at Community College by planning and implementing recruitment fairs for potential graduates and **2000+** alumni from 3 academic divisions, effectively **marketing students** to **45 employers** each year while **increasing participation 20%** at same time.

DEMONSTRATED EXCEPTIONAL ABILITY TO LEARN QUICKLY by completing a **12**-month counselor/advisor training program in **3** months, assuming a caseload of over **100** clients with **zero turnover**.

IMPLEMENTED/TAUGHT JOB SEARCH CURRICULUM for Dislocated Worker program, piloted recareering project for dislocated employees. <u>**Results:**</u> Served and **taught 50** clients in **10** weeks on effective skill identification, job interview preparation, resume formats and job search techniques.

ADMINISTERED ON-CAMPUS/WORK STUDY EMPLOYMENT PROGRAM for over **250** student employees, successfully matching student interests/skills with departmental needs while **monitoring** the **expenditure** of **$200K+** in federal and college **funds** to **prevent over-spending**.

SURVEYED/ANALYZED/WROTE GRADUATE FOLLOW-UP STUDY on an annual basis of over **650** former occupational and transfer students, satisfying the **completion** of yearly **State reports** and internal reporting requirements with follow-up rate in excess of **95%**.

CO-CHAIRED ANNUAL COMMUNITY FUNDRAISER for **5** consecutive years in the planning and coordination of over **20** committees and **400** volunteers, **raising** over **$80K** during that time in a congregation of **5500** members.

<u>**PROFESSIONAL EXPERIENCE:**</u>

Excellent Background in **Career Management** and **Consultation** developed over **25** years in successful positions as: <u>**Senior Career Advisor**</u>, Bernard Haldane Associates, Inc.; <u>**Job Counselor/Workshop Trainer**</u>, Essex County Dislocated Worker program; <u>**Placement Officer**</u>, Essex County Community College; <u>**Vocational/Employment Counselor**</u>, Virginia Bureau of Employment Services.

NANCY R. TYSON   M.A. (Communications & Religious Studies)
                                        B.A. (English/Philosophy)

1800 East 15th Street, Apt. #1502, Washington, DC 20036   (202) 555-1212

OBJECTIVE: ADMINISTRATIVE SUPPORT/SERVICE MANAGEMENT

To Provide Strong Support/Service Expertise Which Maximizes the Efficiency of Administrative and Operational functions by contributing proven ability to:

* **Build Administration and Team Productivity/Morale** by Continually Encouraging Positive Attitudes, Openly and Influentially Communicating/Interacting, Developing Training, Motivational and Leadership Programs.

* **Meet Administration Goals/Objectives/Deadlines** by Independently Managing Special Projects, Organizing Multiple Tasks Operations and Providing Liaison Team and Leadership Coordination.

* **Improve Productivity/Processing Efficiency** by Developing and Coordinating Highly Organized Systems/ Procedures/Team and Leadership Efforts.

QUALIFICATIONS: A dependable and detailed administrative professional offering over 14 years progressive experience with a reputation for:

- Planning/Organizing/Implementing
- Research/Evaluation/Focus
- Leading/Coordinating/Delegating
- Staff Management/Development
- Analyzing/Prioritizing/Completion
- Developing Systems/Procedures
- Organization/Team Support
- Supervising/Motivational Staff
- Strong Interpersonal Rapport

ACHIEVEMENTS:

DESIGNED/WROTE/PUBLISHED MONTHLY NEWSLETTER promoting opportunities of service and action, resulting in a **40% increase** of active **involvement** from an audience of **5000** potential participants.

COMMUNICATED NEW IDEAS/CONCEPTS through effective speaking, attention-getting and participating techniques, providing a **75% increase** of audience **knowledge, awareness** and **understanding** of intricate and perplexing issues.

IMPROVED DEPARTMENT/FACILITY EFFICIENCY by **50%** through evaluation and renovation, providing invigorated perspectives, over-views and multi-functional operations of a **$1.5MM** facility **serving 800 students daily**.

SUCCESSFULLY INITIATED/DESIGNED/IMPLEMENTED a thorough system of self-evaluation by providing a foundation and process for personal growth, self-awareness and productivity, **increasing** student **performance levels 30%** and promoting harmony among faculty, staff, administration and students.

PROMOTED/COORDINATED STUDENT OUT-REACH PROGRAM involving over **900** students from 6 different disciplinary programs, providing "hands-on" experience in **handling daily crisis** while reaching over **1500** families in a 3-county area.

ANALYZED/COMPUTED/PRESENTED COST ANALYSIS for **$800K** budget detailing operational expenditures and maintenance requirements for a **75-100** seat faculty lounge. **Result:** Facility opened **ahead** of schedule and **under budget by 8%**.

PARTICIPATED/CONTRIBUTED TO A SUCCESSFUL CAPITAL CAMPAIGN in the building and construction of a **$10MM** campus library facility, **enlarging** pool of prospective donors by **50%** over a **24**-month period.

PLANNED/ORGANIZED/IMPLEMENTED MAJOR CONFERENCE on self-actualization issues of team leadership, executive communication and personal empowerment, **accommodating** over **900** participants in a 3-day program for **3 consecutive years**.

PROFESSIONAL EXPERIENCE:

Excellent background in **Communications** and **Public Relations Management** developed over **15** years in successful leadership positions as: **Associate Professor of Speech, Theater and Communications; Executive Administrative Assistant to President, Provost and Vice-President; Associate Dean of Students; Director of Theater Arts, Special Services and Functions; Stage Manager/Director of Publicity**, American City College; **Associate Administrator**, District Parish, District Heights, MD, and St. Francis Parish, Capital Heights, MD; **Executive Director**, Washington National Religious Conference.

BARRY A. MITCHELL

1234 Riverwoods Drive
Savannah, Georgia 56321
(404) 555-1212

OBJECTIVE

Health Care Facilities Director position encompassing the administration of multi-site operations; personnel training and staff development programs; and organization providing retirement living with continuing care capability.

BACKGROUND SUMMARY

Over 20 years experience developing expertise in:

- Training
- Recruiting
- Team Building

- Strategic Forecasting
- Financial Management
- Geriatric Assisted Living

- Events Planning
- Customer Service
- For Profit Operations

- State HRS & Federal OBRA Regulations

ACHIEVEMENTS

- Instituted first managed rehabilitation operation in Georgia at Sunset Towers to complement different levels of assisted care including: adult day care services, a geriatric fitness center, and a home care agency.

- Developed a program to assist life care residents who had depleted their funds. By enrolling them in a Medicaid program Sunset Towers was able to relieve their financial obligation while ensuring them continued quality care.

- Effected cash flow turnaround, increased annual revenues form $6.5 million to $14.5 million while increasing customer satisfaction and quality of life benefits for a multi unit retirement facility.

- Chaired a Political Action Committee to assist nursing home administrators lobby representatives and senators to enact nursing home legislation.

- Managed all club operations at Garrison Creek Golf & Country Club the year prior to, and during the 1984, GGA Championship tour event.

EXPERIENCE

SUNSET TOWERS, Savannah, GA   1986 - Present
Executive Director
Manage the activities of this 596 unit retirement community which includes a 150-bed skilled nursing facility. Control an operational budget of $13 million. Establish standards of service to customer while increasing revenues and profits. Supervise a professional staff of 315 employees.

CARMEL'S MANAGEMENT SERVICES, Pasadena, FL   1977 - 1986
Food Service Director
Began employment as a steward. Progressed to area and traveling manager, eventually managed all aspects of contract food services including specialty, hospitality, country club, and health care. Developed policy and procedures manuals for the retirement facilities food service accounts.

EDUCATION

BS, Food Service, The Culinary Institute, Atlanta, Georgia   1974

AFFILIATIONS

The Goodman Association
Georgia Health Care Association
All Saint's Hospital Committee

KEITH CARBON
5632 Cochran Street
West Valley, MA 63542
(517) 555-1212

OBJECTIVE

Communication Instructor/Trainer position involving creating presentations; leading seminars/workshops; writing speeches; and preparing individuals for public speaking engagements for a proprietary seminar or management consulting firm.

BACKGROUND SUMMARY

Over four years experience developing expertise in:

- Training
- Speech Writing
- Public Speaking
- Coaching
- Classroom Instruction
- Proposal Writing
- Creating and Leading Seminars

ACHIEVEMENTS

- Led seminars and workshops on interpersonal skills, multi-cultural relationships, and business communications for Public Speaking, Inc., Pasadena, FL.
- Coached CEOs, television anchors, sales reps, physicians, attorneys, and NFL football player on the art of speaking in front of groups and cameras.
- Created presentations and wrote speeches as both a member and instructor of university speech and debate teams.
- Received national recognition for competitive speaking.

EXPERIENCE

Public Speaking, Inc.   Pasadena, FL
Communications Consultant   1995 - 1996
Created and led training seminars; developed organizational proposals; and instructed/coached/prepared individuals for public speaking engagements.

EDUCATION

Tallahassee University   Tallahassee, FL
Speech Communication Instructor   1994 - 1995
Taught speech courses; evaluated and graded students' speeches, organized and developed lesson plans; presented speeches to be used as references.
Speech and Debate Coach
Organized speech tournaments; constructed competitive speeches and coached speech team members; budgeted for and reported expenditures.

Numerous Restaurants (from deli to fine dining)   1985 - 1994
Bartender/Food Server/Shift Supervisor/New Employee Trainer
Sold and served food and beverages; developed employee work schedules, trained new employees; greeted and seated guests.

COMPUTER & LANGUAGE

MA, Speech Communication, Tallahassee University, Tallahassee, FL   1995
BS, Speech Communication, Florida College, Parkside, FL   1994
AA, General Studies, Springfield College, Springfield, MA   1992

SKILLS

WordPerfect 6.1, WordPerfect Presentations 3.0, Windows 95, Procomm 2.0, Microsoft Word 7.0, Word Works, Page Maker, Corel Draw 6.0, Quattro Pro, ClarisWorks 2.1, MacWrite, MacDraw, MacPaint, Spreadsheet, Database, and Internet & World Wide Web connectors: Netscape, Mosaic, and Indylink. Fluent in Hebrew. Working knowledge of Spanish.

AFFILIATIONS

National Public Speaking Association
American Public Speaking Association
International Communicators Society

JERRY RUDACKER

3645 Calvert Street
Baltimore, MD 20745
(410) 555-1212

OBJECTIVE

General Manager position encompassing golf/proshop/facilities operations; full service food, beverage, and banquet services, personnel training and staff development programs; and capital improvements/expense forecasting and strategic planning for a prestigious member-owned country club.

BACKGROUND SUMMARY

Over 10 years experience developing expertise in:

- Training
- Strategic Forecasting
- Events Planning
- Recruiting
- Financial Management
- Customer Service
- Team Building
- Membership Marketing
- For Profit Operations
- Fine Dining/Banquet/Party Supervision

ACHIEVEMENTS

- Increased membership by instituting an Ambassador program; introduced fine dining, food and beverage quality standards; and established staff structuring at the Bent Tree Country Club.
- Introduced a distinguished lecture program featuring President Gerald R. Ford, Henry Kissinger, David Stockman, Jean Kirkpatrick among others at the Baltimore City Club to the delight of the Baltimore Chamber of Commerce.
- Effected cash flow turnaround, from a $30,000 loss to a profit of $110,000 after first 12 months, and improved revenues by over 9% each year thereafter for National Club Corporation at the Cantonsville City Club.
- One of four individuals representing 60 clubs in the region to be nominated for National Club Corporation Manager of the Year, 1991.
- Created a warm and inviting atmosphere among employees, members, and the Board/Trustees at every club by using a "hands-on" management style.

EXPERIENCE

Links Golf Management   Baltimore, MD
General Manager, Bent Tree Country Club, Baltimore, MD   1995 - 1996
Directed the activities of this former privately owned thirty year old, 350 member club on behalf of a management consulting organization. Prepared the 1996-2000 strategic plan and capital expense forecast. Supervised golf/proshop, course facilities, fine dining, and banquet/party operations.

National Club Corporation (NCC)   Baltimore, MD
Club Manager, Baltimore City Club, Baltimore, MD   1993 - 1995
Managed a prestigious 2,000 member downtown city club to ensure efficient and profitable operation. Actively participated in expanding the membership, improving cash flow, and establishing member equity. Did the financial and strategic planning.

Club Manager, The Cantonsville City Club, Cantonsville, MD   1987 - 1993
Developed the club into a catalyst for business growth in downtown Cantonsville. As the sole employee of NCC, established standards for service to members while increasing revenues and profits. Planned and directly supervised fine dining and entertainment. Established a Distinguished Lecture Series with banquet format.

Associate Club Manager, The River Club, Savannah, GA   1985 - 1987
Completed the associates training program earning NCC rookie of the Year award. Supervised kitchen operations; purchased food products, beverages, and wines.

EDUCATION

BA, Communications, The University of Maryland, Baltimore, MD   1985
Certified Club Management & Operations Trainer, NCC, Catonsville, MD   1994

BRIAN GATEWOOD
5 Central Lane
Chicago, IL 56324
(708) 555-4324

OBJECTIVE

Financial Advisor position involving strategic and economic research; preparing financial plans; and providing quality service and guidance to investors for a major full service brokerage firm.

BACKGROUND SUMMARY

Over 4 years classroom study and outside activities developing expertise in:

• Training	• Strategic Forecasting	• Accounting
• Recruiting	• Financial Management	• Events Planning
• Team Building	• Membership Marketing	• Staff Supervision

• Equity Research: Fundamental, Quantitative & Technical

ACHIEVEMENTS

• Increased membership by instituting a program to introduce potential recruits to individual members with similar interests and goals.

• Directed an after-school athletic program for groups of 25-30 high school students earning the 1993 Youth Leadership Award from the Boy's Club Council of Chicago.

• Elected Executive Board Member of Alpha Epsilon Delta fraternity for four consecutive years; served as Social Chairman Spring 1995, Secretary Fall 1995, Pledge Educator Fall 1996, and President Spring 1997.

• Attended the Northern Illinois University International Programs Abroad program in Frankfurt, Germany which provided a broad exposure to international finance.

EXPERIENCE

Senior Counselor, South Shore Y Camp, Chicago, IL   1996
Directed the activities of a group of First Grade boys. Prepared the weekly activities, scheduled and supervised three staff counselors. Discussed each boy's progress with his parents each week.

Administrative Assistant, Bernard Haldane Associates, Chicago, IL 1995
Summer job provided experience in performing routine office tasks: using telephone, copy machine, fax, calculator, and PC.

EDUCATION

BA, Finance, Illinois University, School of Business, Chicago, IL	1997
Illinois International Programs Division, Frankfurt, Germany	1996
South Side High School, Rockport, IL	1993
Central Baldwin High School, Baldwin, IL	1992

Jose Mendez
708 Glenview Drive
Centreville, VA 22123
(703) 555-1212
josem@anywhere.net

OBJECTIVE

A position utilizing my skills in **Project Management, Leadership, Information Technology, Strategic Planning** and **Logistics** in order to:

- analyze, design and create IT programs to meet organizational objectives
- develop and implement new systems and procedures to their successful and profitable conclusion
- improve operating efficiency through effective management and use of corporate assets.

QUALIFICATIONS

- Project Management
- Leadership/Motivation
- Personnel Management
- Management/Employee Training

- Information Technology
- Systems Analysis
- Technical Documentation
- Representation Liaison Relations

- Strategic Planning
- Logistics Management
- Policies & Procedures
- Problem Solving

WORK HISTORY

Military Advisor
Department of Defense   1996-1997
Commander
82nd Airborne Italy   1984-1997

EDUCATION and PROFESSIONAL

Master of Information Technology   1998
International University, Jonesboro, NC
Bachelor in Military Science/Cavalry   1989
Military Institute, Italy
Languages: English, Italian, French, Spanish
Commendations: For performance as Military Advisor in Paraguay and as Company Commander

COMPUTER SKILLS

DOS O/S, Windows95 O/S, Client/Server O/S (Windows NT 4.0 and NT administration), RDBMS - Access 97 (Access Developers ToolKit and Access Basic), Oracle 7 Client/Server (CDM, JAD, Developer/2000, PL/SQL. Procedure Builder, SQL*PLUS), Visual Basic 4.0, SQL, Web technologies (HTML, MSFrontPage98, CGI, JavaScript, VBScript), IIS, TCP/IP, PowerBuilder 5.0, Java 1.1 knowledge, Software Project Management, MS Office, Crystal Reports, Peachtree Accounting

PERSONAL

- Horseback Riding • Parachuting • Scuba Diving • Tennis • Biking • Jogging • Music

ACHIEVEMENTS

Project Management/Leadership

Prepared Paraguay Military Police Battalion for action on behalf of Italian government as Manager of Technical/ Military Cooperation Project. Convinced officers of need for technical competency; trained; wrote military technical documents including field manual, compilation of laws and standard operating procedures and instruction manual; negotiated with army to move from rural area to capital; persuaded Italian government to fund move; planned and developed budget; designed first Military Police Course. **Results:** Increased project visibility and annual budget by 200%; improved discipline, military status and instruction level.

Managed first Paraguay Operations Other Than War Company to participate in an international Peace Keeping exercise, in Zaire, as Military Advisor. Planned and budgeted program; improvised teaching aids; instructed in NATO's doctrine; developed manual; evaluated performance; supervised field exercises; negotiated with Paraguay Chief of Staff for personnel changes. **Results:** Company accomplished mission and received excellent performance appraisal by all other countries' representatives.

Transformed young recruits into soldiers. Evaluated abilities and capabilities; scheduled and supervised instruction process; guided and motivated; mediated human and job-related conflicts; took corrective measures as needed; delegated administrative and maintenance activities to junior officers; oversaw development. **Results:** Selected as sole representative of branch to attend officers' training in Fort Lennox.

Information Technology

Designed Oracle 7.0 Server database model for virtual software company to track operations, finance and sales as project team leader. Consulted user on needs; evaluated specifications and demands; conceptualized data model; analyzed relationships and systematized entities' relationship diagram; delegated tasks; built and coded forms using PL/SQL and Developer 2000; debugged; modified; wrote documentation. **Results:** Completed on time; met all specifications.

Developed video rental system for video store using Visual Basic 4.0 and Access as project leader. Formulated design strategy; analyzed work breakdown structure; developed project timeline; coached team members; built and programmed database; co-authored user's manual. **Results:** Project completed on time; met client's needs; went on to lead team in developing help desk software system.

Created comprehensive webpage with links to other sites about city of Richmond as project leader. Conceptualized design, navigation flow, links, GUI and other technical aspects; persuaded team members to adopt plan; analyzed project tasks and developed timeline; coached and coordinated team effort; built, coded and programmed website. **Results:** Delivered 47 page site in five languages on time and within project specifications.

Automated Richmond's Swiss Consulate telephone call management system. Consulted on needs and requirements; designed software application to store all phone calls made by consular personnel; programmed application's code; demonstrated and trained on use; tested; modified; drafted user's manual. **Results:** Saved 4 to 5 man hours per month; provided mechanism to charge employees for private international calls.

Strategic Planning/Logistics

Organized downsizing of large organization and merger of two departments. Assessed status and needs; formulated plan to restructure duties, responsibilities and organizational chart; consolidated assets; planned and supervised logistical activities so that parent company of 3000 employees was not adversely affected; established inventory management system; briefed on progress to senior level management. **Results:** Reorganized company had standard to measure inventory; non-productive workers offered retirement; facilities and equipment reached optimum maintenance; morale substantially increased.

Planned Battalion level field exercises to test readiness status of troops. Analyzed level of instruction, weather conditions and terrain constraints; planned tactical maneuvers; assigned missions and sectors; developed and administered budget; delegated tasks (logistical and support plan, communications plan, fire support plan, medical plan, mobility and counter-mobility plan, safety measures); directed and evaluated execution. **Results:** Conducted within budget, heightened readiness condition; received favorable recognition; had 0 casualties.

Coordinated and **organized** delivery of old tanks to depot and reception of new ones within 2 months. Formulated phased plan; supervised inventory and storage functions; documented equipment status; directed teams; provided technical guidance/expertise; devised specialized packing for sensitive instrumentation; trained crews on new equipment; translated technical and field manuals for operation and maintenance; tested vehicles. **Results:** Tanks delivered on schedule; plan and training methods adopted battalion-wide; performed first live "fire while moving" exercise in Italian Army.

Michael P. Neff
2101 Westward Drive
Colchester, VT 05546
(504) 555-1212

OBJECTIVE

A key position as in-house counsel in manufacturing, insurance or healthcare industry utilizing skills in **Business Planning, Organizational Development,** and **Civil Litigation** in order to:

- minimize claims or exposure
- aggressively and effectively represent the interests of company
- develop management and operational strategies
- improve operating performance and profitability
- provide effective management and leadership

QUALIFICATIONS

Qualified by over 20 years professional experience in state and federal courts in:

- Civil Litigation
- Personal Injury
- Workers Compensation
- Negotiations/Settlements
- Industrial Accidents

- Professional Negligence
- Insurance Law
- Products Liability
- Medical Malpractice
- Wrongful Death

- Legal Counsel
- Business Planning
- Organizational Development
- Business Management
- Chemical Engineering

EMPLOYMENT HISTORY

Partner	1981 - Present
Associate	1976 - 1981
Walsh, Snyder, Conlin & Hughes, L.L.P.	1976 - Present

EDUCATION

Juris Doctor, *Cum Laude*	1976
University of Vermont, Burlington, VT	
Bachelor of Science, *Cum Laude, in Chemical Engineering*	1973
University of Virginia, Charlottesville, VA	

PROFESSIONAL AND COMMUNITY AFFAIRS

Past President and Member, Marion County Bar Association

Member: State Bar of Vermont American Bar Association, VT Defense Lawyers Association, International Association of Defense Counsel, Association of Defense Trial Attorneys, Defense Research Institute, American Institute of Chemical engineers

Past President and Board Member: Marion County Unit, American Heart Association

Counsel: Savannah Little Theatre, 1983-1990

REPRESENTATIVE CLIENTS

Towson Tire and Rubber Corporation
MegaDeal Equipment Company
SYDET Companies
Jones Mutual Insurance Company
Complete Union Insurance-Company
King Insurance Company

Total Reinsurance Corporation
Fireman's Friend Insurance Company
Brother Products, Inc.
Morrison Dole, Inc.
Orthopedic Needs, Inc.
Neurosurgical Partners, Inc.

SELECTED ACHIEVEMENTS

Business Planning/Organization Development

Devised plan to improve relationships with existing and prospective clients. Directed creation of complete list of clients; identified those deemed tenuous and made personal contact; set policy requiring insurance defense attorneys to meet clients at least annually; organized annual seminar of new developments in Vermont law; set up open house to familiarize clients with scope of practice; and recommended firm act as host at Vermont Claims Association's annual convention. **Results:** Since 1984, firm's insurance defense practice has tripled in size and net revenues have almost quadrupled.

Developed strategy to increase income and reduce costs in law firm in order to aggressively expand. Evaluated personnel; analyzed financial structure; reviewed recurring and nonrecurring expenditures; implemented semiannual review of staff; set forth recommendations to increase efficiency, developed and implemented budget for receipts and expenditures. **Results:** Improved overall financial performance, developed new practice areas, increased management and support staff, and heightened morale.

Strengthened marketing program for law firm of 15 attorneys. Recommended development of firm brochure; identified potential clients, identified areas of practice not serviced by firm or local community and evaluated need; coordinated redistribution of case loads and developed new areas of practice; participated in continuing legal education seminars to promote firm's expertise. **Results:** Name recognition and business increased.

Chaired recruiting committee for law firm from 1984 through 1989. Evaluated existing professional staff; developed and implemented strategic plan for recruitment; sought candidates to enhance and expand practice areas; promoted firm within local community and to all law schools in Northeastern United States; conducted on-campus interviews; negotiated with all prospective associates or lateral hires; hired/trained new associates. **Results:** The firm doubled in size and is considered one of the most successful and respected law firms in the State.

Created and designed Alternative Dispute Resolution program for the Marion Judicial Circuit. Recognized the need to minimize the current case load; explored preferred methods of dispute resolution; drafted model rules and regulations for a court annexed arbitration program; persuaded judicial acceptance; solicited funds for implementation of the program. **Results:** Created more efficient utilization of judicial resources, provided quicker decisions, saved taxpayers money and heightened stature of firm within legal community.

Civil Litigation

Planned/Directed prosecution of suit in 1986 seeking multimillion dollar award for compensatory and punitive damages against Pilgrim Waterworks Company on behalf of Taylor Contracting Company after a bulldozer struck a high pressure underground diesel fuel line. Reviewed available information the day of the accident; directed on-scene investigation with all responding agencies; designed strategy for discovery; retained all necessary expert witnesses; developed multiple theories of liability; demonstrated egregiousness of Pilgrim Waterwork's conduct; tried case to judgement. **Results:** Verdict for $5.1 million in favor of plaintiff, the largest verdict in Marion County and one of the largest in the State of Vermont.

Planned/Directed prosecution of suit in 1990 seeking multimillion dollar award for wrongful death as a result of an industrial accident. Filed extensive and detailed discovery to each defendant seeking to uncover the facts leading up to rupture of warm liquor accumulator; compiled and cross-referenced all discovery to document knowledge of events; retained expert witnesses; evidenced gross misconduct. **Results:** Negotiated settlement of claim for $1.75 million, the largest settlement in Southwest Vermont as of that date.

Avoided multimillion dollar award against Snyder Truck Rental for catastrophic injuries of plaintiff. Scrutinized information; canvassed neighborhood; coordinated investigation and deduced grounds upon which plaintiff's liability claim would fail; retained expert witnesses; assessed injuries and medical issues; orchestrated strategy to neutralize adverse witnesses; tried case to judgment. **Results:** Proved lack of liability on part of Snyder Truck Rental and received additional cases from client.

Uncovered fraud on behalf of defendant Quaker Confection Company. Counseled client not to settle claim; investigated and discovered collusion between parties; argued that pregnant plaintiff conspired with Quaker's driver, brother of her boyfriend and unborn child's father. **Results:** Verdict for client; saved client $250,000 it was prepared to offer and received further defense work from client.

Professional Negligence

Represented general surgeon in multimillion dollar medical action arising out of the alleged wrongful death of a 17-year-old who died of a ruptured aorta ten hours after arrival at emergency room. Collected medical records; identified and clarified certain discrepancies; consulted with all attending medical practitioners; analyzed available information and eliminated alternative courses of action suggested by plaintiff's counsel; deposed plaintiff's expert witness and convinced him my client had conformed to prevailing standard of care. **Result:** Summary judgment in favor of general surgeon.

Represented orthopedic surgeon in multimillion dollar medical malpractice action seeking damages for alleged negligent casting of a severe leg fracture with-resultant sciatic nerve impairment. Evaluated medical records; resolved discrepancies; compiled office records, including records of treatment, phone calls, prescriptions for medications and super bills; prepared a detailed time line and analysis of patient complaints. **Results:** Demonstrated patient could not have reported alleged symptoms to surgeon on the dates alleged, resulting in defense verdict for the orthopedic surgeon.

Saved insurance company one million dollars of two million dollars designated for settlement in the death of a 24-year-old female after developing a condition known as status epilepticus. Analyzed and rationalized conflicting medical record entries; prepared a detailed time line of events leading to death, formulated alternate theories for etiology of death and demonstrated mitigating factors; convinced plaintiffs to mediate the claim. **Results:** Avoided punitive damages and physician retained medical license.

Chandler M. Taylor
246 Lightning Avenue
San Jose, CA 99876
(876) 555-1212

OBJECTIVE

A position utilizing my skills in **Business and Commercial Law, Strategic Problem Solving, Market Analysis** and **Market Development** in order to:

- represent clients to maximize business potential while safeguarding interests
- identify, avoid or troubleshoot potential impediments to organizational profitability
- assess and expand growth in marketplace.

QUALIFICATIONS

- Business/Commercial Law
- Contract Negotiations
- Insurance/Property Law
- Litigation Strategies
- Risk Management

- Strategic Problem Solving
- Project Management
- Consulting
- Motor Sports Industry
- Writing/Editing

- Market Development
- Research & Analysis
- Client Relations
- Leadership/Supervision
- Agency Agreements

WORK HISTORY

Billings, Johnson & Morgan, LLP, San Jose, CA	1996 - Present
Attorney	
Young, Goldman & Schmidt, Springfield, VA	Summer 1995
Summer Associate	
Miller, Jones, Simpson & Delp, San Jose, CA	Summer 1994
Summer Associate	
MicroTech, Boulder, CO	Summer 1993
Marketing Representative	
Miller-Jenkins Corporation, Waco, KY	Summers 1989 - 1992
Marketing Intern	

EDUCATION and PROFESSIONAL

Juris Doctor   1996
  University of California, School of Law. Los Angeles, CA
  Notes Editor, *California Journal of International & Comparative Law*
  Bill Davis Moot Court Team

Bachelor of Arts in Psychology, *Cum Laude*   1993
  Parkside Junior College, San Diego, CA
  President, Class of 1993

Invitation to Serve: Advisory Board for Sports Business Program at San Jose Technology Institute
  Parker Business School, Global Affairs (official appointment pending final program formation).

Member: American Bar Association: State Bar of California; San Jose Bar Association (Sports Section).

Admissions: Superior and State Courts of California. Court of Appeals of California; Supreme Court of California; U.S. District Court for the Northern District of California; U.S. Tenth Circuit Court of Appeals.

PUBLICATIONS

Identifying Agents for Depositions Under Federal Civil Procedure Rules. CIV Journal, Vol. 8, No. 2 , May 1998.

Proper Investigatory Surveillance. CIV Journal, Vol. 10, No. 32, March 1997.

Advantages of a Limited Liability Partnership (LLP), Intra-law firm publication, May 1994.

Flood Relief Manual. FEMA inspired source book for volunteer attorneys to assist 1994 earthquake victims.

COMPUTER SKILLS

- Windows 95 • WordPerfect ,7.0 • Lotus 1-2-3 • Microsoft Word • Excel • PowerPoint • Westlaw • Lexis

ACHIEVEMENTS

Business and Commercial Law

Negotiated Sponsorship Contract between USAUTO All Pro Team client (Sunny Racing Group) and union-automotive nonprofit entity (UAF-HM). Assessed proposed contract; utilized motor sports and legal knowledge to explain ramifications and implications; recommended changes to protect team interest and enhance marketability position; negotiated changes with sponsoring entity. **Results:** Secured favorable terms: improved team visibility and changes increased market exposure through sponsored show-car exhibits at USAUTO Salem Cup race events.

Defended lawsuit against large insurance clients for breach of contract, fraud and tortious interference with business arising out of complex off-shore captive insurance devised litigation approach; deposed numerous parties and witnesses; researched, analyzed, prepared and argued full range of motions; assisted in mediation, settlement negotiations and trial. **Results:** Obtained full defense; saved clients over $3 million dollars; shielded sensitive internal business operations from public eye and scrutiny; reduced risk of further litigation.

Reduced potential multi-million dollar exposure for large client sued for breach of contract, fraud, bad faith and retention. Analyzed client's business practices; designed approach to receive immediate response from client; formulated defense strategy; drafted and argued discovery motions; evaluated and appraised discovery requests from opponent on client's business; determined extent of compliance. **Results:** Client prevailed on every discovery motion; significantly reduced client expense and employee time and energy required to locate, evaluate and produce documents, computer print-outs and other requested materials; protected client from public dissemination of extremely sensitive internal information.

Strategic Problem Solving

Generated state-by-state compendium of law regarding methods of wine promotion for international wine marketing; including use of store coupons, in-store division of large beverage campany. Identified promotional categories, in-store tastings, sweepstakes, combination packaging and supermarket sales; researched laws of all fifty states; applied laws to promotional and sales methods; designed comprehensive quick glance chart with appended supporting statutes and regulations. **Results:** Wine division saved time and resources by relying on information to develop permissible promotional activities in each state; reduced potential fines stemming from noncompliance.

Prevented plaintiff from obtaining products liability judgment against large appliance manufacturer client. Evaluated merits of complaint; investigated case and statutory law: determined client had been sued without justifiable cause; demanded dismissal. **Results:** Obtained dismissal, saved client time, legal expense and potential damage award; guarded client from inevitable negative product publicity and corresponding adverse market reaction.

Defended large insurance client in coverage lawsuit seeking over $3 million in alleged damages for environmental clean up of two EPA sites. Researched and analyzed case history; determined winnable defense that would not adversely affect client in future; convinced client not to settle as had 5 other defendants: pursued strategy. **Results:** Court granted summary judgment; established new California caselaw for late notice defense in insurance claims coverage disputes.

Market Analysis/Development

Recruited USAUTO Late Model Stock driver for management by USAUTO All Pro Team client. Interviewed and assessed driver's accomplishments and potential; discussed marketability of driver and recommended consideration; advised client on duties, responsibilities and scope of authority over driver; drafted letter of intent, negotiated and prepared agent contract between client and driver. **Results:** Created mutually beneficial and successful professional relationship; client saved recruitment expense by having attorney with motor sports knowledge assess driving skills and marketability.

Advised NHRA Pro Stock Truck Team (SunCoast Motors) on implementing effective marketing strategies to maximize sponsorship opportunities. Researched alternative methods; assessed opportunities: prioritized strategies: presented tactical sponsorship plan to owner and implementation team. **Results:** received several promising sponsorship leads for 1999 race season.

Marketed computer equipment and services for MicroTech. Initiated contact: consulted on current utilization: developed rapport: educated prospective and existing clients on advantages of upgrading current computer systems and utilizing support services: persuaded on value of company's products and services: briefed technical sales force on needs. **Results:** Elevated interest in computer system upgrades and support services: increased company leads.

Ashley L. Johnson
2200 Lincoln Drive
Fairfax, VA 22345
(703) 555-1212

OBJECTIVE

A position utilizing my skills in **Information Technology Management, Strategic Problem Solving, Consulting** and **Business Liaison Relations** in order to:

- improve operating efficiency and effectiveness through management, staff development and fiscal accountability
- design and implement cutting edge technology to increase organization's profitability
- maximize business affiliations through enhanced service and sophisticated negotiations.

QUALIFICATIONS

- Information Technology Management
- Software/Hardware Engineering
- System Crash Prevention
- Systems Analysis/Procedures
- Contingency Systems Planning
- ISO-9002

- Business Liaison Relations
- Government Relations
- Customer/Client Service
- Organizational Development
- Leadership/Motivation
- Training/Presentations

- Strategic Problem Solving
- Crisis Management
- Consulting
- Operations Management
- Business Operations Analysis
- Budget Management

PROFESSIONAL EXPERIENCE

Technology Source, Inc.   1998 - Present
  Computer Operations Manager
AppleMac   1996 - 1998
  Americas Field Development Unix Program Manager
ACI   1995 - 1996
  Regional Operations Senior Systems Administrator
TWN International   1995 - 1995
  Information Technology Manager
Applaud Systems   1993 - 1995
  Business Recovery Specialist
All Seasons Hotel   1988 - 1990
  U.S. Secret Service Security Liaison

EDUCATION, HONORS and CIVIC

University of Richmond, VA
  Bachelor of Science in Criminal Justice, *Magna Cum Laude*

Virginia Technology & Training Center
  Unix Systems Administration Certification

Recognition Society of the Handicap Student (RSTHS)-Co-Founder
National Health Corps-CPR/First Aid Instructor, Disaster Relief Volunteer

COMPUTER SKILLS

Operating Systems: SCO, HP-UX, AIX, SOLARIS, SYSTEMS V, DYNIX, DG-UX
Servers and Mainframes: HP, IBM, Sequent, DEC, Data General, Sun
PC's: IBM, NEC. HP, AT&T, DELL, MICRON
Networks: TCP/IP, TSO/IMSP PES, MAUS, SQL, DECNet, CCMail, MSMail
Software Applications: ENCORE Property Management Systems. MSWord, EXCEL, Windows for Workgroups, ECCO, Quicken, Peachtree Accounting for Windows, Lotus 1-2-3, Access, HP Service Guard. HP LVM. Corel WebMaster.

ACHIEVEMENTS

Information Technology Management

Initiated maintenance programs to stabilize data center for value added reseller. Designed and implemented software to alert users of problems; scheduled quarterly hardware system checks; renegotiated support agreements; managed staff and third party vendors; coauthored ISO 9000 Disaster Recovery Plan. **Results:** Improved and stabilized servers reducing system downtime; increased system performance.

Developed, customized and implemented technical training program for AppleMac. Assessed training requirements; motivated staff; designed Unix and DMIL curriculum; engineered career development plans; initiated new course content; scheduled instructors; purchased supplies. **Results:** Educated approximately 2000 employees at all levels.

Negotiated hardware/software contracts within three months after being named Unix Program Manager. Evaluated needs; designed and updated hardware configurations; recommended and implemented support processes and procedures; trained personnel; monitored quality assurance and contractual agreements. **Results:** Purchased & leased and initiated new hardware and software configurations below budget; enforced default clause of contract netting approximately $25,000 in refunds.

Led team in evaluation of prereleased operating systems to avoid conflicts with existing software products. Collected and analyzed data from participating departmental members; identified problem areas; conducted meetings to formulate solutions; recommended improvements and enhancements; monitored implementation of suggested changes. **Results:** Prevented issuance of insufficient technology.

Analyzed and **recommended** strategies to systematize technology updates in workplace for increased employee retention as member of AM senior level task force. Assessed work environment; investigated past and current documentation relating to job distress; conceptualized matrix for ranking complexity of software changes or releases; recommended proprietary software tools to facilitate knowledge and understanding. **Results:** Strategies accepted and being implemented.

Strategic Problem Solving/Consulting

Implemented phase one of server upgrades for Technology Source within 5 days of hire. Assessed status; made time line recommendations; delegated tasks; identified potential problem areas; scheduled third party vendor to assist; oversaw and troubleshot. **Results:** Enhanced system performance.

Investigated software product that caused system to crash (core dump). Gathered data from system network and customer; formulated core dump pattern; researched calls and source code; performed tests; coordinated resources to resolve issue; spearheaded labs in redesigning source code in high availability software. **Results:** Corrected software's interaction with kernel within 6 months.

Managed down systems for high availability customers in large technology firm. Diagnosed problems; designed recovery plans; coordinated resources to resolve issues; generated reports; interpreted data; monitored system activity; recommended customers purchase higher service level agreements. **Results:** Reviewed and stabilized between 150-200 customers' machines per month; saved millions of dollars for customer and company; increased service revenues by 5-10%.

Reduced theft 72% within 3 months of transfer for major retailer. Reviewed theft detection; purchased surveillance equipment; educated employees; readjusted schedules; initiated network among other retailers. **Results:** Increased apprehension of shoplifters and dishonest employees; increased employee awareness regarding internal and external theft.

Business Liaison Relations

Facilitated meetings to resolve hardware compatibility issues between third party vendor, prominent customer and major computer company. Diagnosed problems; developed alternative scenarios; scheduled and conducted meetings between CEOs and senior level management initiated and monitored action plan. **Results:** Hardware replaced; customer satisfaction increased; customer purchased higher service level agreement.

Conceptualized, designed and **implemented** procedures to increase customer satisfaction for governmental and secured site customers. Consulted with customers; researched needs and available resources; developed standard operating procedures; presented both internally and externally. **Results:** Facilitated expedited transfer of information; enhanced corporate image; increased revenues.

Coordinated interaction between Secret Service, Special Forces, hotel staff and other agencies during 1988 Presidential Campaign. Researched employees' background; scheduled staff coverage; established/implemented timelines and routes; installed special communications systems; facilitated meetings; surveyed and conducted control during diplomatic movements. **Results:** Successfully transported President and candidates, their spouses, families and staff.

Directed development of first 300 hour Security Officer training course for technical school. Developed course guidelines; evaluated content; motivated development staff, obtained state certifications without modification; coached on instructional techniques; created benchmarks. **Results:** Successfully deployed state certified course for Security Officers in 47 states.

Jocelyn Hendrickson
4404 Portsmouth Road
Atlanta, GA 30063
(707) 555-112

OBJECTIVE

A position utilizing my skills in **Public Relations, Advertising, Promotions, Strategic Planning** and **Market Development** in order to:

- project a positive business image through use of multi-media communications
- increase market awareness and sales of products or services by designing creative programs to capture consumers
- improve efficiency, increase revenues and streamline operating procedures to achieve organizational goals

QUALIFICATIONS

- Public Relations
- Media Utilization
- Crisis Management
- Image Development
- Presentations/Training
- Administrative Management

- Advertising/Promotions
- Project Management
- Sales Management
- Writing/Editing
- Event Planning
- Leadership/Motivation

- Strategic Planning
- Market Development
- Business/Operations Analysis
- Customer Development/Service
- Budgeting/Goal Setting
- Computer Skills

WORK HISTORY

Director of Public Relations and Special Projects
Marietta School of Massage   1988 - 1997

Massage Therapist
Just Chiropractic, Inc.   1988 - 1992

Director of Operations
Management Trainer
Manager
Hospitality Industry   1976 - 1987

EDUCATION and PROFESSIONAL

Bachelor of Science, College of Health and Human Development
Georgia State University, Athens, GA

Massage Therapy Certification (Licensed in FL)
Marietta School of Massage

Neuromuscular Therapy Certification

M. Peter Sech Community Building Training Workshop

PERSONAL

• Willing to relocate and travel • Cycling • Cooking • Bird-dog training • Camping •

ACHIEVEMENTS

Public Relations

Created Speakers Bureau to address community need for knowledge on wellness issues. Developed action plan; interviewed; presented mission; selected speakers to match needs of targeted audience; acquired personnel to operate audio—video equipment, observe, coach and critique mock presentations; scheduled performance feedback. **Results:** Educated public on techniques for stress management, blood pressure reduction and circulation improvement; developed community good-will; increased business for student clinic.

Convinced production team for Gilda Radner Telethon to include and televise massage therapy services given to volunteers and participating breast cancer patients. Conceived idea; presented to management; served as liaison to production staff; participated in planning meetings; recruited and trained therapists; oversaw event set-up; troubleshot. **Results:** Requested to provide services at annual event; received free publicity for school; recognized by community for public service.

Planned one-day massage therapy classes targeted at couples, parents, athletes and fitness-conscious individuals. Identified and responded to needs; developed curriculum; interviewed and contracted faculty; composed and designed several promotional brochures; formulated marketing plan; drew from growing database; published newsletter article; set up canvas of neighborhood. **Results:** Achieved 60% commitments weeks prior to classes; produced model for future community classes; arranged educational in-service programs for medical professionals in 11 area hospitals.

Initiated breakthrough in corporate policy by introducing public relations program to enhance sales at Dexter's restaurant, a $4 million operation. Noted lackadaisical attitude of staff, convinced area director of need to stimulate and motivate; conceptualized idea for first birthday event; solicited prizes from area merchants and vendors; generated promotional materials; established team meetings; scheduled and ran event. **Results:** Attracted over 200 attendees; increased employee enthusiasm; gained customer loyalty; increased sales; named Manager of Public Relations; developed on-going PR and management training programs.

Advertising/Promotions

Produced promotional material to launch 620-hour massage therapy certification program. Managed production team: designer, writer, photographer, models, printer; evaluated design options; coordinated team meetings; oversaw production calendar to meet deadlines; negotiated design, copy and layout. **Results:** Created 4-color brochures; came in 15% under budget; received national recognition from competitors and colleagues.

Convinced CCN "Headline News" to cover local business as part of its coverage of National Convention. Created action plan; coordinated coverage with reporter and camera crew; oversaw filming; agreed to on-air interview. **Results:** Received national and international coverage; increased interest calls by 50%; praised by competitors; segment used as lead-in at next National Convention; contacted by channels 5 and 11 and cable station for additional interviews.

Launched graduate newsletter to reach audience of 1,900 plus. Recognized need; submitted proposal to senior management; conceptualized, developed, wrote, edited, designed, and published; emphasized graduate accomplishments and school activities; created vehicle to gain advertising dollars. **Results:** Ran biannual mailings of 8-page newsletter; increased participation in school activities; improved public relations and communication.

Administered 3-day educational conference for internationally recognized sports massage instructor. Designed advertising plan; developed system for enrollment management; organized transportation for students; provided on-site troubleshooting; set up evaluation process to drive business plan for future conferences. **Results:** realized profit; received positive feedback from participants; planned additional conference.

Strategic Planning/Market Development

Developed 5 year strategic plan to expand continuing education department at nationally accredited school. Evaluated existing program; presented proposal to management; recruited and interviewed potential instructors; negotiated and drafted contracts. **Results:** Increased net department revenue by 85% in 4 year expanded program from 20 to 50 courses; improved quality of courses.

Redirected advertising budget for business with $1.9 million in annual revenue. Researched and analyzed statistics on effectiveness of existing advertisements; evaluated demographics for optimum placement; expedited changes; designed strategic calendar to track spending. **Results:** Reduced spending by 50% in 1 year with no reduction in sales.

Reduced publishing production budget by 50%. Audited expenses of producing 2 public relations publications; researched design feasibility in combining; evaluated timing and scheduling needs; implemented merger. **Results:** Produced higher quality, more effective marketing tool.

Authored articles for national professional journals to promote interest within compatible industry. Convinced editors of need and benefit of coverage; researched topics; collaborated with and interviewed colleagues; composed documents; submitted manuscripts. **Results:** Opened new market for services; invited by editors to write additional articles; wrote newsletter articles for State Chapter of national organization.

Nicole Ashby
1234 Kings Island Drive
Hagerstown, MD 22342
(410) 555-1212
nicole@anywhere.net

OBJECTIVE

A position utilizing my skills in **Training, Organizational Development, Facilitation, Strategic Planning, Public Speaking** and **Advocacy** in order to:

- design and implement programs to maximize management and employee potential
- consult on effective methods of retaining and establishing long range client relationships
- direct planning to establish long range and short range strategies to improve organizational effectiveness
- represent organization to enhance public support and expand impact.

QUALIFICATIONS

- Training and Facilitation
- Organizational Development
- Board Development
- Motivational Speaking
- Government Relations

- Strategic Planning
- Executive Training
- Leadership Development
- Client Relations/Retention
- Start Up Operations

- Public Speaking
- Advocacy/Representation
- Community Relations
- Consulting
- Networking

EXPERIENCE

Consultant/Facilitator/Trainer
The Hilltop Group   1995-Present
Marketing/Event Planner
Yourself Care, Inc.   1996-1997
Facilitation Specialist/Trainer
Management Strategies   1995-1996
Executive Director
Directors of Technology Association   1990-1995
Southeast Regional Director
CTS International, Inc.   1988-1990
Assistant Director/Manager of Planning
National Friends Association   1983-1988

EDUCATION

Graduate Studies in Communication and Education Administration
Maryland State University
University of Maryland
University of Virginia

Bachelor of Arts Degree in Education - 1978
Roanoke College

PROFESSIONAL and CIVIC

National Society for Training
ConsultingTrainers Network

The MAP Foundation: Board of Directors
Maryland School Age Care Association: Board of Directors
The Junior League of Baltimore. Inc.: Board of Directors
United Nations Society - Baltimore Chapter: Past President, Board of Directors

ACHIEVEMENTS

Training and Organizational Development

Taught classes in *Presentation Skills for Technical Managers* and *Decision-Making Skills for Executives*. Assessed target audiences; developed and adapted curriculum for specific groups, introduced concepts of communication styles and skills in interactive setting; demonstrated effective techniques to achieve desired results, including effective project management, team building and critical thinking; evaluated and critiqued participants. **Results:** Received excellent evaluations citing material and instructor very helpful; enabled Technical Mangers to translate and present technical information to non-technical audience and Executives to adapt decision-making styles to specific situations.

Trained literacy program directors in *Meeting Effectiveness* for Meeting Strategies, Inc. Consulted with group; facilitated planning sessions; assessed needs; recommended course and formation of new organizational structure; edited and refined preexisting course to fit specific group needs; presented seminar. **Results:** Participants empowered with skills in meeting-time-management and results driven agendas; taught similar class to government employees.

Designed and **organized** start-up association for 28 Boards of Directors of state-owned technical institutes. Consulted with founders; developed action plan; established policies and procedures; created and implemented models for board member development programs; co-authored manual; created newsletters, annual reports; planned and orchestrated annual and regional conferences, board meetings and training sessions; marketed and promoted to statewide institutions and public officials. **Results:** Elevated image of vocational training; increased public awareness and funding.

Orchestrated and **supervised** over 100 international citizen exchanges for National Friendship Association, begun by President Ronald Reagan. Served as representative to Nancy Reagan's office and liaison to Board of Directors; coordinated communications with embassy personnel and foreign representatives; researched individual organizational exchange histories, spoke internationally to promote organization, created and implemented master plan. **Results:** Exchanges implemented with China, Russia, New Zealand, Australia, Germany and England.

Facilitation and Strategic Planning

Directed expansion of scope and services of international professional exchange organization. Selected and instituted development of Board of Advisors; founded International Career Forum; developed training sessions and newsletters for clients and members; spoke publicly; facilitated overseas exchanges for training professionals; implemented strategic plan to increase visibility to highly recognized international associations. **Results:** Promoted international careers to students and young professionals; enabled seasoned professionals to interact with foreign counterparts.

Led planning session for state-wide group representing 12 organizations with 10,000 members. Identified need to bring divergent interests to common goal, facilitated discussion on public policy issues, directed group in consensus skills; developed evaluation mechanism to prioritize; established parameters for group undertaking. **Results:** Group agreed to unify in project to elevate Maryland's position on child welfare.

Facilitated strategic planning sessions for Baltimore Regional Commission - Vision 20/20 citizen collaborative. Directed groups of interested citizens in public forum in determining issues in health, housing and transportation; trained on developing strategies and action plans to encourage civic participation and responsibility for future of Baltimore Region. **Results:** Enabled citizens to interact effectively with regional leaders in critical issues.

Public Speaking/Advocacy

Inspired, motivated and **captivated** audiences across all segments of business from junior to executive levels. Identified hot buttons; innovated methods to open audiences to new ideas; presented on topics including: board development, public advocacy presentation skills, decision making, team building, meeting planning, networking and strategic committee effectiveness, influenced and persuaded to try new techniques. **Results:** Received numerous requests for repeat speaking engagements; impacted way people conducted business and life.

Lobbied and **impacted** legislation on local, state and federal levels representing various civic organizations. Polled constituency; analyzed proposed legislation; researched congressional intent; attended hearings and committee meetings; met with governor's staff, city council members, state and U.S. representatives; presented positions. **Results:** Funding appeared for organization for first time in governor's budget; other legislation passed or defeated as recommended; developed long term relationships/access to elected officials.

Presided over international banquets and special events for over 10 years. Researched speakers, audience and situational needs; introduced speakers and guests including Patrick Moore and other former United Nations Ambassadors, controlled pace; facilitated question and answer sessions; presented recognitions. **Results:** Fostered international goodwill; attendance grew each year.

Planned and **organized** legislative receptions for candidates and elected officials including U.S. Speaker of the House. Determined guest list: designed invitations; booked space. selected caterers and menus: oversaw decorations: prepared briefing papers on political issues for host organization: coordinated with security personnel: chaired events: met one-on-one with government representatives to discuss policy issues. **Results:** Receptions well attended: organizational interests and concerns communicated.

Kaitlin Pendleton
8813 Porter Street
Durham, NC 23465
(651) 555-1212

OBJECTIVE

A consulting position utilizing my skills in **Financial Analysis, Business Analysis, Project Management** and **Business Liaison Relations** in order to:

- identify and implement strategies to increase operating efficiency and profitability
- improve an organization's financial and business practices
- enhance relationships with clients, customers and industry professionals to maximize business potential.

QUALIFICATIONS

• Financial Analysis	• Project Management	• Business Liaison Relations
• Business Analysis	• Reports Development	• International Relations
• Accounting	• Currency Exchange	• Leadership/Supervision
• Consolidations	• Financial Management	• Banking Relations
• Due Diligence	• Training/Motivation	• Executive Presentations
• Forecasting/Budgeting	• Information Management	• Policies & Procedures

WORK HISTORY

Stars Are Us, Inc.   1998-Present
  Executive Assistant to the President

Dorsey-James, Inc.   1991-1998
  International Financial Analyst
  Financial Analyst
  Assistant to the Vice President of Finance
  Staff Accountant

EWA (*joint venture between EDL and Wallace, Akins & Co. PC*)   1992-1993
  Staff Accountant

EDUCATION, PROFESSIONAL and CIVIC

Bachelor of Arts   1992
  American University, Washington, DC
  Accounting G.P.A. 3.9

Certified Public Accountant, North Carolina   1998

Overnight Volunteer Coordinator: St. Patrick's Night Shelter
Crisis Hotline Volunteer: League Against Domestic Harm

COMPUTER SKILLS

- Windows 95 • Microsoft Excel • Microsoft Word • Lotus 1-2-3 Peachtree Accounting Lotus Notes PCFAS -JD Edwards G/L Package, including FASTR • AS400 •

PERSONAL

- Willing to travel • Spanish lessons • Tennis • Roller Blading • Dancing • Aerobics •

ACHIEVEMENTS

Financial/Business Analysis

Consolidated financial results of 38 international manufacturing and distribution companies. Designed multiple linked spreadsheets; reviewed and resolved problems; determined, supported and booked US GAAP adjustments; analyzed and eliminated inter-company balances and transactions, analyzed debt and fixed asset roll-forwards, amortization and depreciation expense, and currency fluctuation effects for consolidated cash flow statement; prepared footnotes pertaining to debt, accrued liabilities, fixed assets, and inventory; established and documented procedures for future considerations. **Results:** Cut consolidation time by 80% despite 153% increase in number of reporting companies.

Created financial reporting package for multi-company, multinational organization. Determined required information for consolidated financial statements and for tax reporting and financial analysis purposes; developed reporting formats, designed automated spreadsheet links; wrote detailed user instructions and accounting guidelines; established deadlines; trained financial managers; arranged for electronic submission of packages. **Results:** Provided timely and consistent financial information from 18 countries for financial statement reporting and management decision-making; reduced reporting costs.

Analyzed financial performance of international subsidiaries and acquisition targets for senior management. Visited foreign sites, reformatted foreign reporting to US accounting standards; made spreadsheets with analytical tools; summarized key financial indicators from P&L, balance sheet, and cash flows, compared to budget, forecasted prior period results; wrote commentaries on performance. **Results:** Management utilized information to evaluate operations, to close unprofitable manufacturing plant and to make acquisition decisions.

Leveraged currency fluctuations to sell inventory at reduced price with no adverse effect on profitability. Noted trend in foreign exchange rates; presented idea to marketing and finance senior management to have promotional sale of slow-moving inventory; analyzed profit points; set necessary variables; consulted bankers to lock in forward contract. **Results:** Increased revenues; moved excess inventory; improved customer and supplier relations.

Project Management

Designed financial statement data warehouse on Excel for multinational company. Identified alternative ways to show information for internal and external reporting and for analysis; analyzed and conceptualized format to address needs and be user friendly; created database with three ways to ensure data integrity; supervised input of historical information; trained employees. **Results:** Warehouse manipulated to report quarterly or annual information, including actual, budget or forecast and "as if" analysis; provided faster, more accurate reporting.

Supervised outside auditors in due diligence at foreign acquisition target. Researched due diligence work programs from previous acquisitions; determined activities to work, formulated questions to be discussed with auditors and target's management; conducted independent analysis; explained key benefits and potential issues with recommendations to Manager of Business Development. **Results:** Acquired innovative design leader in industry at lower price than anticipated.

Managed budget process for manufacturing/distribution company with 145 cost centers at 24 remote locations. Formulated strategy; created schedule and got management sign-off, developed Excel spreadsheets and instructions for budgeting managers, trained end users; troubleshot problems; linked cost center budgets into databases; presented results. **Results:** For first time in company's recent history, budget completed and approved before beginning of fiscal year, surveys showed 98% overall user satisfaction with new procedures, improved efficiency in reporting and analysis.

Directed international operations in providing financial information for public offering. Consulted outside accountants, researched information requirements; created spreadsheets; communicated needs and time-sensitive deadlines, resolved discrepancies; organized information into summary spreadsheets and graphs; kept managers focused. **Results:** Work completed on time, outside analysts priced company competitively; determined ongoing reporting needs, developed new analysis tools; enhanced relationships with managers.

Business Liaison Relations

Solidified relationships with foreign managers. Visited operations in Germany, Sweden, Finland, Czech Republic, and England; kept in constant contact with all locations via telephone, fax and e-mail; analyzed business practices; identified areas of concern; consulted on financial management and reporting methods, introduced new procedures and systems; provided training; allayed concerns. **Results:** Developed trust; managers sought assistance at onset of issues rather than after the fact; eased transition of newly acquired entrepreneur organization.

Served as contact point for auditors, outside tax accountants, attorneys, bankers and insurance brokers. Worked with auditors during audit of year-end consolidated financial statements, provided tax accountants with information to complete tax returns, conferred with attorneys on various issues, e.g., corporate structure, setting up and closing companies; dealt with bankers to negotiate loans, establish letters of credit, trade currency, hedge position and report loan compliance status; coordinated documentation to brokers to ensure appropriate insurance coverage. **Results:** Complete and accurate information provided on time to keep business operating at peak performance; reduced expenses by minimizing time of outside service providers.

Negotiated exclusive contract with travel agency. Sought proposals from multiple agencies; analyzed and compared responses; negotiated best deal, presented findings and recommendation to Vice President. **Results:** Concluded exclusive deal with one full-service travel agency with potential to save company tens of thousands of dollars.

Jeff B. Tatum
45 111th Street, Apt. 202
Washington, DC 20027
(202) 555-1212

OBJECTIVE

A position utilizing my skills in **Sales and Marketing, Program Development, Project Management, Promotional Events** and **Presentations** in order to:
- increase sales through refining services and heightening market penetration
- expand organization's impact, profitability and client base
- plan and implement programs to enhance public awareness and company image.

QUALIFICATIONS

- Sales/Management
- Market Development
- Customer/Client Relations
- Negotiations
- Key Account Management

- Project Management
- Program Development
- Leadership/Motivation
- Staff Development
- Recruiting/Interviewing

- Promotional Events
- Presentations
- Coaching/Training
- Community Relations
- Image Development

WORK HISTORY

Owner
Depend on Us, Inc., VA — 1997 - Present
Account Executive
Washington Pistols Arena Football, League, DC — 1996 - 1997
Head Men's Basketball Coach / P.F. Teacher
East Riverside High School, DC — 1993 - 1996
Basketball Scout
Berkley Scouting Service, VA — 1992 - 1993
Assistant Basketball Coach
Mason College, VA — 1990 - 1992
Head Basketball Coach
Dunham Junior College, MD — 1986 - 1990
Assistant Basketball Coach
University of Maryland at College Park, MD — 1983 - 1986

EDUCATION

Master's Degree in Physical Education
Dupree University
Bachelor of Science Degree in Physical Education
Maryland State University

PERSONAL

• Willing to Travel • Willing to Relocate • Golf • Coaching • Biking •

ACHIEVEMENTS

Sales and Marketing

Convinced National Life Health Corporation to be corporate sponsor for professional football organization. Researched company; initiated contact; developed presentation; sold on value of product and added benefits of exposure on ECCN; made visual demonstration; fielded questions and overcame objections; generated excitement; offered professional athlete and prior recipient to announce "Mr. Football," College Park High School player of the year. **Results:** Sold 8 game corporate package, increased revenues.

Negotiated three-year contract for corporate sponsorship together with group transportation for all team and league events with number one bus line in city. Researched and analyzed competition; determined needs; made sales calls; sought services for our team and opposing teams; presented proposal; came to terms; persuaded owner to accept. **Results:** Value of contact approximately $70,000.

Persuaded division one prospective student-athletes to attend university within months of being hired as assistant coach. Evaluated existing product and system; formulated, targeted and implemented recruiting strategy; coordinated camp visits; stimulated interest calls; interviewed and sold prospects and parents; developed, maintained relationships; made offers; supervised signing of contracts. **Results:** Recruited seven all-state players; turned around 6 season losing streak and became highest rated basketball class in campus history; product seen on national TV; increased financial contributions to program and university.

Created and **marketed** *Depend on Us* home improvement business. Conceived idea; conducted market research; identified need; designed name, logo, flyers and business cards; implemented sales strategy; initiated contact; made presentations; wrote business. **Results:** Company successful since inception.

Program Development/Project Management

Planned and **administered** ALNA men's basketball program as head coach. Assessed skills and abilities of staff and players; coordinated recruiting efforts; supervised scheduling; controlled budget; coached and instructed; lectured on personal development both athletically and socially marketed. **Results:** Improved product 300% in first year within budget; enhanced image of program which led to higher contributions and ability to upgrade facilities.

Invited by national championship coach to evaluate program and talent level of university sports team. Observed performance; assessed strengths and weaknesses as team and as individuals; planned meetings, counseled and offered group and individualized instruction; supported program's philosophy; made recommendations. **Result:** Received favorable feedback from players and staff; team Anderville had successful season; appeared in ALNA tournament.

Spearheaded projects to build sidewalk and daycare playground. Reviewed existing plan; designed walkway; convinced community leader to have city build sidewalk; analyzed organization budget; interviewed contractors; investigated costs, services and materials; evaluated bids; selected firm; persuaded Board of Directors of feasibility; led development; oversaw progress. **Results:** Raised funds, playground made out of recycled Keds shoes in use today with safe access enjoyed by parents and children.

Designed, managed and **sold** new program targeted to niche market. Identified need; developed marketing strategy; planned budget; advertised product and services; spoke to large and small audiences; generated interest; created enthusiasm; hired, trained staff; supervised daily activities. **Results:** Program operated at full capacity within budget; produced revenues; program received favorable feedback.

Promotional Events/Presentations

Taught, instructed, coached and made presentations to large and small groups across country on topics including:

• basketball	• selling	• time management
• football	• promoting programs	• self improvement
• recruiting	• motivation	• team building

Pitched "hot tub in the end zone program" to local business. Conceptualized promotional events at home football games; presented idea to owner together with full marketing strategy; convinced owner to donate hot tub; coordinated production; recruited personnel to participate; coached through events. **Results:** Obtained corporate sponsorship in addition to tub; generated high level of enthusiasm at games; increased ticket sales.

Promoted historic East End neighborhood of Baltimore, MD, on city's number one rated television talk show. Collaborated with personnel: discussed issues; conducted house tour; provided neighborhood history; turned five-minute segment into entire program. **Results:** Enhanced neighborhood image; spearheaded restoration movement in area which increased property values; shown in classrooms in local schools to stimulate community pride; organized and coordinated home tour of neighborhood which generated revenues for association.

Organized fund-raiser for local organization. Took existing framework and developed new ideas, directed committee delegated duties; promoted all day events; sold tickets. coordinated set up; motivated people to participate: encouraged volunteers. **Results:** Raised most funds in 12 year history of organization: improved image: increased sales.

Margaret Stanton
72 Backview Drive
Seattle, WA 55443
(514) 555-1212

OBJECTIVE

MANAGEMENT: Career opportunity in a stable, challenging corporate environment which will utilize extensive and demonstrated skills of research, consultation, training, supervision and public relations.

PROFESSIONAL CORE COMPETENCIES

TRAINING/Personnel Development
EXTENSIVE RESEARCH EXPERTISE
EFFECTIVE oral/written communication
Effective Team **BUILDING**
Multi-project coordination
Marketing products/services
INNOVATIVE MANAGEMENT
GOAL SETTING/attainment
Decisive organizational **LEADERSHIP**

PROFESSIONAL ACHIEVEMENTS

PROVIDED LONG-RANGE PLANNING. Developed and presented programs on state-wide basis. Identified weaknesses; encouraged changes; sought speakers; arranged locations; evaluated workshops: improved subsequent presentations; detailed successes in regular reports. **Results:** Strengthened services/planning programs; recognized as professional planning consultant. **Learned importance of setting goals and objectives.**

LEADERSHIP DEMONSTRATED. Interviewed, hired, trained, and managed staff, explained implemented staff directives; revitalized with new procedures; promoted client services; updated professional resources. **Results:** Significant increase in resource usage; expertise requested and respected: received promotion for innovative/effective methods. **Learned to delegate with enhanced supervisory responsibilities.**

SUCCEEDED AS REFERENCE LIBRARIAN. Applied skills acquired in library school; learned equipment use; performed reference, referral, and research services for businesses and general public; planned programs and events; displayed books and other media; learned from other department heads and staff. **Results:** Skills and abilities enhanced by hands-on experience; promoted to **Branch Manager** position. **Learned that learning everything I could about library work would benefit me with transferable skills.**

SUPERVISED MULTIPLE DEPARTMENTS. Managed multi-function staff; assigned responsibilities; pinpointed problem areas; effected changes in morale; enabled staff to broaden horizons; promoted mutual communication patterns; provided guidance and encouragement to stimulate client skill/usage. **Results:** Attained exceptional reputation; received promotion. **Learned to trust judgement and act upon client needs.**

Stanton   Page 2

EXPERIENCE

Metropolitan School District of Suwanick Township (WA)   1995-Present
Substitute Teacher
Taught pre-K through 6th grade in six elementary schools, assisted in
learning disabled, emotionally handicapped, and multiple disabilities
classes.

Seattle-Pohawk County Public Library (WA)   1987-1995
P.T. Adult Librarian (1992-1995)
Supervised up to staff of seven; trained/evaluated staff, selected adult
materials; merchandised adult collection; planned and promoted programs
for adult and family audiences.

Agency Manager (1987-1992)
Supervised Children's Librarian, and staff of seven; interviewed, hired,
trained, scheduled, and evaluated staff, promoted client services;
provided community programming.

Washington State Library (WA)   1985-1987
Planning Consultant/Extension Division
Provided long range planning and consultation services; identified
weaknesses; encouraged changes; planned, promoted, and conducted statewide, long-range planning conferences; increased awareness of need to
market services.

EDUCATION/ADVANCED TRAINING

Advanced training in:
Supercare Management Seminars,Strong Communication Skills For Women,
Employee Assistance Programming, The Manager's Job Today-Management
Retreat

Washington Library Certificate I   1987
A-M-L,S. Library Science   Seattle College   Seattle, WA   1980
B.A. (Journalism)   Rialto College   Rialto, NV   1975

AFFILIATION

Suwanick Township Site Based Planning Committee (96-97)
Suwanick Township Elementary School Redistricting Committee (95-96)
North Suwanick Elementary School PTO Volunteer (94-Present)

PERSONAL CORE COMPETENCIES

Dedicated to competent **PROFESSIONALISM**
WILLINGNESS TO ACHIEVE and motivate others
INTENSE WORK ETHIC to benefit employer
THOROUGH, capacity for effective detail work
SELF-STARTING ATTITUDE
DYNAMIC MOTIVATIONAL METHODS

BETTY JOHNSON
52 Old Country Road
Braintree, MA 02854
(517) 555-1212

OBJECTIVE

A sales representative position leading to management using proven skills in the areas of communicating, overcoming, negotiating and achieving in a progressive, growth oriented company.

QUALIFICATIONS AND BACKGROUND

14 years progressive responsibility and experience in:

- Achieving
- Overcoming
- Organizing
- Focusing

- Communicating
- Negotiating
- Preparing
- Learning

SELECTED ACHIEVEMENTS

NEGOTIATED eight computer reservation system contract renewals. Analyzed wants and needs of the client; developed specific proposals that met client needs without expensive incentives. **Results:** Renewed seven out of eight contracts within a four month period with one pending; attained 87.5% retention.

MANAGED all daily operations of a $4m travel agency. Arranged all travel concerns for corporate travel; initiated and maintained communication with corporate representative; oversaw 3 employees; hired and trained agent. **Results:** Successfully arranged travel for 800 corporate executives generating $4m in sales.

ACHIEVED full time account representative status from a part time customer service agent position. Independently learned **all** aspects of account representative position; initiated training from managers for responsibilities needed in position; undertook additional job responsibilities; initiated an on call status for existing position. **Results:** Promoted to account representative position in less than three years competing with employees who had as much as 15 years seniority.

OVERCAME concerns of a group of customers based on comments by competitors. Listened to the concerns; identified product; informed superiors; persuaded customers to meet with superiors to examine the benefits of the product. **Results:** Re-established open communication; secured opportunity to discuss renewal of contract.

EXPERIENCE

One Star Systems (MA)   1997-Present
Sales Manager
Maintained agency base of 44 accounts in Massachusetts and New York; prepared proposals; negotiated renewal and new computer reservation system contracts; processed amendments to contracts; resolved problems for customers; advised and sold various products; organized seminars and training.

EXPERIENCE

Worldwide Blower Pac   1997
Sales Support/Customer Service
Contacted engineers to get planholders' lists; called contractors to determine bidding intentions on upcoming projects; taxed scopes and quotes to contractors; made changes on computer for scopes and quotes for the estimating engineer; produced blue prints; compiled EXP quotes for engineers; answered phones and directed calls; called travel agent for air fare; computed freight charges for inbound and outbound; posted invoices on computer.

St. Francis (MA)   1989-1997
Certified Dietary Manager
Ensured that special therapeutic diets were prepared by the Massachusetts Diet manual; purchased food and supplies according to need; negotiated price points with vendors; directed and supervised dietary personnel in the preparation and serving of an adequate diet while meeting nutritional needs; controlled food inventories by maintaining adequate records for donated, purchased and government commodities.

El Tacolleta Restaurant   1988-1989
Bar Manager
Presented in store training program which increased operational efficiency; conducted performance evaluations/salary reviews and coordinated pay increases based on merit.

El Tacolleta Mexican Restaurant   1985-1988
Service Manager
Supervised, scheduled and trained a staff of 60 employees; planned and scheduled large parties and banquet reservations; maintained customer and employee relations which enhanced the product quality, service and customer satisfaction.

EDUCATION

B.S. Restaurant Hotel and Institutional Management	Boston University	1985
Certified Dietary Manager	New York State University	1991

HONORS AND ACTIVITIES

Sports Scholarship 1980
Starter Scholarship 1984

Adam Winston
48 Paul Street
Brunwick, ME 03918
(302) 555-1212

OBJECTIVE

Customer Service Management position using proven skills of organizing, planning, record keeping and succeeding in a fast paced, growth oriented company where customer satisfaction is a top priority.

QUALIFICATIONS AND BACKGROUND

Over 9 years of progressive responsibility and expertise in:

- Team Building
- Record Keeping
- Organizing Meetings
- Planning

- Purchasing Raw Materials
- Inventory Management
- Scheduling Production
- Forecasting

ACHIEVEMENTS

PLANNED and **COORDINATED** all responses to sales and customer service inquiries. Answered questions about manufacturing, shipping, quality control, and special orders, quoted pricing and availability, confirmed information on orders; analyzed production schedules, backlogs, and production forecasts; negotiated production schedule on behalf of customer; proposed alternatives as needed. **Results:** Helped to increase sales representatives' new business by an average of $500,000 per representative; received customer service appreciation award.

ORGANIZED scheduling of daily plant production. Analyzed pending orders and due dates; schedule production and product mix to meet customer delivery requirements and maximize efficiency of plant resources; scheduled communication meetings; planned future production; tracked shipping of orders; processed requisition of critical materials to meet customer demands as well as Just In Time inventory objectives. **Results:** Increased production efficiency, decreased down time and 10% reduction of critical materials inventory.

PRODUCTION of highest quality product by directly overseeing that IS09000 and specific company quality standards are met on every manufacturing run. **Results:** Low rate of customer complaints and credits while promoting the quality abilities of our company to current customers as well as new prospects. Less than 1% of manufacturing credits as a percentage of sales. Established new 8 hour production benchmark for division.

SUCCEEDED in the implementation of an outsourcing program for a difficult manufacturing run. Determined ergonomic liability for our employees; sought outside vendors who could perform work safely; calculated outsource cost versus retaining work in house; chose select vendors; implemented program; maintained business relationship. **Results:** Decreased cases of reported Carpal Tunnel Syndrome; allowed machines to run at faster, more productive speeds, allotted time for more orders in production scheduling, promoted positive community image.

EXPERIENCE

Eastco Corporation (ME)   1995-Present
Production Control Manager   1998-Present
Schedule Plant production equipment. Requisition all packaging, paper and miscellaneous production materials. Create daily and long range schedules; direct production control meetings to stimulate communication, maximize production and meet customer demands.

Production Supervisor   1996-1998
Served as Second Shift Production Supervisor for Envelope Department. Duties included direction and management of unionized employees to ensure that customer satisfaction, safety, quality, productivity, and maintenance goals were maximized.

Customer Service Representative   1995-1996
Customer Service Representative for Bangor Envelope Plant. Responsibilities included coordination with customers, sales, and plant personnel of quotations, orders, order status, scheduling, artwork and deliveries.

Agricultural Insurance (ME)   1990-1994
Insurance Agent
Served as licensed property, casualty, life and health insurance agent. Duties included the solicitation and closing of new business as well as providing customer service assistance for existing clients.

Franklin Inc. (VT)   1992
Intern
Product and sales analyst for engineering plastics and polymers. Produced timely sales and data reports for production planning and forecasting. Developed computer program in Dbase IV which enabled marketing to determine the profitability of various product pricing strategies.

Franklin Inc. (VT)   1991
Intern
Responded to information needs within rubber department. Maintained marketing information systems facilitating effective managerial planning and decision making, using the corporate mainframe, Lotus 1-2-3, SAS, and various other PC software applications.

EDUCATION/ADVANCED TRAINING

Advanced training in:

Safety Standards	ISO9000	Interviewing Skills
Public Speaking	SAP	Warehouse Management
Diversity Training	Lotus 1-2-3	International Finance
Customer Service	D-Base III & IV	French

B.S. Management	University of Vermont	Burlington, VT

AFFILIATIONS
United Way

Cindy Billings
18 Bark Street
Brockton, MA 02195
(516) 555-1212

OBJECTIVE

Operations management position using proven skills of researching, writing, compiling and succeeding in flexible, fast-paced, multi-task environment where progressive thinking is appreciated and rewarded.

QUALIFICATIONS AND BACKGROUND

- Research Alternative Solutions
- Writing Proposals
- Succeeding

- Winning New Accounts
- Editing Publications
- Managing Departments

MANAGED department of 100 employees and 5 managers. Redesigned workflow to provide customer service; administered $3,000,000 annual departmental budget; analyzed financial data for profitability and efficiency; oversaw high volume transaction processing; monitored quality of work using Statistical Process Control; appraised performance of managers; recommended candidates for first and second line management positions; approved performance appraisals of clerical employees and appropriate pay increases; enhanced team building, participated in Team Management with Employee Involvement; provided leadership during budgeting and planning process for entire division. **Results:** Earned cost control bonuses; improved customer service; increased company business.

AUTHORED response to Request For Proposal. Analyzed components of request; responded to each requirement; created first draft; edited first draft creating succinct, precise proposal; circulated draft to senior managers and company officers; evaluated comments and corrections; created second draft; upon approval, shipped final proposal to requesting company. **Results:** Won $500 million annual contract.

SUCCEEDED in streamlining department personnel and back log of work to be done. Analyzed personnel responsibilities; identified areas for cross-training; implemented training; analyzed cause of work backlog; provided education and training; evaluated effectiveness of information provided. **Results:** Reduced personnel, saving 11% of department's original budget; reduced processing backlog by 90%.

RESEARCHED telecommuting problems and possibilities. Recognized space and productivity problems; brainstormed possible solutions; analyzed benefits of telecommuting; evaluated individual work loads and anticipated increase in productivity; created proposals for hourly employees to work at home. **Results:** Proposal saving space, cutting costs and improving employee productivity and morale submitted to management.

EXPERIENCE

Flagstaff Inc. (MA)   1997-present
Project Manager
Analyzed pros and cons of outsourcing benefits administration (including financial, operational and systems aspects), and made recommendation; benchmarked company's total comp practices against national; redesigned comp and benefit practices based on findings; designed and implemented process to effect incentive payouts for all employees; served as liaison with Corporate IT ensuring Year 2000 compliance for all HR systems; designed system-generated Total Compensation Statement to be distributed to all employees; negotiated contract terms with vendors; authored Requests For Proposal to solicit bids on work to be outsourced.

American Star Administration   1995-1997
Medicare Part B Appeals Manager
Organized resources to meet goals within budget; complied with Federal regulations; planned and budgeted for the department; hired employees; arranged training; communicated company policies, departmental procedures, performance expectations; appraised performance; monitored quality of work produced.

Donald L. Rueben Corporation   1983-1995
Directory Processing Manager II
Managed various departments in company including Order Processing, Billing and Copy Editing; hired employees; oversaw training of new hires; appraised performance of employees; monitored quality using SPC techniques; planned and budgeted for the department; organized resources efficiently to accomplish stated goals within time and budget constraints.

EDUCATION/ADVANCED TRAINING
Advanced training in:
- Excel
- PowerPoint
- WordPerfect
- Lotus 1-2-3
- FileMaker Pro
- Employee Relations
- Family Medical Leave Act (FMLA)
- Business Writing
- Time Management
- Team Management
- Performance Evaluation
- Interviewing Techniques
- Americans with Disabilities Act (ADA)

B.S. Business Administration   St. Catherine's College   Boston, MA

AFFILIATION

Who's Who of American Women

Lamar Philips

16 Riverton Street, Daytona, FL 33954 • (814) 555-1212 • email: lphilips@writeme.com

OBJECTIVE

To provide a medium-sized business or large division with executive leadership that stimulates growth, improves returns and enhances profitability by focusing on customer satisfaction.

SENIOR MANAGEMENT PROFILE

- $200M P&L Responsibility
- Multi-Location Facilities
- Creating Organizational Cultures
- Joint International Ventures
- Global Operations
- Improving Returns
- Building Teams
- Strategic Planning
- Stimulating Rapid Growth
- Improving Operations
- Intensive Customer Focus
- Enhancing Profitability

CORE COMPETENCIES

Leading Teams

- Directed operations of $175M-plus repair and overhaul division. Division consisted of 42 like-product business teams in 11 different facility locations with 1,100 employees. Division overhauled, repaired 50,000 different aircraft components.
- Led $50M-plus autonomous division with 175 personnel in eight facilities located in the U.S., England and Singapore.
- Led implementation of joint venture with Han-Ling Airplane Manufacturing Company which was completed on schedule and 20% under budget.
- Developed, communicated and implemented common culture and expectation initiatives to solidify the consolidation of four previously-independent business units.
- Conceived and consistently communicated an expected "Customer First" culture that enabled the organization to rank among the leaders in Smithson in growth, returns and customer satisfaction for four consecutive years.
- Implemented development program for division employees in personal leadership, listening, salesmanship, presentations, personal development, time management, group dynamics and process improvement methodologies for team development.

Stimulating Sales Growth

- Doubled sales in three years in a division that was projected to be flat. Developed a sales strategy that shifted the focus from providing a product to providing solutions.
- Redefined mission and approach of a product support and services organization, moving Smithson in two years from a distant third to first in service according to customer surveys.
- Improved win ratio on sales proposals from 40% to 80% by creating an initiative to understand the customers' strategies, activities and philosophies and by redefining the role of the sales force.
- Created a "Characteristics of Excellence for a Sales Force" profile that was applied across the entire Aerospace segment.
- Reduced service cycle time of customer-owned assemblies 80%, saving customers over $20M in inventory and providing a sustainable competitive advantage.
- Received the NatEx Supplier of the Year award for excellence in customer support—the only company in the maintenance and overhaul industry to be recognized.

Improving Returns

- Increased return on investment from an above average 20% range to more than 50% for four straight years—the highest in Smithson Aerotech.
- Doubled inventory turns by improving material planning tools while doubling business volume.
- Achieved receivables of 28 days sales outstanding in an industry averaging over 50 days by providing total solutions tied to prompt payments.

Enhancing Profitability

- Doubled business volume in three years with only 40% increase in direct labor and 20% increase in net capital employed.
- Created multi-facility, business councils for manufacturing methods, quality, employee services, business computer systems and environmental/safety to share best practices.
- Improved product quality by reducing customer returns 90% through increased training and establishing a proactive measurement/reward system.
- Reduced backlog 50% by implementing 42 like-product business teams at 11 facilities with 1,100 employees, overhauling/repairing 50,000 different aircraft components.
- Designed, implemented an artificial intelligence-based scheduling system that reduced the time to reschedule the facility from five days to two hours.

EXPERIENCE

Smithson Aerotech, Marrieta, FL
Vice President - Operations, **Component Services Division.** Division overhauled/repaired 50,000 different aircraft components and assemblies. 1996 - Present
General Manager, **Wheel & Brake Services Division.** Business serviced the world-wide aircraft wheel, tire and brake maintenance needs. 1993 - 1996
Sales Manager, **Airline Wheel & Brake Division**. Directed world-wide sales force of $15OM-plus airline wheel and brake division in a highly-competitive environment. 1991 - 1992
Product Support Manager, **Commercial Wheel & Brake Division**. Responsible for maintaining world-wide end-customer satisfaction. Accountable for technical services engineering, field service, customer service, technical publications, advertising, customer relations. 1989 - 1990
Manager, **Management Information Systems**. Led information technology team in the development and maintenance of manufacturing and financial business systems. 1987 - 1988

Miller Aerospace Corp.(Laurel), Miami, FL
Section Manager, Information Resource Management. 1986 - 1987
Program Manager/Business Development Representative. 1983 - 1985
Engineering/Engineering Computer Systems. 1978 - 1983

Westin Films, Ft. Lauderdale, FL
Systems Analyst 1978

EDUCATION

M. B. A., *Management.* Florida State University
B. S., *Computer Science,* University of Miami

William Ronner
95 King George Drive
Chicago, IL 63897
(775) 555-1212 • Email: wronner@anywhere.net

OBJECTIVE

To provide executive leadership in a medium-sized business and create superior shareholder value by growing market share as well as improving revenues, profitability and customer satisfaction.

PROFESSIONAL QUALIFICATIONS

Experienced senior manager accustomed to P&L responsibility for single and multi-location organizations with revenues up to $300,000,000. Led underperforming company to national market presence through creative marketing. As executive with Fortune 1000 corporation, directed marketing and product management of leading-edge product portfolios. Skilled leader capable of identifying and resolving challenges organizations encounter in determining correct environment and processes and converting those challenges into opportunities. Demonstrated passion for finding, serving and keeping customers. Successful at establishing multi-party business alliances and negotiating positive business relationships.

ACHIEVEMENTS

Led an underperforming computer technology company confronted with diminishing resources and insufficient skill sets to develop positive national recognition. Created sales force, developed strategic initiatives, implemented operational plans, introduced new products, built business relationships and established a winning culture and successful record the company today enjoys. Grew net revenues 28% and net market share 32%.

Chaired acquisition/assimilation team during negotiations for $55,000,000 (net revenues) business. Concluded purchase 30 days ahead of plan and 17.9 % below financial model target. Saved $7,600,000 in acquisition costs.

Formed third-party alliances expanding product placement for the company and two major customers. Increased product sales for all parties and enabled one of the company's wavering product lines to profitably continue in the market .

Developed sales/marketing plans and incentive programs for field operations that improved net sales and profits while providing increased financial/professional rewards for the sales staff. Reduced sales personnel turnover 30 % and lowered sales training costs for new staff.

Drove customer retention 19% over a 30-month period by developing industry surveys, analyzing processes and establishing baseline customer satisfaction index. Introduced improvements leading to increased customer focus.

Established alliance with nationally-recognized development company to provide program design and implementation tools, leading to improved product quality and time-to-market and saving $155,000 in direct costs.

Developed long-range needs assessment and business plans during formation of new business which improved order accuracy of 200-person team 35% within the first six months of implementation.

Improved average time-to-market for product line by 21.4 % and reduced business unit costs to serve customers by more than $2,000,000 for the fiscal year.

William Ronner
Page 2

ACHIEVEMENTS CONT'D

Cross-trained and assimilated over 400 employees into parent company operations, matching experience/skill sets to key positions. Reduced operating costs 21% first year and avoided duplication.

Achieved sales club status the first year assigned to the corporation's poorest performing sales territory where its largest competitor was headquartered.

Established open communications in a company with history of organizational conflict. Initiated weekly meetings, encouraging employees to express ideas and other solutions. Created newsletter to inform work force of the company's progress and celebrate "wins." Demonstrated how information positively supported the efforts of everyone.

Identified opportunity and led re-engineering processes enabling company to emerge among the first operations to automate field sales activities. New technology expedited order processing and improved accuracy.

Acquired high profile, class "A" office facilities in major technological development center for 61% of average cost plus no-cost leasehold improvements. Saved $149,000 over five-year term.

Founded organization to provide support to family members and others experiencing loss during child custody proceedings. Grew local membership to 300 persons first year, appearing on numerous television and radio news/human interest programs and creating national recognition for the organization.

EXPERIENCE

President & Chief Operating Officer, **CarCom Technology**, Chicago, IL

Led $3,000,000 company during period of unprecedented growth by revising business objectives and plans in accordance with current conditions and initialing and directing marketing alliances with key business leaders.

The Miller & Miller Company, Springfield, IL

> *Director & General Manager,* **Marketing, Retail Sales Enterprise - Automotive Systems Division,** Springfield, IL. Determined marketing product management strategies for dealership sales applications and services for $400,000,000 division of $1.2B corporation.

> *Director*, **Management Systems and Services - Automotive Systems Division**, Springfield, IL. Created, staffed new operation to re-engineer corporate processes and procedures for warehousing, manipulating, using data supporting targeted marketing/sales initiatives.

> *National Director,* **Administration, Planning and Statistics - Automotive Systems Division,** Springfield, IL. Managed sales administration/planning staff. Developed, implemented sales compensation plans, objectives, sales tracking/analysis processes for 200 sales representatives, managers, officers.

> *Regional Sales Manager* - **Chicago Region**. Directed 21 field sales representatives in six-state territory.

> *Assistant General Sales Manager,* Springfield, IL
> *Marketing Manager* - **Parts & Service Applications**, Springfield, IL
> *Sales Representative,* San Diego, CA
> *Manager* - **Customer Service & Support**, Bowling, IN
> *Instructor* - **Parts Inventory Control Systems**, Bowling, IN
> *Assistant* **Manager - Customer Service & Support**, Bowling, IN

Daryl Easton
~Business Consultant~

P.O. Box 262
Fairfax, Virginia 22185 (703) 555-1212

A **Logical, Realistic Manager** who handles multiple tasks competently, offering strong abilities in areas of:

- Leadership & Team Building
- Critical Thinking / Problem Solving
- Recommending & Managing Change
- Budgets / Financial Analysis
- Criteria Standards / Compliance
- PC's & Technical Tools
- Operations Management
- Negotiating Business Deals
- Project Management

OBJECTIVE:

To provide a consultative service that facilitates managing on-going business analysis, oversee project teams, and develop improvement plans, utilizing proven ability to:

- **Resolve problems efficiently and design / manage change**
- **Communicate effectively at all levels and assemble natural work groups**
- **Plan & manage business projects, handling all negotiations and implementations**

AREAS OF EXPERTISE	PERSONAL AWARDS
PROJECT PLANNING / MANAGEMENT	**COMMUNITY AWARENESS AWARD 1995** VIRGINIA STATE SENATE
PROBLEM SOLVING	**WHO'S WHO REGISTRY 1991**
FINANCIAL ANALYSIS	
STATISTICAL PROCESS CONTROL	**NATION'S BEST MILL 1990** NATIONAL TREE AND PAPER ORGANIZATION
INVENTORY MANAGEMENT	
ENVIRONMENTAL COMPLIANCE ISSUES	**THREE YEAR SAFETY RECORD 1985** MORACO PRODUCTS
SAFETY ANALYSIS / TRAINING	
PROCESS IMPROVEMENT STUDIES	**MOST IMPROVED SALES TERRITORY** MORACO PRODUCTS COMPANY
QUALITY ASSURANCE	**LOWEST INJURY RATE 1986** MORACO PRODUCTS COMPANY
CUSTOMER SERVICE	

EDUCATION AND TRAINING

Bachelor of Science, Education
State College, Annapolis, Maryland

Statistics
University of Virginia

Finance
University of Virginia

Effective Executive Workship
Meade Business School, Mason College

Stein Solutions and Decision Making

Principles of Selling

The Versatile Salesperson

PROFESSIONAL EXPERIENCE

<u>VICE PRESIDENT / GENERAL MANAGER</u>   Virginia Paperworks Corporation

Managed all operational aspects of a $20MM business including budgeting, P&L, manufacturing, compliance issues, and staffing. Orchestrated $10MM rebuild in less than 24 months, while maintaining ongoing operations. Developed staff and employee base to accommodate increased production capacity while maintaining cost containment goals.

<u>PRESIDENT/CEO</u>   Mayfair Recycling Inc.

Created new budget and five year plan incorporating capital spending plans. Created a sales and marketing group and developed new marketing plan. Implemented cash management policies and recovered $700M in 30 days. Developed quality and safety guidelines while improving productivity.

<u>PLANT MANAGER</u>   Moraco Products Company

Developed budgets and capital spending plan resulting in a 62% increase in productivity. Implemented 100% guaranteed quality program, managed National award winning safety program.

<u>PLANT SUPERINTENDENT</u>

Managed newly acquired facility to profitability in 9 months. Implemented new quality and safety programs. Improved productivity by 42%.

<u>QUALITY CONTROL/PRODUCTION SUPERVISOR</u>

Developed and implemented quality program. Created inventory tracking program reducing raw material storage costs.

ACHIEVEMENTS:

ORCHESTRATED **$1OMM**, 6-PHASE REBUILD of OPC **$11MM** facility of **$750MM** national paperboard company in less than 24 months, causing minimal operational stoppages.

RETAINED **100%** OF BUSINESS RELATIONSHIPS as well as maintaining confidence from **101** employees, **21** staff, and **75** vendors during Chapter 11 procedures.

SOLVED CRITICAL CASH SHORTAGE for a **$20MM** paper manufacturer by analyzing finished goods inventory and surplus equipment, developing **2** part plan (export sales and returned goods) to recover **$700K** cash in **30** days.

IMPLEMENTED PRODUCTION PERFORMANCE EVALUATION SYSTEM in operational and quality areas, reducing product variability by **76%**, provided an increase in operating time of **6%**, improved operating performance of major customers up to **67%**.

CREATED NEW MARKETING PLAN which eliminated flawed product mix, created annual operating budget for FRP, creating cost guidelines which in turn successfully reduced operating costs by **10%**. Also, planned and managed **$20MM** operating budget for another manufacturer.

PLANNED SIMM PROCESS SYSTEM for **$9MM** location of **$1B** international paper company that on completion yielded a **62%** increase in productivity.

NEGOTIATED ARRANGEMENT WITH MAJOR FUEL SUPPLIER to invest in the change of energy source, resulting in an operating savings of **$245K** and eliminated the need for a **$3MM** overhaul of existing equipment arrangement used as model for **3** subsequent deals, saving over **$1MM**/year.

MANAGED EXPANSION PROJECT, selecting and placing **32** staff into new responsibilities also improved overall productivity **15%**.

CONSULTING PHILOSOPHY

I believe most organizations already have the talent and staff to be able to solve many of their difficult problems. The real problem is that daily activities don't allow sufficient time to focus on solutions.

The role of the consultant is to provide an experienced resource to examine specific organizational problems, create and develop the system / process that the staff can implement, then train them to do so.

While I possess effective problem solving skills, I enjoy helping others find their own solutions by asking questions and sometimes playing "the Devil's Advocate". I attempt to create an environment where they can learn how to solve problems always with an eye on what's best for the organization as a whole.

Frequent meetings are necessary and important tools to communicate and reinforce the operations' goals and they are also effective problem solving venues when several departments will be affected by the result of policy decisions. I also encourage, particularly key staff members, to discuss issues and concerns one on one. I believe that this personalized attention serves as an effective learning environment.

I prefer to foster an atmosphere of openness and honesty where failure only exists when someone fails to ask for help when it becomes necessary, in a timely manner, or no action is taken when it is required. I believe in taking responsibility for all of my actions and I expect others to do the same. When an organization is doing well it is because the people are free to do the things that they do best.

I suppose I could be described as someone who enjoys a challenge and gets things done by encouraging the best from others.

WHAT HAVE...

Harry Williams, COO, Outfromt
Bill Benton, former Executive VP, Moraco Products Co.
Graham Bobson, Former Regional Manager, Moraco Products Co.
Ashly Harris, Division Controller, The Watson Group
Jack Russell, Regional VP, The Watson Group

SAID ABOUT DARYL EASTON

- Daryl has achieved a goal in safety that has set a new standard for our Company and our industry,

- He manages the lowest cost operation in the Company!

- Daryl and his staff have had excellent results improving productivity, quality, and customer relations.

- He has the ability to quickly analyze areas for improvement both operationally and financially.

- Understands the manufacturing from both micro and macro perspectives.

- Negotiated remarkable results for Mayfair's shareholders.

RICHARD PARKER
~Litigation Services & Business Consultant~

254 N. Columbus Avenue   (614) 555-1212
Burke, Virginia 43310   fax (614) 555-7777

A Results Oriented, Knowledgeable Executive with a keen insight into complex
business operations, offering strong abilities in areas of:

~ Finance & Accounting   ~ Analytical Problem Solving   ~ Effective Communication
~ Strategic Planning   ~ Organizational Relationships ~ Information Analysis
~ Business Valuation   ~ Systems & Process   ~ Expert Testimony

OBJECTIVE:

To provide a consulting service that enables attorneys and business owners to focus on
real issues and problems while developing approaches that achieve necessary objectives,
utilizing a proven ability to:

~ Communicate effectively at all organizational levels
~ Develop strategies based on critical analysis
~ Plan and manage business projects

AREAS OF EXPERTISE	PERSONAL AWARDS
FORENSIC ACCOUNTING	SERVICE TO YOUTH Phillip Kent Council, BSA
CONCEPTUALIZATION	
FINANCIAL ANALYSIS	SILVER OTTER Phillip Kent Council, BSA
PROBLEM SOLVING	
BUILDING RELATIONSHIP	
PROJECT PLANNING/MANAGEMENT	LEGION OF MERIT US Navy
BUSINESS ACQUISITION	
BUSINESS RECOVERY	
BUSINESS GROWTH PLANNING	MERITORIOUS SERVICE MEDAL US Navy
INCENTIVES SYSTEMS	

EDUCATION AND TRAINING

Bachelor of Arts	Philosophy	Parkside College
Masters of Accountancy	Accounting	University of Virginia
Certified Public Accounting	State of Virginia	

PROFESSIONAL EXPERIENCE

BUSINESS CONSULTANT   Miller, Jones, Potter & Hendricks
Conduct research and investigation of business matters and their legal ramifications. Provide expert testimony related to investigation. Provide written analysis and documentation of business practices.

                                            PlastiCare Inc.
Developed recovery plan for a financially stressed manufacturing company, interviewing management and supervisory personnel, reviewing technology and operations of three plants. Revised divisional budgets and eliminated unprofitable product lines. Re-engineered organizational structure and recommended change in business ethics. By the end of the fiscal year, recovered losses and generated $1.5 million in profit.

EXECUTIVE VICE PRESIDENT   Monk Foods, Inc.
Managed five vice presidents, six departments and had CFO responsibilities for a regional food service distributor. Developed many systems that complemented corporate goals and enabled the company to sustain rapid growth in a competitive environment. Sustained productivity rates substantially higher than industry average. Managed business acquisitions to include evaluation of business "fit," due diligence, pricing and transition.

SENIOR ACCOUNTANT   Leland & Wayne
Responsible for audits of businesses in a variety of industries including manufacturing, distribution, real estate, recreation and non-profit. Trained staff accountants in auditing techniques, business cycles and accounting theory. Prepared financial statements and governmental reports.

BATTALION COMMANDER   Navy Reserve
Commanded a supply and service battalion. Reorganized entire battalion due to downsizing then recruited and trained personnel for the change in mission. Selected in first year of eligibility for the rank of Captain.

ACHIEVEMENTS:

BUILT $11MM COMPANY TO **$130MM** in sales within **18** years, acquiring **5** other companies, and managing **5** senior executives.

ACQUIRED & DEVELOPED **5** small to mid-sized companies in the range of **$5-15** million, increasing sales over **40%** and propelling the company to regional status **40%**.

PLANNED AND SUSTAINED DYNAMIC GROWTH RATE of **25%** per year through high volume warehousing, specialized distribution methods, and information systems designs.

DEVELOPED INFORMATION SYSTEMS to parallel growth of **$130MM** company; coordinated the data processing support; procured "cutting edge" computer hardware and software.

MANAGED 5 EXPANSION PROJECTS of warehouse and office facilities, increasing from **20,000 SF** to **198,000 SF**, developing operational and architectural plans, coordinating with contractors; met all budgets.

ENGINEERED RECOVERY OF FINANCIALLY STRESSED COMPANY through analysis and restructuring, creating **$1.5MM** of profit in **6** months.

UNCOVERED **$2MM** IN HIDDEN BUSINESS PRACTICES and corporate shelters that were the basis for client's legal claim by performing detailed forensic accounting audit.

CONDUCTED ANNUAL LOGISTICAL MOVEMENT of **4,000** personnel and heavy equipment involving air, rail and ground transportation with a strong, successful emphasis on safety.

CONSULTING PHILOSOPHY

BASIC PARADIGM: Every organization should be guided by their mission statement. Each individual has a personal responsibility to support that mission by doing their job to the best of their ability. To be successful everyone must do more than just manage, they must take the initiative and anticipate requirements before they happen.

MIND SET: All members of the organization should be aware of the customers needs. To do one's job is the minimum to be expected and does not require an awareness of the customer's needs. To excel at one's job requires an intensity and urgency to plan for and satisfy the customer.

PROFESSIONALISM: In order to create a positive working environment, everyone must manage, not monitor. Managing implies controlling the situation and directing it to a desired outcome. This means using known policies and procedures at all times, and making conscious, documented decisions to support the organization when policies and procedures do not meet the common sense test.

PLANNING: Current operations must be guided by a strategic plan. Each manager and supervisor must incorporate the plans for their area into the overall plan. Only then will each person understand their role in the accomplishment of the strategic plan. Managers should not get caught in the trap of working hard and accomplishing little. Time must be spent to analyze what should be done. When putting a plan into action, do what is right because it is the right thing to do. Doing what is easy in the short run will create greater problems in the long run.

LEADERSHIP: Time must be taken to mentor individuals. The results will far exceed the efforts. A good leader listens and guides the ideas and concerns of others. The most important contribution we can make is to develop individuals to their maximum potential.

The greatest compliment you can pay yourself is to work your way out of a job. Those who work for you should desire to become so capable that they require little direct guidance. This does not mean to be a friend rather, than a boss. Expect a lot from those who work for you, and they will generally live up to your expectations. Set worthy goals that are both measurable and obtainable, and then expect them to be accomplished.

Leadership is a process of influencing others. It is carried out by applying varying leadership attributes such as beliefs, values, ethics, character, knowledge and skills. When someone new to the organization is deciding if he respects you, he does not think about each of these attributes. He watches what you do so then he can tell what you are. The basis of effective leadership is honorable character and selfless service.

- Bad news does not get better with age.

- Talk to the source, not someone interpreting the source.

- Don't treat symptoms; go for the disease.

- Try to be a synergistic thinker. Look at how the parts affect the whole.

Parker Robertson
9987 Oakenshaw Drive
Miami, FL 33765
(817) 555-1212

OBJECTIVE

A position utilizing my skills in **Financial Analysis, Planning, Market Development, Sales, Problem Solving, Training** and **Presentations** in order to:

- devise and implement strategies to enable an individual or organization to make money, save money and avoid undue liabilities
- identify and resolve issues to achieve organizational objectives and goals
- improve profits through leadership and staff and client educational programs
- increase revenues through enhanced services and target marketing.

QUALIFICATIONS

- Financial Analysis/Planning
- Financial Services
- Investment Analysis
- Market Development/Sales
- Territory Management
- Project Management

- Problem Solving
- Consulting
- Staff Management
- Business Analysis
- Tax Laws/Codes
- Strategic Planning

- Training
- Executive Presentations
- Customer Service/Relations
- Leadership/Motivation
- Event Planning
- Computer Skills

WORK HISTORY

Consultant
  Parker Robertson, CHFC, FL   1997 - Present
Financial Planner
  Jones Mutual Financial Services, Inc., FL   1995 - 1997
Financial Planner
  Namesake Financial, FL   1989 - 1995
Financial Planner/Owner
  Zolan, Inc., SC   1981 - 1988
Medical Sales Representative
  BioMed Laboratories, Inc., SC   1979 - 1981
Medical Sales Representative
  Othello Diagnostics, Inc., SC   1974 - 1979

EDUCATION and PROFESSIONAL

Bachelor of Science Degree, South Carolina State University

Series 7 NASD License
Life and Health Insurance Licenses
Series 63 License

Chartered Financial Consultant   1989

ACHIEVEMENTS

Financial Analysis and Planning

Structured financial plans for group of 17 doctors which saved them $.40 in income taxes for each $1 earned. Gathered financial data; analyzed individual conditions; consulted on needs and goals; investigated tax savings and investment programs, services and products; customized plans; persuaded each client to adopt and implement comprehensive plans to match objectives. **Results:** Increased retirement income by 35%; avoided tens of thousands of dollars in future income and estate taxes; protected assets from potential liabilities.

Designed multi-faceted estate plan for wealthy client looking to maximize his only child's inheritance. Collected estate and investment details; made comprehensive analysis of current and future tax liabilities; trust arrangements; identified most tax efficient and cost-effective products; presented detailed gameplan to client. **Results:** Reduced future estate taxes by $1.7 million; eliminated $420,000 in capital gains taxes; created $3 million gift to charities; increased inheritance and social prestige for child.

Detailed "recovery" program for professional client to save pension plan more than $130,000 in income and penalty taxes. Scrutinized new tax laws relating to retirement plans; consulted with outside pension expert; assembled financials; selected best product; initiated and synchronized document filings and investment timing; educated client as to purpose and impact of plan implementation. **Result:** Client redirected $110,000 in taxes and $22,000 in penalties into his own retirement account at a total cost of $10,000.

Restructured client's portfolio to generate $1 million additional retirement income. Analyzed investment portfolio; identified discretionary funds capable of being sheltered and better managed; involved client in long range planning and goal setting; chose program; educated client. **Results:** Avoided 45% tax liability on earnings; saved client $260,000.

Coordinated reorganization of elderly client's savings in excess of $500,000 into tax sheltered investments. Evaluated risk tolerances and income requirements for lifestyle; found safest and most effective alternatives and companies to accomplish goals; taught client about tax control methods; persuaded to reposition away from certificates of deposit. **Results:** Saved over $12,000 in taxes yearly for rest of life; had open access to his money; increased inheritance to beneficiaries by $80,000.

Problem Solving/Consulting

Solved future capital gains tax problem, enhanced annual income and secured tax deduction for professional client. Consulted; accumulated financials; calculated current liabilities; investigated programs that would contribute to tax savings and increased income; made recommendation; educated on implementation. **Results:** Saved $40,000 in income tax and $88,000 in estate taxes; received $35,000 income tax deduction; realized $110,000 additional income during lifetime; donated $320,000 to charity.

Set up system to alert clients to crucial tenth year premium anniversary dates to take advantage of reduced costs. Researched peculiarity in contract; identified clients at risk developed strategy; demonstrated need to amend cost structure; coordinated with plan provider. **Results:** Secured 33% rate reduction annually for each client; maintained full coverage.

Maximized efficiency of mortgage loan operation to accelerate loan processing and closing times. Delegated underwriting, processing and closing functions for quick preparation of loans; organized program to pre-sign documents before actual closing date; oversaw 1 to 3 day turnaround of closed loans to companies that purchased loans and provided proceeds. **Results:** Reduced closing time by 2 weeks; builders received proceeds of sale 2 to 4 weeks sooner than industry average.

Spearheaded multi-committee "Great Days of Service" for volunteer force to perform service projects for disadvantaged families and family service organizations. Coordinated and oversaw project selection, liaison relations with county officials, staffing equipment and supplies, conducted meetings; managed 150 to 250 volunteers for each day of service. **Results:** Completed more than 24 projects to aid people and organizations in need.

Sales/Training Presentations

Presented series of financial planning seminars for physicians and teaching staff at South Carolina College of Medicine. Researched programs provided by state and facility, designed seminars to address goals at various career stages; coached on prioritizing needs; instructed on income and asset protection; offered services. **Results:** Received requests for services; illustrated potential savings to $190,000 for several attendees.

Created "road show" seminars geared to service organizations including Key Club, Lions and Chambers of Commerce as well as to retirees. Contacted service organization chairpeople; persuaded to schedule program; negotiated hotel space for general audience seminars; designed and mailed invitations; determined topics based on targeted needs; wrote scripts; produced slides, overheads and handouts; made presentation; sold. **Results:** Increased business; demonstrated ability to adapt style to any audience in any setting.

Produced sales training manual for regional sales force for new Westall product line. Investigated applications; compared competitors' products; studied features and benefits; organized method of presenting to customer base, designed manual; conducted work-shop and training sessions. **Results:** Provided for easy assimilation of information; eliminated need for extensive training program; hastened ability to effectively sell line.

Developed training manual for elders of church in need of guidance in dealing with communities and ministries. Analyzed activities and works; studied purpose of each committee and ministry; conceived format; wrote text; laid out and produced manual; trained elders. **Results:** Became primary reference for working effectively within organization.

Brian D. Jenkins
8806 Cather Avenue
Ft. Lauderdale, FL 33456
(775) 555-1212

OBJECTIVE

A management position utilizing my skills in **Financial Management, Portfolio Analysis, Strategic Planning, Business Development, Problem Solving** and **Decision Making** in order to:

- improve profitability through fiscal accountability and strengthening of internal controls
- research, develop and implement systems and procedures to improve operating effectiveness while increasing market share
- identify weaknesses to eliminate fraud, waste and mismanagement
- enhance personnel performance through leadership and staff development.

QUALIFICATIONS

Qualified by extensive experience in:

- Financial Management
- Portfolio Analysis
- Budget Development
- P&L Analysis
- Investments
- Administrative Management
- Strategic Planning
- Problem Solving/Decision Making
- Negotiations
- Policies and Procedures
- Business Analysis
- Sales and Marketing
- Business Development
- Executive Presentations
- Organizational Development
- Leadership/Motivation
- Liaison Relations
- Consulting

WORK HISTORY

BDJ Consulting, FL	1997 - Present
Consultant	
Myers Computer Supplies, FL	1992 - 1997
President	
Wilson James Hughes, FL	1988 - 1991
Vice President	
Bass Brothers, FL	1982 - 1988
Vice President, Mortagage Sales and Trading	
American Mortgage Association, TX	1971 - 1982
Director of Mortgage Backed Securities	
Accounting Manager	
Murphy Foods, Inc.	1967 - 1971
Controller-Office Manager	

EDUCATION

Florida State University, FL
BA Studies in Mathematics
The University of Miami, FL
ABA Accounting

COMPUTER SKILLS

- Microsoft Word - PowerPoint - Excel - Access -

PERSONAL

- Willing to Travel and Relocate - Golf - Deep Sea Fishing - Writing "How to" Book -

ACHIEVEMENTS

Financial Management/Portfolio Analysis

Uncovered fraud involving mortgage originator and government employees. Diagnosed anomalies in foreclosure files; analyzed data; determined violations were occurring; identified magnitude of problem; notified authorities. **Results:** $200 million scam was discovered and shut down.

Led 90 person loan accounting department through reconciliation, centralization and system conversion. Identified deficient procedures; analyzed manpower requirements; formulated organizational structure; budgeted for optimum conversion completion. **Results:** Multi-billion dollar conversion completed and reconciled on budget.

Conceived and **developed** automated reports analysis system to assist in client audits. Observed difficulty in manually analyzing volume of monthly reports; highlighted areas in need of attention; conducted cost/benefit analysis; coordinated system development effort; established monitoring mechanism; implemented program. **Results:** Doubled monitoring capacity; found illegal use of custodial cash accounts; reduced operating costs while improving efficiency.

Predicted failure of large southern financial institution. Analyzed low interest rate portfolio and proposal for change; evaluated present status; produced data and reports demonstrating future performance under alternative economic scenarios; briefed Board of Directors; recommended against liquidation of portfolio and purchase of high interest rate investments; prescribed counter-strategy; was ignored. **Results:** Institution failed as direct consequence of pursuing its original course of action.

Raised capital for start-up golf wholesale distributing operation. Evaluated opportunity; consulted with entrepreneur; negotiated interest; co-authored business plan; targeted financial institutions and outside investors; made presentations; negotiated funds. **Results:** Within 3 years business grew to $5 million; made profit since inception.

Strategic Planning/Business Development

Educated financial institution executives on value of new security return on capital. Analyzed portfolio holdings; identified range of products to enhance earnings; determined funding options; consulted with staff; formulated presentation strategies; made recommendations to Board of Directors and Chief Investment Officers at institutions including: Pier Savings, National Home Savings, All Life, Home Bank, EastBank. **Results:** Company led Wall Street in mortgage security sales for five years.

Created FNMA Mortgage Backed Security. Researched mortgage security availability; identified range of structures; evaluated; authored issuer guidelines; consulted with Wall Street experts including Pascal Brothers, First Miami Corp, SkyCorp, St. Germain; determined guarantee fee levels; conceived implementation strategy; introduced securities to capital markets. **Results:** FNMA is largest single issuer of mortgage securities; generated several billion dollars net profit.

Controlled data management of 25,000 plus foreclosures per year. Conceived and instituted automated foreclosure analysis system to analyze collection results, recognize unacceptable write-offs, determine causes and uncover payment deficiencies; formulated plan to reduce miscommunications among interested parties. **Results:** Eliminated annual loss of $3 to $5 million of uncollected proceeds; reduced staff by 30%; increased profits.

Invented wrist pad for prevention or relief of pain from carpal tunnel syndrome. Anticipated work place need; consulted with doctors and therapists; organized sales and distribution business around product; directed design engineer; arranged for production; developed marketing/advertising plan to include television commercials. **Results:** Product well received by doctors and users.

Problem Solving & Decision Making

Solved dilemma of how to sell mortgage portfolios and simultaneously issue guaranteed mortgage securities. Analyzed accounting requirements; identified and evaluated procedural options; crafted solution; educated principals as to how and why would work. **Results:** GNMA conducted successful $53 billion sale of mortgages at better than normal market rates; purchasers able to market new securities at profit and avoid timing risk; transaction catapulted "Ginnie Maes" to prominence in capital markets.

Negotiated $250 million loan Street Dealer to "sell short" for delivery in forty-five days. Determined amount needed and timing; surveyed market availability; convinced dealer to commit; followed up to assure delivery. **Results:** Met for issuance; generated $2.5 million profit.

Perceived plan to eliminate legal and political impediments to accessibility and construction of golf course clubhouse. Diagnosed difficulty of crossing land financed by Washington Savings and Loan and under control of RTC; surveyed government contacts to identify appropriate person to address issues; negotiated deal for road construction on RTC land in exchange for sub-division lots and removal of other restrictions preventing construction. **Results:** Impediments removed; clubhouse built; grant of property compensated club for its extraordinary expenditures.

Carl L. Benton
2258 Old Apple Road
College Park, CO 87654
(656) 555-1212
carlb@anywhere.net

OBJECTIVE

A Management Position with a growth oriented company utilizing my skills in **Distribution Management, Warehouse Management, Operations Management** and **Employee & Customer Relations** in order to:

- direct and coordinate most effective and economical modes of transportation
- evaluate methods of packaging, warehousing and loading
- coordinate with production, sales, records and purchasing in order to increase operating efficiency
- provide effective leadership, motivation and staff development to achieve organizational goals

QUALIFICATIONS

- Distribution Management
- Warehouse Management
- Inventory/Loss Control
- Transportation
- Logistics

- Operations Management
- Cost Control
- Business Liaison Relations
- Problem Solving
- Customer Relations

- Employee Relations
- Personnel Management
- Budget Development
- Food Product Knowledge
- Training/Presentation

EXPERIENCE

Rocket Associates, Inc.		1997 - Present
Sales Associate		
Gentle Soap Company		1995 - 1996
Distribution Operations Analyst		
Jones & Parker Manufacturing Company		1971 - 1994
Southeast Regional Soap Distribution Manager	1991 - 1994	
Distribution Center Liaison Manager	1987 - 1991	
Plant Liaison Manager	1981 - 1987	
Shortening & Oils Department Manager	1978 - 1981	
Employee Services Manager	1975 - 1978	
Team Manager	1971 - 1975	
US Army		
Captain, Missile Combat Crew Commander		1967 - 1971

EDUCATION

Masters of Science Degree in Business Management
Sunset University (Formerly Albany Methodist University), TX
Bachelor of Arts Degree in Physics
Colorado Springs Institute, CO

Training in: TQM, Human Resources, EPA, Real Estate

COMPUTER SKILLS

Electronic Data Interchange (EDI), SAP (Inventory, Order Shipping), Microsoft Word, Excel, Lotus, PowerPoint, Windows 95, Netscape

ACHIEVEMENTS

Distribution/Warehouse Management

Devised plan to circumvent French price controls by distributing foreign produced Parker & Jones products through three US distribution centers. Identified need to control distribution and create market to supply French living in US, sent shipments from international to domestic centers and sold to wholesale trade. **Results:** Increased customer satisfaction; brands showed 11% profit with no adverse impact on distribution costs.

Incorporated distribution expansion of experimental brand nationwide from my plant while continuing normal distribution of a total brand family in the Southwest. Formulated plan to contract local distribution facility, trained 40 employees in less than six months, provided on-site and participated in and monitored data system set-up. **Results:** Transfer of stock was accomplished without negative customer impact; no shipment shortages occurred; distribution costs decreased by $0.05 per case due to increased volume; contract facility costs saved customer $0.04 per case.

Managed distribution center operations during 5-week disaster clean-up following 100-year storm. Saved and shipped 185 trailer loads prior to road closings, determined number and value of lost cases, provided data for claims and took extraordinary safety precautions. **Results:** Saved $2,552,000 by rescuing 232,000 cases.

Persuaded sales, customer service and manufacturing managers to sell "Customer Pick-up Plan". Set up strategy sessions, explained benefits of backhauling for both company and customers and methods of operation. **Results:** Saved company $1.2 million.

Developed production plan to cover customer shipments in Denver shipping territory following manufacturing failure at northeast site. Reorganized southeast operations to facilitate distant coverage, scheduled weekend extended hours and notified sales and manufacturing of changes. **Results:** No shorted customer shipments occurred from Colorado to Nevada by plant changes; non-plant customer shipments were not delayed.

Operations Management

Conducted several seminars for carriers and customers to explain conversion to SAP and interlinks via EDI. Created handouts, diagrams, chartpads and audio-visual aids, presented materials and "what-if" scenarios and followed with question and answer period. **Results:** System in place within 6 weeks; surpassed old system capability and reliability.

Scheduled packing bin and line to eliminate at least one brand changeover semi-weekly. Reorganized production plan to maximize run times and coordinated with material suppliers. **Results:** Saved, at minimum, $440,000 annually.

Directed/Planned operation of shipping dry goods from Washington to Panama to reduce transportation costs. Evaluated existing route, designed re-route of vans on flat cars through Eastern Lake,Tennessee, and coordinated with new carrier. **Results:** Saved $100,000 annually in transportation costs; saved $.15 per case in distribution costs; no lost delivery time.

Managed edible oil line changeover from glass to plastic containers with no disruption of service. Scheduled off-hour times, trained technicians on safety prior to installation of hot-melt technology, cleaned out lines, changed equipment, coordinated changeover with rails, tracks and bottle-feed supply and instructed on weights and volume measurements and on new stacking methods. **Results:** Line operational 3 days ahead of schedule.

Employee/Customer Relations

Chaired Denver plant sixtieth year Open House celebration for 1800 plus employees, customers, local government officials, friends and family. Brainstormed with staff, set up committees, allocated manpower, devised plan to permit all employees to participate, established rotating visitation system, mapped tour route and coordinated transportation. **Results:** Reaffirmed and strengthened good will; demonstrated plant's environmentally friendly operation; came in below budget.

Led intra-department effort to empower 93 technicians and five managers. Identified need to increase efficiency, recommended technicians assume responsibilities and make decisions on-site rather than rely on off-site planner and persuaded management to accept plan. **Results:** Improved morale; heightened productivity.

Reorganized interview process of non-management plant positions for 450 employees to incorporate Total Assessment Guidelines and meet diversity targets. Directed and managed staff, screened applications, oversaw test administration, interviewed, reviewed confidential background checks and hired. **Results:** Caliber of employees improved with 93% eligible to further develop their careers within organization.

Selected to represent Parker & Jones' college recruitment program for five of its manufacturing operations. Coordinated with placement office personnel, professors and plant personnel managers, recruited, interviewed and recommended potential new hires. **Results:** Stimulated interest in company; one-third of suggested applicants accepted positions.

Kevin M. Beckwith
9804 Robnel Avenue
San Diego, CA 98798
(775) 555-1212

OBJECTIVE

A management position utilizing my skills in **Environmental Technology and Engineering, Environmental Law** and **Risk Management** in order to:

- ensure an organization achieves compliance using the most cost-effective means
- interpret laws so that an organization understands what it needs to do and not do to be in compliance
- assess and mitigate environmental health and safety risks through strong leadership and fiscal accountability.

QUALIFICATIONS

Qualified by 16 years experience in:

- Environmental Engineering
- Hazardous Waste Treatment
- Biochemical Engineering
- Analytic Chemistry
- Fluid Dynamics
- Control Systems

- Environmental Law
- Litigation Investigation
- Compliance Audits
- Negotiations
- Governmental Liaison
- Policies and Procedures

- Risk Management
- Remedial Management
- Property Audits
- Project Management
- Training/Presentations
- ISO - 14000

WORK HISTORY

President
  Beckwith, Trevor & Burke, Inc.   1993 - Present
Regional Manager, Hazardous Waste
Manager, Technical Services
Engineer
  Kendrick Environmental Services, Inc.   1985 - 1993
Attorney/Project Engineer
  MicroTech Engineering Corp.   1981 - 1985
Attorney
  Kevin M. Beckwith, Attorney at Law   1980 - 1981

EDUCATION and PROFESSIONAL

Juris Doctor   1979
  Eton University School of Law, San Diego, CA
  Legal Research Assistant
Bachelor of Arts   1976
  Eton University College of Liberal Arts, San Diego, CA
  Biochemical Engineering Research Assistant, Eton School of Medicine, San Diego, CA

Admitted to State Bars of California (1980) and Oregon (1982)

Registered Environmental Manager   1992

COMPUTER SKILLS

• Microsoft Word • Excel • PowerPoint • DOS • Windows • MacDraft •
• MacDraw • Gridzo • Statworks • PageMaker •

ACHIEVEMENTS

Environmental Technology and Engineering

Fixed groundwater model prepared by another firm for consortium of insurance companies stuck with costly cleanup to fit site with state requirements. Identified problems (groundwater above ground, uphill flow, and inapplicable statistical procedures, etc.); corrected them by incorporating ditches into model; wrote computer program to calculate optimal input parameters. **Results:** State accepted model as centerpiece in complex action plan and later used to limit scope of damages in related class-action suit brought by families using down-gradient, contaminated water; estimated savings greater than $1 million.

Invented algebraic method for graphic display of water table elevations which reproduced judgment of experienced geologists. Combined two mathematical techniques: calculation of best-fit surface through series of points in space and inverse-square weighting to smooth differences. **Results:** Reduced substantial amount of senior-level time to mechanical process which could be performed by clerk; eliminated arguments over "professional opinion"; resolved interpretive problems.

Designed electrical controls for miniature wastewater treatment system for vibratory deburring industry. Analyzed problems stemming from variable flow; integrated electrochemical treatment portion of process with flow control mechanisms; enabled system to speed up, slow down, and turn itself on and off in response to changes in upstream production without lapsing into inefficient batch-mode operation. **Results:** Cut number of components necessary for device; dropped its price by several thousand dollars per unit which made it practical.

Managed design development and permitting for first bioremediation systems in California (Hollywood Naval Shipyard) and Oregon (tank site in Portland). Convinced regulatory community of viability of using naturally occurring soil microbes to petroleum; demonstrated process. **Results:** Achieved two cleanups; eliminated need for dig and haul alternative; saved each location several hundred thousand dollars.

Environmental Law

Persuaded three federal and state agencies to accept cyanide contamination as harmless after all had ordered cyanide to be cleaned up to limits of detection. Analyzed relevant agency policy directives and guidance documents; showed that cyanide concentrations met functional equivalent of drinking water standards; found series of obscure agency policies requiring agencies to grant relief requested. **Results:** Saved cost of cleanup with estimated savings of $0.5 million; avoided need to secure Resource Recovery Act permit eliminating need to cleanup several solid waste management units with estimated savings greater than $2 Million; was first successful Alternative Concentration Limit petition in EPA's West Region VI.

Convinced state that toxic metals observed in some wells in and near spill site were not part of spill and did not need to be cleaned up. Used statistical means; showed that metals rose and fell whenever organic acids were present regardless of whether spilled or naturally occurring. **Results:** State dropped request for additional metals assays; eliminated need for cleanup order; estimated savings greater than $1 Million.

Developed emergency and spill response plan for hazardous materials transportation and processing facility covering DOT, EPA, and OSHA. Reviewed and dissected preparedness and response planning requirements that could apply to any facility; constructed plan from modules capable of expansion; provided for easy customization. **Results:** Plan did not become obsolete as conditions or regulations changed; estimated savings of $1000 per year per facility; trained members of firms on plan; firm used plan to generate business with several clients and potential clients.

Drafted comprehensive assessment of environmental compliance for major lighting manufacturer in California and its Utah headquarters. Reviewed, compared and contrasted state and federal regulations; identified areas of over and under compliance. **Results:** Resolved conflict between plant and headquarters; cut costs in enough areas to pay for remediating shortcomings; achieved net cost reduction.

Risk Management

Built and **defended** complex risk assessment for EPA covering controversial PCB processing plant proposed by Carbine shortly after Zaire disaster. Gathered data on predicting occurrence and effects of potential spill scenarios of earthquakes, airplane crashes, fire, trucking accidents, etc.; quantified exposure to PCB's under worse case conditions; listened and responded to public concerns while defending EPA's official position. **Results:** Analysis formed basis for EPA's permitting decision; generated goodwill; eased tensions; facilitated consensus.

Coordinated development of portable system for washing oil and grease covered railroad ballast (rocks). Identified method to recycle rocks; combined system used for washing rock for landscaping purposes with traditional waste water treatment technology (gravity settling followed by inorganic coagulation, polymer electrolytes and dispersed air flotation) to separate contaminants from rock. **Results:** System met all state and federal requirements at cost which averaged 20% less than cost of landfilling; saved money by recycling rock.

Performed comprehensive assessment of environmental compliance at national firm in textile rental laundry industry. Found many plants having trouble meeting wastewater regulations; reasoned certain provisions were either useless or counterproductive and probably would be changed in-due course; characterized to senior management noncompliance as reasonable and necessary under circumstances. **Results:** Resolved conflict between senior management and corporate environmental staff; avoided millions of dollars for unnecessary compliance costs.

Wrote comprehensive environmental compliance audit report for chemical formulator in Montpelier, VT that explained how to comply with spirit and intent of law when it conflicted with strict letter of applicable requirements. Reviewed purposes behind law and history of plant's relationship with local sewer authority; demonstrated that drafters did not intend to apply law to inconsequential violations; made recommendations to keep certain chemicals out of lines and change time of discharge to eliminate other violations. **Results:** Avoided need for treatment system; estimated savings of $70,000.

Daniel Carson
9876 Bedlam Circle
Houston, TX 30556-9834
(770) 555-1212

OBJECTIVE

A position utilizing my skills in **Project Management, Image Improvement, Business Development** and **Problem Solving** in order to:

- expand an organization's impact and profitability
- employ effective methods to improve quality and cost control
- plan strategies to achieve objectives and goals

QUALIFICATIONS

- Project Management
- Image improvement
- Customer/Client Relations
- Advertising

- Business Development
- Sales &Marketing
- Multimedia Development
- Color/Concept Management

- Problem Solving
- Quality Control
- Management
- Employee Training

EMPLOYMENT HISTORY

Owner, Consultant, Colorist	
Daniel "The Man" Carson, Houston, TX	1997 - Present
Senior Colorist	
Super Video Associates, Athens, TX	1995 - 1997
AdExec, Inc., Yuma, AZ	1994 - 1995
On The Edge, Rialta, NM	1993 - 1994
Eastern Imaging, Tiana, NM	1991 - 1993
Visual Effects, Centerville, NM	1990 - 1991
Color Concepts, Inc., El Paso, TX	1987 - 1990
Telescribe, Houston, TX	1985 - 1987
Audio Engineer	
Audio Effects, Houston, TX	1983 - 1985
Production/Stage Manager, Audio Engineer	
Pot of Gold Music Hall, Houston, TX	1982 - 1984
Owner, Audio Engineer	
Carson, Inc., Houston, TX	1976 - 1983

AWARDS AND RECOGNITIONS

Finalist for Spirit Award for Christian Music Video of the Year (Randy Pitt)	1996
Finalist for Spirit Award for Christian Music Video of the Year (The Newton Boys)	1995
Won Patra Award for Best Televised Commercial (Cyclo)	1995
Finalist for TNS Best National Televised Commercial (CarFast)	1993
Finalist for TNS Best National Televised Documentary (DocuChannel)	1993
Finalist for ARV Country Music Video of the Year Award (Mandy Parker)	1989

EDUCATION AND PROFESSIONAL

Bachelor of Arts Studies, Valentine State College
Member: Association of Movie & TV Engineers, National Television Society, Navy Association, Telecom Internet Group, TX Veterans Alliance

COMPUTER AND TECHNICAL SKILLS

PC, Unix, Macintosh, DOS, Windows, Microsoft Works, Word

Proficient with Rank telecines and Phillips datacine, DaVinci and Colorvision color correctors and supporting equipment. Work in both NTSC and PAL.

ACHIEVEMENTS

Project Management

Contributed to the successful marketing campaigns of over 2500 projects encompassing products and services for television, the music industry, advertising agencies, major corporations, industrial manufacturers, public service organizations and the Internet through visual enhancement. Analyzed and improved images using hi-tech, state-of-the-art motion picture film and digital video equipment, increased resolution, manipulated images, transferred film to tape, coordinated and consulted with directors, directors of photography and advertising agency personnel. Representative projects include commercials or advertisements for:

NationCom (Needle Drop), River Spray, Pepso, Cola Phiz
BDM, Milky's, Moore Beer, MicroTech, Chiplets, PineTree Inc., Doughboy
Monda, SegaMasters, SmartLink, Bike, Sneakers, McDaniel's, BellNorth, CCI, Button's
Happy's, StateLife, The Universal Channel, The Toons Network, VTV
Curtaintime, Smithson Barnnet, MVM, Hooch Home Entertainment.

Devised and designed special effects to capture mood and essence of project and improve quality:

* Innovated technique of slowing down and smearing image for Randy Jackson video
* Applied the color tints to black and white film simultaneously for Lauren Tay music video
* Created velvet-like texture to flat film and perceived idea to overlay various facial parts on different faces to make new faces for Newton Boys award winning video
* Imposed vibrant colors, image warping and alternate speeds to create unique effect for Texas State Insurance.

Business Development

Marketed services as only free-lance colorist in South and introduced clients to services offered by Creighton Communications, Inc. Networked, contacted prior clients, explained benefits of using extended services, acted as liaison and troubleshot. **Results:** Both ventures have grown; brought in over $25,000 in first month for company.

Established first film transfer department at Southern Images, a post production facility in Texas. Patterned department after successful midwest state-of-the-art operation created the year before, selected equipment, conducted seminars, trained and cross-trained employees throughout facility, developed, organized and planned site, launched grand opening, promoted services and created marketing tools, recruited new clients, troubleshot, managed, evaluated, and improved overall operation. **Results:** New department generated $1 million revenue first year and $1.5 million in second year; became "beta" site to test new hardware and software; effected changes in design and/or software.

Guided company out of bankruptcy. Established new policies, procedures and systems to operate, marketed, persuaded and negotiated with clients, supervised and trained employees and directed operation. **Results:** Revenues grew to $750,000 annually.

Published articles in international trade magazine to promote business. Emphasized need to improve images through use of digital rather than analog technology and explained how operation employed state-of-the-art equipment. **Results:** Client base grew.

Problem Solving

Modified procedure to simplify and streamline film to tape post production path for "The Chronicles of Zenon" television series produced by Luke Sanders. Reviewed and analyzed system, calculated time, cost, quality and complexity and conceived an alternative method of operation. **Results:** Achieved better quality at lower cost; clarified direction and reduced problem areas.

Delayed aging in burn pattern on CRT. Analyzed problem, designed strategy to prevent premature aging, tested, modified, evaluated, and sold engineering department on procedure and implemented new strategy. **Results:** Saved $25,000 a year in maintenance or replacement; decreased man-hours to correct; increased revenue.

James L. Parker
62 Bellview Drive
Pittsburgh, PA 11876
(455) 555-1212

OBJECTIVE

A position that will utilize my skills in **Investments, Acquisitions, Management, Business Development** and **Strategic Business Planning** in order to:

- explore expansion growth opportunities domestically and internationally
- enhance an organization's impact, image and client base
- maximize legal, financial and managerial background to optimize performance and profitability
- design and communicate long range and short range goals and objectives

QUALIFICATIONS

Qualified by extensive experience in:

- Investments
- Mergers & Acquisitions
- Business/Real Estate Law
- P&L/Operations Analysis
- Lender Relations
- Negotiations

- Management
- Business Development
- Financial Management
- Marketing & Sales
- Problem Solving
- Customer/Client Relations

- Strategic Business Planning
- Franchise/Start-up Operations
- Venture Capital
- Consulting
- Image Development
- Leadership/Motivation

WORK HISTORY

Chief Executive Officer	1987 - Present
Parker & Associates	
President and Chief Executive Officer	1987 - Present
Milo Title Insurance, Inc.	
Senior Vice President and Chief Financial Officer	1984 - 1986
B&J Insurance Services. Inc.	
Financial & Legal Affairs Vice President	1981 - 1983
Johnson Farm Foods, Inc.	
Executive Vice President	1978 - 1981
ECC Holdings Inc.	

EDUCATION and PROFESSIONAL MEMBERSHIPS

Juris Doctor Degree	1978
Radford University	
Masters Degree in Business Administration	1975
Bachelor of Science Degree in Finance	1973
University of Pennsylvania	

Member: Pennsylvania Bar Association, Virginia Bar Association, Maryland Bar Association

Member: Mortgage Brokers Association, American Land Title Association

PERSONAL

• Golf • Greens Committee, Country Club of the South • Boating •

ACHIEVEMENTS

Investments and Acquisitions

Established and **marketed** law firm/title agency franchise that handles over $700 million worth of real estate transactions annually. Perceived idea; designed operational protocol; analyzed markets; identified qualified attorneys; negotiated terms and conditions; purchased leased office space with equipment; handled client development/ relations. **Results:** Grew business to 10 locations with revenues in excess of $12 million.

Invested in retail shopping center in Pennsylvania resort area. Evaluated business opportunity, conducted due diligence; formulated action plan; reviewed and approved architectural plans; prepared construction budget; negotiated with lenders; drafted tenant lease agreements; oversaw project. **Results:** Project in progress.

Orchestrated establishment of mortgage banking business specializing in non-conforming mortgage products. Conceived idea to solidify business relationship for title company and assist mortgagee owners in obtaining requisite licensing; presented proposal; negotiated agreement; facilitated reception of warehouse credit lines. **Results:** Primary business became vendor of choice for title and transactional services; generated over $400,000 in annual gross revenues for title company.

Raised venture capital for start-up waste management company. Consulted with founders; evaluated merit of business; directed preparation of business plan prospectus; arranged for and attended meetings with potential lending institutions and private investors. **Results:** Raised needed $3 million in one month.

Launched aggressive acquisition plan to maximize corporate growth. Targeted smaller rivals; met with CEOs and accountants: analyzed acquirees' financial statements and books of business; made decision to go forward; negotiated terms, conditions and price; coordinated staff changes; guided transactions to conclusion. **Results:** Acquired 6 companies within 2 years; added $100 million premium volume; increased productivity and profitability, added major restaurant, construction, franchise operations, etc., to account base.

Management/Business Development

Managed operation and **expanded** client base for $12 million business. Initiated policies and procedures; established accounting system; staffed; recruited franchise operators; oversaw client development; built relationships; organized events and implemented marketing strategies to promote organization; networked with lenders; real estate agencies etc.; offered enhanced services. **Results:** Company had continuous growth over 10 year period; continues to grow.

Oversaw financial acts pertaining to construction of multi-million dollar food processing and office complex for Johnson Farms Foods. Negotiated interest rates, financial and legal covenants, draw schedules, collateralization issues, and Industrial Development Bond aspects with bank; drafted/reviewed numerous documents. Petitioned local, state and federal agencies for appropriate permits; selected contractors; monitored and approved payment schedules; coordinated transition from old office and processing complex to new; reviewed and approved equipment installation agreements; reconciled environmental claims brought by local and federal governments. **Results:** $10 million construction project completed on time and numerous ancillary, but critical issues successfully resolved, enabling smooth transfer and minimal disruption of company's business; increased profitability.

Took over troubled trucking company. Negotiated with IRS and secured creditors to release seized assets: filed suit to collect delinquent accounts; persuaded drivers to return to work; secured credit line to make repairs and continue operations: bid for new projects, improved internal bookkeeping system. **Results:** Restored profitability; paid off creditors; eventually sold company for profit.

Directed accounting staff as CFO for insurance company. Provided technical guidance/expertise; participated in strategic planning meetings; prepared capital and operating budgets for company; analyzed financial statements; supervised payroll, payable, receivables, auditors, etc.; integrated accounting systems of acquired companies. **Results:** Improved flow of financial information to CEO, allowing for more informed decision-making and evaluation.

Strategic Business Planning

Developed legal strategy to extricate company from multiple lawsuits filed following adverse Federal Court verdict. Analyzed financial and legal comprehensive management agreement with potential investor; researched law; formulated plan to take case to U.S. Circuit Court and eventually U.S. Supreme Court and to change venue of next lawsuit; identified expert financial witnesses to contest key issues that resulted in initial adverse verdict. **Results:** Company dismissal of other suits; saved several million dollars; case established legal precedent in many other cases.

Facilitated national distribution strategy to accommodate market growth. Developed plan to establish regional and local distribution centers throughout country. Oversaw site selection; reviewed or drafted commercial lease documents and negotiated lease terms for offices; warehouses, equipment, computer systems. **Results:** Reduced long-haul trucking costs; improved delivery scheduling; increased customer satisfaction.

Spearheaded efforts to counter union organizing efforts by Teamster's Union. Established policies and procedures for management to follow: spoke with employees to explain company's position; designated company's collective bargaining representative. **Results:** Company lost initial election, but employees voted union out after one year.

Patricia Eller
202 Locksly Court
Fairfax, VA 22134
(703) 555-1212

OBJECTIVE

A position utilizing my skills in **International Marketing, Export Trade, Market Research** and **Project Management** in order to:

- implement multiple techniques to enhance company image, optimize product exposure and increase revenues

- improve manner and method of moving product worldwide

- conceptualize and direct results-driven strategies to meet key business objectives.

QUALIFICATIONS

- International Marketing
- Market Research
- Product Positioning/Distribution
- Image Development

- Export Trade
- Documentation Analysis
- Government Relations
- PC Skills

- Project Management
- Event Planning/Promotions
- Presentations
- Customer/Client Relations

EXPERIENCE

Merlin Brokers, Alexandria, VA Real Estate Agent	1996 - Present
Redcoat Industries, Klopman Division, Chantilly, VA Product Development Manager - Export	1990 - 1996
U.S. Department of State, Washington, DC Intern	1989 - 1990
Graphics Design and Costume Production, Springfield, VA Independent Contractor	1976 - 1983

EDUCATION and PROFESSIONAL

Towson State University, MD Bachelor of Science Degree in Management Towson Fellowship Tradition Award	1989

Fashion Technology Institute, DC
Textile Technology Program

Seminars: Center for Creative Leadership
Communismus

Published: *Costumes by Computer*, Costume! Magazine. November, 1989

Member: Fairfax Women in Business, Fairfax Women in International Trade,
Eastern Center for International Studies

Language Skills: Read Business French

Award: Most Promising Agent of the Year (1997)

ACHIEVEMENTS

International Marketing

Extended and **enhanced** company's image in international marketplace. Analyzed foreign fashion trends, products and buying patterns; forecasted future trends; consulted with worldwide sales force to design and customize sales collaterals; created innovative tools; coordinated joint visits to international clients including Sparks & Button, Flair and Expression (Bolivia); educated clients on technical value of product line; produced reports; recommended marketing and product assistance for individual clients and agents. **Results:** Assisted sales in generating higher revenue; developed stronger relationship with clients; improved understanding domestically of needs of global clients.

Presented fashion and product seminars to worldwide sales agents at annual sales meetings in S. America. Planned and organized meetings; researched trends country by country; identified slides to emphasize state-of-the-industry; wrote and produced speech and supporting collateral which integrated communication of current trends with introduction and promotion of new products. **Results:** Sales force better equipped to sell products and overcome objections.

Managed division's first international trade show (New York City) promoted and hosted by U.S. Department of State. Consulted with shipping departments to assess duty requirements; coordinated shipping; designed booth; directed assemble/disassemble of booth; selected products for display; created sales aids and graphics; assisted customers at show. **Results:** Show produced high volume of orders; enhanced company recognition; produced additional shows in S. America for both apparel and activewear segments of division.

Developed all sales collateral to increase revenues and heighten market awareness:

- Image intensive brochure - produced company's first brochure for export division
- Technical brochure - conceptualized, wrote and had translated into four languages
- "Concept" boards - promoted company's products through illustration
- Color cards and seasonal brochures - designed or updated on continual basis.

Export Trade

Launched international business segment of major corporate division as member of three person team. Conceptualized organization and systemization of new marketing materials sent to export agents; consulted with sales and product development managers; analyzed requirements of sales staff, budgeted project requirements; directed outside agency; produced aids in assembling and shipping. **Results:** Export business grew to $40 million within five years and accounted for 18% of division's revenue; improved company's system of selling; increased knowledge base of sales agents.

Spearheaded release of company's product line semiannually to worldwide agents. Identified all products to be included in seasonal line (150-200); explained and promoted products; directed manufacturing plant technicians in assembling samples; wrote, produced and organized sales aids to accompany shipment; directed employees in shipping finished product to offices around the world. **Results:** Delivered on-time and within budget; increased profitability.

Analyzed export requirements of small businesses for Department of Commerce (Washington, DC). Evaluated product's potential for success in particular export market; informed companies of Department of Commerce's services; advised companies on required licenses and documentation; consulted with U.S. embassies overseas on political climate in particular countries. **Results:** Increased exports adding to growth and revenue of small and medium sized companies.

Project Management/Market Research

Oversaw implementation of international garment care labeling for export division. Researched and analyzed European labeling; interviewed and consulted with academic expert infield; organized required laboratory tests to simulate European procedures; systematized procedure to apply new adopted labels to every product sample shipped to Europe. **Results:** Produced uniformity with international labeling system to communicate universally understood laundering instructions through icons; lowered incidence of product returns; improved image of company by demonstrating willingness to adopt European standards.

Researched and **evaluated** garment and fabric trends in Europe for domestic adaptability. Identified unique designs and garment silhouettes; analyzed qualities of high end fabricator development of more moderate version; Collected samples from several sources including consultants, retail stores, European sales agents and customers; made samples available to division product development managers in U.S. **Results:** Improved level of aesthetics in domestic product; heightened awareness of European market, making it possible for company to continually produce unique products in highly competitive industry.

Planned and **produced** costumes for theater production. Researched historical period; analyzed sketches; prioritized time schedule; managed technical preparation; directed workers in construction; evaluated quality of finished product. **Results:** Produced aesthetically appealing production on schedule and within budget; developed full range of costumes for Broadway and regional theater, opera, dance, and film projects.

JONATHAN WINTERS
55 Chippendale Avenue
Mallets Bay, NJ 11876
(212) 555-1212

OBJECTIVE

A CEO/COO position with emphasis on diversification and expansion of markets and organizational reengineering to improve company growth.

QUALIFICATIONS AND BACKGROUND

Over ten years of PAL experience in all areas of management including finance, operations, marketing and sales. Proven track record of success conducting negotiations with large lenders, state and local agencies and financial institutions. Demonstrated ability to expand sales and markets. MBA with entrepreneurial track record and hands-on management skills.

DEMONSTRATIONS OF EFFECTIVENESS

- **Built** a small, local contracting business into a major general contractor within Mallets Bay, New York. Expanded and diversified markets; broadened base of operations from Mallets Bay to include all of the greater New Jersey metropolitan area; recruited, hired, trained, and supervised professional, administrative and field staff, oversaw the activities of as many as 12 sub-contractors and their employees. **Results:** Company has achieved average annual growth of 30-40%.

- **Developed** marketing strategies for the successful penetration of the residential new building and renovation markets. Identified markets complementary to current business; created direct mail campaigns, including collateral materials; designed highly visible in-home promotional materials; instituted Total Quality Management program, *Commitment to Quality*. **Results:** New markets now comprise 70% of sales and are sustained exclusively through referrals and repeat business.

- **Managed** and **coordinated** multiple, complex construction projects. Prepared bids and project budgets; advised clients on project financing; scheduled and supervised in-house tradesmen and sub-contractors; provided full project management control through PERT; established project checkpoints to ensure client satisfaction. **Results:** Projects completed on time and within budget, and consistently generated referral business.

- **Diversified** company into counter cyclical businesses. Researched investment opportunities; identified market niches; created joint ventures and partnerships with other investors; projected and allocated funds available for outside investment. **Results:** Diversification program has consistently generated an average return on investment of 30%.

EXPERIENCE

RENT-US-NOW, Mallets Bay, NJ   1986 - Present
President/CEO
Full responsibility for a multimillion dollar general contracting company. Founded business
and built it to the present size. Expanded into complementary markets and maintained state-
of-the-art knowledge of construction techniques enabling the company flexibility in new
construction, renovation, residential/commercial and light commercial building. Established
a management team of Project Managers and supervisory staff. Maintained company
profitably since its inception. Marketed company services resulting in a consistent annual
growth pattern through diversification program.

STORK EXPRESS, Jersey City, NJ 1984 - 1986
Senior Account Executive
Called on the corporate market: Fortune 500 and smaller companies selling Stork Express'
overnight express services. Established four new national account programs, each of which
generated more than $1 million in annual revenues. Was one of the leading producers in the
New York metropolitan area generating a 200% increase in 15 months, a company record.
Awarded two Metro Sales Awards.

RIVERVIEW COMMUNITY COLLEGE, Talbott, NJ   1992 - Present
Adjunct Professor
Appointed Adjunct Professor and established a new course, *Small Business Management*,
emphasizing the development of business plans for new and existing small businesses.
Course is now one of the leading offerings of the college. Class provides students with
theoretical and practical approaches.

EDUCATION

MBA, Finance, PICANTE UNIVERSITY, LINTA GRADUATE SCHOOL OF BUSINESS   December 1990
BA, Business and History, FISHKILL COLLEGE, Fishkill, NY   June 1984

INTERESTS

Progressive Martial Arts
Tae-Kwon-Do Karate School
Instructor, 2nd Degree Black Belt Rank

DARLA S. MILLER
11908 Stevens Court
Milton, VA 22165
(703) 555-1212

OBJECTIVE

An Information Technology position involving client server testing, evaluation, monitoring systems, and systems application.

Profile: Highly skilled professional with more than 17 years experience testing, and monitoring systems, migration of software within production and project development. Expertise includes the ability to prioritize projects, coordinate teams and operate within strict timeframes. Background supported by an A.A. in Computer Programming.

CAREER HIGHLIGHTS & ACHIEVEMENTS

- **Designed** plans for each project created for the system application. Organized projects and evaluated necessary changes to the application. Analyzed data to determine whether requirements written in the general design and analysis work correctly in the final application.

- **Formulated** plans to determine how and when projects should be processed. Prioritized the order of projects in order to meet specific deadlines. Organized internal and external status meetings with all staff involved to determine the progression in each project. Evaluated staffing needs to meet the implementation dates required by clients. Produced test plans for each project.

- **Coordinated** all changes that occurred for individual projects. Organized all necessary information relating to the projects and developed plans to test the projects. Attacked the analysis and general design for Mac and Windows '98 projects. Determined what types of accounts needed to be created. Tested new procedures for clients to ensure that all requirements were met within specific timeframes and successfully migrated to clients.

- **Monitored** several applications. Discovered and solved any problems as they occurred. Presided over each project to ensure that jobs ran successfully. Clients received product on time, meeting all specifications and each application produced the necessary reports.

- **Developed** plans to determine testing needs of projects. Organized and educated all team members on project specifications. Evaluated input and output files and utilized regression process to ensure accuracy. Developed process to efficiently transmit files to vendors. Streamlined procedures to save time from startup through implementation of each project.

- **Analyzed** design documents to determine whether projects could utilize existing data or whether new data needed to be created. Evaluated all information received from vendors. Met with vendors to evaluate needs and complete projects to client satisfaction.

DARLA S. MILLER ... Page 2

PROFESSIONAL EXPERIENCE

CDI, INC., Springfield and Manassas, VA   1979 - Present

Quality Assurance Tester, Manassas, VA   1996 - Present
* Responsible for writing test plans testing batch changes in the acceptance environment. Involved in system, interface, integration, vendor, and regression testing.

Migration Release Coordinator, Manassas, VA   1992 - 1996
* Migrate software within the acceptance and production libraries utilizing the endeavor process for the fulfillment/network/provisioning/Diamond/global and CADB groups. Responsible for migrating natural modules using syspac, used for the CADB application. Responsible for Change Management Record (CMR) for all applications.

Lead Production Scheduler III, Manassas, VA   1988 - 1992
* Work concurrently on the operation of Multiple Large IBM computer platforms via remote work platform. Responsible for monitoring the production systems and attempting first level resolution before referring to other organizations. Daily responsibilities included job set-up and reconciliation associated with production batch processing.

Production Analyst, Springfield, VA   1987 - 1988
* Responsible for reviewing and setting up jobs and new applications in the CA-7+ database.

Data Processing Group Leader, Manassas, VA   1985 - 1987
* Responsible for the overall efficient operation of all off-line equipment in support of or affiliated with general-purpose computers.

Production Coordinator, Springfield, VA   1983 - 1985
* Responsible for operation of multiple large IBM computer platforms via remote work platforms. Monitored the production systems and attempted first level resolutions before referring to senior staff or other organizations. Involved in startup of three additional data centers, ensuring that jobs continued to run smoothly in the expansion process.

Computer Peripheral Operation, Springfield, VA   1979 - 1983
* Responsible for operating two online printers as well as printing invoices and payroll checks. Coordinated jobs into the production stream to achieve best utilization of computers.

EDUCATION

A.A., Computer Programming   1978
PHILLIP CHANDLER COLLEGE, Hazleton, MD

COMPUTER SKILLS

SMTF (Migration Tool), Endeavor (Migration Tool), OS-JCL, IBM 360/370 JCL, File-Aid DB2, Connect Direct (NDM), COBOL, ASSEMBLY, TSO, WYLBUR, CA-7, ISPF, SYNCSORT, MICROSOFT WORD/EXCEL, LOTUS NOTES.

KIRSTEN L. DANST

11856 Pier Circle • Sutton, DE 22982 • (914) 555-1212 • email: kirstens@anywhere.net

OBJECTIVE

Executive or Consultant position, preferably with an international focus, involving
Research & Analysis ... Project Management ... Strategy Development ... International Liaison
and using proven skills in

- Conceptualization & Analysis
- Initiation & Innovation

- Organization & Development
- Oral & Written Communication

- Problem-solving
- Teaching

PROFILE

Over ten years of research and work experience including: social and organizational analysis; research interviewing; economic and business analysis; project development and management; recruiting and training; diplomatic negotiation and representation. A focused, persistent professional who thrives in environments that require innovative solutions and independent action. Possess ability to establish and maintain excellent relations with people of varied cultures and backgrounds. Fluent in Russian, Slovene, and Serbo-Croatian; reading knowledge of Macedonian.

SELECTED ACCOMPLISHMENTS

- Analyzed factors blocking changes in the way CIA assessed its regional performance. Mapped the flow of information and identified sources of delays and distortions. Efforts enabled division to institute a series of targeted, timely reviews. Result: staffing dropped by ten and executives were refocused.

- Directed review of CIA call-site performance. Researched CIA commitments to Congress, compared performance of Social Security call-sites, and developed questions to ask top executives. Result: briefing piloted efforts to push reform in the CIA.

- Led development of a new software application by a team of contractors. Drafted specifications, programmed portions of the prototype, and shepherded product to completion. Result: application facilitated timely performance review.

- Served as acting economic officer of US Liaison Office in Talinsk. On own initiative, recruited the largest national contingent to attend a development conference and drafted a substantial share of the post's total reporting; substance of one report was briefed to the President.

- Negotiated first grain agreement with a country not fully recognized by the US. Kept Chief of Mission informed and explained each step to the Romanians. Result: exchange of letters took place prior to fund expiration deadline thus ensuring full funding of project.

- Successfully implemented and coordinated a major diplomatic event in Romania involving 600 officials and diplomats with only three weeks notice.

- As head of Consular Section in Deriany, reorganized visa and passport processing. Result: increased number of visas processed per day despite the loss of two of the three interviewing officers and local staff turnover.

- First American since World War II to study at Spartan University in Helgarth (1990).

- Since age of 15, have helped to instruct a multitude of internationals, both here and abroad, in a better understanding of America.

EXPERIENCE

UNITED STATES DEPARTMENT OF STATE, Deriany, Romania   1997-1998
Independent Contractor/Researcher
> Organized diplomatic representational events ranging from small luncheons to dinner for 80. Supervised permanent staff of six. Served on Executive Board of Dignitaries' Club.
> • *Edited manuscript on inter-ethnic marriages in Serbia that has generated interest from publishers.*

Chief of Consular Section, US Embassy
> Prepared reports of visa fraud that triggered criminal investigations. Rationalized visa and passport processing operations.

CENTRAL INTELLIGENCE AGENCY   1995-1996
Operations Research Analyst, Analysis and Studies Division, CIA
> Led assessment of telephone call-site performance. Critiqued process by which CIA evaluated overall regional and servicewide performance and drafted alternative approach focusing on bottom-line results. Managed design and programming of new software application.

UNITED STATES DEPARTMENT OF STATE, Talinsk, Slovakia   summer 1994
Acting Economic Officer, US Liaison Office
> Researched and wrote over 15 economic and political reports; substance of one report was briefed to the President. Negotiated grain agreement. Secured corporate support for major diplomatic event.

THE UNIVERSITY OF DELAWARE, Dover, DE   1993-1994
> Taught two undergraduate discussion seminars on the former Soviet Union. Researched census data for publication in a new history of Bosnia and Hercegovina.

FULBRIGHT GRADUATE FELLOWSHIP, Prague, Czech Republic   1992-1993
> Conducted sociological study on inter-ethnic relationships in the former Czechoslovakia. Interviewed over twenty married couples, analyzed and obtained corrected statistics on marriage and divorce. Researched change in Czech and Slovak family law. Organized outings and activities for teenage Kosovo refugees.

MicroTech, Winston and Hazlett, NJ   summers 1991,1990,1988,1987
Thomas J. Watson Memorial Scholar
> Conducted analyses of scrap cycle and production data discrepancies. Assisted co-workers to refine computer skills. Wrote in-house manual for the Freelance graphics package. Trained new expediter.
> • *Won "Suggestion Award" for recommendation regarding safety improvement.*

EDUCATION

MA, *University of Maryland, Center for East European Studies,* Temple Hill, MD   1996
Concentration in 19th and 20th century Balkan history
Awarded two Foreign Language and Area Studies (FLAS) Fellowships

MPP, *University of Maryland, Institute of Public Policy Studies,* Temple Hill, MD   1995
Emphasis on Applied Economics and International Trade Law

BA (*cum laude*), **College Scholar/Russian,** Princeton University, Princeton, NJ   1991

MASON A. LITTLE

8876 Grouper Court   Springfield, Massachusetts 66045   (617) 555-1212

Career Objective

Senior level Executive Management with emphasis on Sales, Marketing, Engineering and Consulting global markets.

Strong management background in sales, engineering and manufacturing, specifically:

— Directing the future of the organization.
— Restructuring and turning around businesses.
— Integrating acquired companies.
— Developing business plans and successful implementations.
— Building and leading result-oriented teams.
— Providing innovative and dynamic leadership.
— Skillful in negotiating contracts.
— Developing successful business relationships on the global market.

ACHIEVEMENTS

— Started in the USA as Executive Vice President with $2 million in annual sales and 7 employees. Successfully integrated two newly acquired companies which grew to over $200 million and a 250 employee organization.

— Restructured the High Temperature Technology Division, Sales, Engineering and developed business strategies. Turned the division around and increased sales 500% within 3 years. Established the group by increasing gross margins from minus 10% to plus 35%.

— Directed the successful development of Opaque Powder Coating and marketed the application in the USA, Guatamala and South Africa. Established state-of-the-art engineering solutions and increased market share within 3 years to 40%.

— Innovated new solutions in material handling and automation in applications for the high temperature division. Established the company as a turnkey supplier and successfully penetrated the market in the USA, Britain and Hong Kong.

— Standardized design for high temperature kilns and reduced engineering costs from 25% to 6% or less. Dominated the market for technical ceramics with this equipment up to 80% of the market share.

— Restructured the clean air technology group and worked with key accounts (OEM). Transferred technology from Europe; improved the standardized design and successfully expanded applications into new markets. Established the company as the leading supplier with state-of-the-art capital equipment to the semiconductor and printing industries. Increased sales 400% within 3 years and established this group as one of the top performers.

MASON A. LITTLE...PAGE 2

ACHIEVEMENTS
(continued)

— Installed representatives to penetrate markets in US, Hong Kong, Guatamala, Thailand and South Africa. Results: Expanded business opportunities, increased proposal generation which led to increased sales and profits.

— Established program of outsourcing having capital equipment built in Mexico. Presented company with a low cost extension of their domestic capacity, set up the organization to provide timely management and accomplished the task by reducing cost of manufacturing to 30% of original cost by maintaining higher quality and schedule.

— Changed engineering and project management procedures in order to gain ISO 9001 certification.

EMPLOYMENT HISTORY

WESTMAN INDUSTRIES, Crystal, MA   1994-Present
Division Vice President
Assigned to expand core business, build the business plan and expand to Pacific Rim countries. P&L responsibility for Sales, Marketing, Engineering and Installation for 6 capital equipment non-automotive product groups.

Division Vice President   1988-1994
Assigned total P&L responsibility for Sales, Marketing and Engineering. In charge of 4 capital equipment groups, including an automotive group.

Vice President, Engineering   1985-1988
Promoted to Vice President Engineering and Project Management for all product groups, including material handling.

Vice President, Sales   1984-1985
Retained to reinforce and regain sales for 4 product groups including High Temperature Technology.

Vice President, Engineering and Operations   1982-1983
Appointed to integrate two newly acquired companies into one organization including the restructuring of all engineering, manufacturing and installation activities.

WESTMAN INDUSTRIES, Brandeis, NY   1980-1982
Vice President
Appointed Executive Vice President by the owner, Mr. Westman, started the office with $2 million in sales and 7 employees.

ELLIOT TESCH
41 Spring Brook Drive
Yorktown, VA 22376
(804) 555-1212

SALES/MARKETING EXECUTIVE
-over 25 years proven experience-

Senior level sales management with a proven record for setting and meeting profit goals. Skilled in organizing a sales operation that generates sales increases. Particularly strong interpersonal skills that build rapport and trust with the customer and create a cooperative team approach in the company to meet the customer needs and bottom line profits.

QUALIFICATIONS
-experience encompassing-

- Dealer/Distributor Networks
- Sales Management
- Marketing Programs
- New Product Development
- National Account Development
- Sales Training & Development
- Customer Relations

- Trade Shows
- Sales and Promotions
- Territory Development
- Product Launch
- Budget Management
- Quality Control
- Foreign Market Development

CAREER PERFORMANCE HIGHLIGHTS

- **Developed a New Distributor Division.**
  Set up solid marketing direction through distribution channels; developed an aggressive and structured program to reward distribution for sales efforts by creating stepped-up commissions and product specials. **Results:** 30 qualified distributors to represent our product with coverage in 13 states and sales volume of $500,000.00 in 18 months.

- **Directed a Sales Management Staff to a positive Forecast and Business Plan.**
  Evaluated all department functions, streamlined procedures; established solid leadership in all sales department areas; directed suppliers' inventory levels and reorder points; formulated an attainable forecast for a 12 month period. **Results:** An accurate inventory record; a 10% reduction in inventory space and a 12% increase in bottom line profit.

- **Guided the Introduction of New Products.**
  Organized procedures and market studies for 3 new products; galvanized a management team to produce a master plan to control the development effort from beginning to end and launch products into the marketplace. **Results:** Product introduction came in under budget; produced immediate market acceptance and added $2 million in 12 months to company sales volume.

- **Increased Market Share and Distribution Awareness.**
  Scheduled National, Regional and Territory meetings with salesforce and distribution to coordinate training programs; developed all sales & operation manuals for distributor support in the field. **Results:** A better trained salesforce and a more confident distributor network which led to an increase of 30% in sales and a 5% market share.

ELLIOT TESCH . . . Page 2

CAREER PERFORMANCE HIGHLIGHTS (continued)

- **Coordinated Trade Show Presentations and Advertising Campaign.**
  Planned trade show design and booth layout; developed floor plan, scheduled people, established delivery schedules for products, organized installation of booth and product at site and directed the scope and nature of the advertising campaign for the show. **Results:** Obtained qualified leads from end-users and increased sales by 15% annually for 3 years.

- **Set-up Foreign Market Agent Network.**
  Initiated a market study to find potential; created a marketing direction and sales strategy to penetrate targeted areas. Hand picked the right agent to get our product stocked and sold in the market areas. **Results:** 6 stocking agents in 3 foreign markets with combined sales of $2 million in 15 months.

PROFESSIONAL EXPERIENCE

VIDEO SOLUTIONS
National Sales Manager   1994 - 1998
- Recruited by President to set-up distribution network and national sales-force along with all programs to develop product line.

PARKER INDUSTRIES
Product Manager   1991 - 1994
- Served as the catalyst to establish a sales and marketing team of distributors; increase market share and introduce a new product line to the marketplace.

X Y Z PACKAGING MACHINE CORPORATION
District Manager   1988 - 1991
- Hired to promote and sell product to direct accounts in the East. Maintained $1 million account base for 2 years.

THE ROBERTSON CORPORATION
Regional Manager   1983 - 1988
- First manager assigned to organize and train a distributor network on a new product line and form a strong sales base.

ZEBRA METAL WORKS
Marketing manager for New Products   1973 - 1983
Export sales manager
Regional sales manager
- During my 10 years of tenure I was called on to develop 2 different divisions; the export sales division and the division of new product development. Both departments performed under budget and above quota and I was recognized by the company for my contributions.

EDUCATIONAL BACKGROUND

SPRINGFIELD COLLEGE, Springfield, Illinois   1982
  Business Management Degree

References and Further Data Available Upon Request.

WILLIAM CONNOLLY

8879 Scrabble Road
Oakdale, CA 67089

(338) 555-1212
bconnolly@contactme.com

OBJECTIVE

Communications manager responsible for all internal and external communications in relation to public affairs, community relations and media relations. Special skills include editorial and opinion writing, and news management.

QUALIFICATIONS

Award-winning writing, editing and communication skills. Proven team leader, organizer and consensus builder. Creative problem solver and innovator. Short and long-term planner and project leader. Effective manager and motivator. Teacher, trainer and mentor. Proficient at analyzing and simplifying complex issues. Efficient and decisive, especially under deadline pressure. Comfortable with issues of diversity.

SELECTED ACHIEVEMENTS

- Directed investigation into campaign spending in California. Organized reporters, developed story ideas, established deadlines and edited all copy. Won first place award for investigative reporting from the Metropolitan Newspapers of America. Submitted in the Pulitzer competition.

- Wrote hard-hitting weekly editorials analyzing local policy and taxation issues and recommending course of action. Editorials shaped public policy and won eight professional awards, including five first place, in eight years.

- Analyzed staffing organization following corporate downsizing reducing staff by 25 percent. Reorganized assignments and shifted work load for more efficient and improved news coverage. Won three awards for general excellence, including one first place.

- Won Journalist of the Year Award in 1994 from among 125 editorial employees. Cited for staff reorganization and development, readership development plan, four individual awards, publication of eight special projects and community leadership in five organizations.

- Analyzed spending patterns at Oakdale High School before a tax referendum. Published series of stories and editorials detailing patterns of overspending and taxation. Tax referendum was defeated resulting in a tax savings for residents.

- Researched and wrote an investigative report on the environmental dangers of Leaking Underground Storage Tanks after an underground vault exploded due to leaking gasoline. Won two awards for investigative reporting.

- Directed breaking news coverage of the flood of the Los Valjos River which was honored for best breaking news story by the California Sun.

WILLIAM CONNOLLY ... Page 2

SELECTED ACHIEVEMENTS
(continued)

- Planned annual Reader Development action plans by surveying readers, conducting focus groups, resulting in improved news coverage, op-ed pages, new feature ideas and continuing reader involvement and marketing.

- Initiated an employee recruitment program, including minority recruitment, by attending numerous job fairs and conferences. Leadership resulted in establishment of a recruitment committee and appointment as chairman of committee on diversity.

- Trained up to 12 reporters on improving reporting and writing skills. Focused on story organization, clarity, editing, research and investigation. All became award winners for reporting and writing.

- Motivated two experienced reporters who were not performing up to their abilities by increasing responsibilities, performance expectations and training. Both have won awards and are performing to their abilities.

- Managed day-to-day operations for two editorial offices publishing 17 newspapers with 33 employees and a combined circulation of 70,000 readers.

EMPLOYMENT HISTORY

PIONEER PRESS, Oakdale, CA   1986-Present
Associate Editor, Northwest Group, 1996-present
Managing Editor, Tree Bark , 1990-present
Managing Editor, Fall Leaves, 1986-1990

METRO LIFE CITIZEN, Wacan, CA   1981 - 1986
Assistant City Editor, 1984 - 1986
Sports Editor, 1982 - 1984

LIFETIME PAPER, Berwyn, CA   1979 - 1981
News Reporter

EXPERIENCE

DAVIEN UNIVERSITY, Riverton,CA   1996 - Present
Adjunct Professor of Journalism

EDUCATION

CALIFORNIA UNIVERSITY, Springbrook, CA
Master of Science, Journalism
State House Beat; Editor for Illinois Courant, Graduate School publication.

OAKDALE COLLEGE, Oakdale, CA
Bachelor of Arts, English
Daily Sun news staff for three years; Sigma Pi Rho Honorary Society

245 Birch Dr.
Engle, KY 45123
(463) 555-1212

MORGAN MCLAIN

OBJECTIVE: An influential, market-oriented position in a leading edge company providing products and/or contracted services to fulfill corporate development and promotional needs.

SUMMARY: Increasingly diversified successes with experiences including:

- For profit and non-profit management
- Executive management and Board of Directors reporting
- Strategic planning
- Generating operational funds
- Grant writing, program development
- Multiple complex project management and administration
- Fiscal budgeting and reporting
- P & L responsibilities
- Legislative process, lobbying
- Organizational development
- Publishing and printing background; maps, books, newspapers
- Multi-media presentation, promotion, and advertising
- Hiring, training, and supervising
- Public and professional presentations
- Major conference sponsorship
- Internal and external publications
- Curriculum development

ACHIEVEMENTS:

- **Raised** funds, **developed** marketing strategies, and **generated** contracts between state agencies and non-profit organizations.

- **Reconfigured, directed**, and **managed** a non-profit organization with a Board of Directors chartered to improve safety and access for bicyclists in Kentucky.

- **Authored** TQM procedures for corporate pursuit of ISO 9000 certification.

- **Tripled** the size of a statewide advocacy organization by implementing improved marketing and fund raising programs.

- **Generated** awareness, **solicited** members, and **established visibility** for a non-profit organization through a highly successful direct mail marketing program.

- **Authored** legislation and lobbied a bill through committees into law on behalf of statewide constituency.

- **Organized** coalitions to design, implement, and secure funding for community recreational trails.

- **Designed** a unique, low cost method for statewide constituency to be mobilized for public hearings and meetings.

- **Launched** a regional newspaper, establishing a forum for a major recreational user group in Kentucky.

MORGAN MCLAIN . . . Page 2

ACHIEVEMENTS: (continued)

- **Developed** grant-winning programs to implement safety training procedures.

- **Collaborated** with state officials to establish a major new recreational use for state parks and forests.

- **Supervised** a 60 member Control Data publications department producing proposals and product related support literature.

- **Authored** articles and published newsletters, newspapers, and speech support documentation.

- **Directed** city, county, and regional organizations to collaborate on the revision, production, and distribution of a major transit map.

- **Promoted** special events, taught seminars, and made presentations at major national conferences.

- **Convinced** state officials to broaden available trail mileage for major user group by implementing local control of state parks facilities.

- **Established** a statewide annual conference for recreational users to examine funding, design, and conflict resolution issues.

- **Designed** an easy to implement, low cost method of tracking the effectiveness of a university writing laboratory; developed tutorial modules to assess and improve student writing.

- **Awarded** grant by international organization in recognition of outstanding advocacy efforts.

- **Developed** guidelines and maintenance procedures for trail use in state recreation areas.

EXPERIENCE:

KENTUCKY BICYCLE COALITION	**Executive Director**	1994 - Present
SPERRYDALE PRODUCTION	**Editor**	1989 - 1994
MILLENNIUM DESIGN	**Contract Editor**	1982 - 1989
UNIVERSITY OF KENTUCKY, Louisville	**Supervisor**	1980 - 1982
RUDOLPH HIGH SCHOOL	**Instructor, Coach**	1976 - 1980

EDUCATION:

UNIVERSITY OF ARIZONA	**Mini MBA Non-Profit Mgmt.**	1996
UNIVERSITY OF KENTUCKY, Louisville	**ME, Education**	1982
UNIVERSITY OF KENTUCKY, Lexington	**BS, English**	1977

PROFESSIONAL TRAINING:

- Corporate Leadership
- Counseling and Management
- Collaborations: Making Partnerships Work
- Corporate Networking Strategies
- Stress Management
- The Responsibility of Leadership
- Building Coalitions to Change
- Performance Appraisals/Reviews
- Leadership and Empowerment

12 Wreath Road
Kuai, HI 99447
(325) 555-1212

STEVEN CARUTHERS, P.E.

OBJECTIVE: A key management position in the service or manufacturing industry utilizing my experience and expertise in applications technology and engineering.

SUMMARY: More than 20 years of experience in engineering and technical management and problem solving including:

— **Design and implementation of specialized machinery**
— **Process system design, installation and start-up**
— **Facility layout and design**
— **Technical product sales and marketing**
— **New product development**
— **Executive and team level responsibility**
— **Technical problem solving**
— **Excellent leadership skills**
— **Strong organizational ability**
— **Successful project management**
— **Environmental compliance responsibilities**

ACHIEVEMENTS:
- **Created** an animated computer presentation for one of the south's largest service industries. Informed officers of quality and production improvements available through factory floor automation. Received contract for all of their control requirements.

- **Worked** on a team in the preparation of a proposal to a major supplier in the health care industry for a chemical delivery system having major quality control impact. National customer purchased die system and was pleased with the overall operation. Additional orders followed.

- **Obtained** U.L. listing for a commercial product and implemented necessary quality control measures required to maintain certification.

- **Developed** and **implemented** test plans for identifying the mechanical configuration required to optimize electrical performance of an antenna feed network. Performance criteria were met and the parts could be manufactured with commercially available technology.

- **Prepared** budget estimates for the construction of a large recycling center in Nebraska. Resulted in allocation of corporate funds.

- **Responsible** for the design and fabrication of the mechanical systems for the upgrade of multiple antenna systems for leading government contractor. After rigorous testing the government accepted and deployed the systems.

- **Developed** contracts with local architect and contractors for design and construction of a major recycling center. Prevented any construction delays due to permit and code compliance issues.

STEVEN CARUTHERS . . . PAGE 2

ACHIEVEMENTS:
(continued)

- **Directed** and **assisted** with a major rebuild of specialized equipment imported from Italy. Met deadlines for the equipment to be operational for a grand opening presentation to local dignitaries and customer representatives.

- **Assessed** the manufacturing capabilities of companies providing fabrication services. Selected vendors who met schedule, price and quality goals. Patented a method for improving the life of a major component used in the continuous casting of copper rod for the nation's largest privately held wire and cable manufacturer.

- **Participated** in a corporate planning process which resulted in the redefinition of the company's direction and goals.

- **Developed** a computer program to create an AutoCad drawing file directly from output generated by a surface design software package. Reduced drafting time by 1 1/2 months and ensured accuracy of the final drawings.

- **Managed** the import and implementation of European technology and equipment for the recovery of CFCs from polyurethane foam. Successfully established the only U.S. demonstration project for this technology.

- **Worked** with Klinehauser National Laboratories in the development of a proprietary process for the separation and recovery of valuable plastics. Pilot plant is under construction.

WORK EXPERIENCE:

APPLIANCE SCRAPPERS OF AMERICA **Vice President of Technical Services**	1991 - Present
RIESEN ENTERPRISES **Director of Engineering**	1989 - 1991
UNIVERSITY OF HAWAII **Research Engineer**	1979 - 1989
PALMSTRING COMPANY **Design Engineer**	1977 - 1979
HONOLULU LINEN SERVICES **Project Manager** **Draftsman**	1972 - 1977

EDUCATION: **B.S., Mechanical Engineering Technology**   1977
Maui Technical Institute, Maui, Hawaii

PERSONAL: Registered Professional Engineer
Who's Who in Technology Today
Who's Who in the Extended States
Past Director of the Maui Tech National Alumni Association

ANN BENSON

9410 Sanford Blvd. • Washington, DC 20038 • (202) 555-1212 (h) • (202) 555-1234 (w)

OBJECTIVE

Software Engineering position involving
Program Design ... Training ... Project Development
and using proven skills in

- Research & Analysis
- Written Communication
- Creativity & Innovation
- Conceptualization & Implementation
- Development & Evaluation

PROFILE

Ten years of research and software engineering experience including creation, mathematical and statistical model development, program and report writing, presentation and supervision. Adept at recognizing potential problems, creating and developing alternatives, and presenting simplified solutions. Functional knowledge of German and Italian.

SELECTED ACCOMPLISHMENTS

- **Created and developed** suite of programs in the C language and under the UINIX operating system to perform communications algorithm that enabled engineers to build working hardware model for military use.

- **Produced** suite of C language programs in both regular and multiple precision formats enabling easier calculation for programming staff. Program ran on a Sun station using the UNIX operating system.

- **Improved** existing number theoretic C language by eliminating dependence on external software packages thus producing a more widely usable program. Implemented program in parallel using the MPI (Message Passing Interface) language. Program ran under the UNIX operating system.

- **Saved** several thousands of dollars in computer time by using statistical analysis in an innovative way to estimate program completion time. Program was written in Fortran in a UNIX environment for use on a large computer.

- **Created** teaching material including lecture notes and examples for a "Mathematics of Cryptology" course. Wrote, in a limited time, tests for several courses that were within the capabilities of the students yet challenging.

- **Discovered** theorem that related terms in a certain polynomial to entries in a specific matrix that enabled completion of a C language computer program.

- **Discovered and documented** major inaccuracy in a statistical model which was in general use; led to alternative model to ensure data accuracy.

- **Researched** algebraic number theory in order to write a program that set a world record in computational number theory. Wrote scholarly paper for use in the workplace.

- **Researched and wrote** an expository paper on a new technique to perform a certain mathematical operation more quickly.

RELATED EXPERIENCE

DEPARTMENT OF JUSTICE, Washington, DC   1988-present
Mathematician
>   Apply sopisticated mathematics to communications problems to develop software. Write
>   programs in C, C++, and FORTRAN in the UNIX operating system; produce documenta-
>   tion of work and give oral presentations describing it. Interact with engineers in implemen-
>   tation of algorithms in hardware. Supervise students from summer co-op program.

ADDITIONAL WORK EXPERIENCE

PHOENIX COMUNITY COLLEGE, Phoenix, AZ   1986-1988
Mathematics Instructor
>   Taught Algebra and Calculus; developed lecture materials and tests.

THE UNIVERSITY OF ARIZONA AT PHOENIX, Phoenix, AZ   1985-1987
Teaching Assistant in college mathematics courses.

INTERNATIONAL RECTIFIER, Albuquerque, NM   summer 1984
Intern
>   Engaged in statistical quality analysis; ran future analysis tests on chip samples and wrote
>   program to catalog it.

EDUCATION

Master of Arts, Mathematics, *The University of Arizona at Phoenix,* Phoenix, AZ
Bachelor of Science, Mathematics, *The University of Arizona at Phoenix,* Phoenix, AZ

Currently hold TOP SECRET Security Clearance

MARTHA C. MOORE
1109 Old Saw Mill Road
Colchester, VT 05673
Phone: (515) 555-1212
Fax: (515) 555-7777

* OBJECTIVE *

A key position of responsibility in a design department utilizing my knowledge/skills in **Art Directing & Conceptualization, Project Planning/Oversight, Art Editing/Quality Control,** and **Interpersonal Communications** in order to:

- provide leadership/supervision in achieving departmental/organizational objectives
- plan/implement creative/innovative techniques to solve graphic design problems
- establish/institute effective procedures to maintain high quality control standards.

* QUALIFICATIONS *

Qualified by over 15 years of increased responsibility/experience in:
Art Directing/Conceptualization * Project Planning/Oversight * Art Editing/Quality Control
Problem Solving/Decision Making * Administrative Management * Staff Development
Supervision/Performance Evaluation * Goal Setting * Budget Development/Administration
Customer/Client Relations * Contract Negotiations * Image Development * Time Management
Design/Layout * Color/Type Design/Specifications * Interpersonal Communications

* EMPLOYMENT HISTORY*

Consulting Art Director/Freelance Designer	1995 - Present
Martha by Design, Burlington, VT	
<u>Clients included:</u> BakerHarper; Wishcraft Press	
Parker House; Gateway	
Senior Art Director	1994 - 1995
Young Families Digest, Essex, VT	
Art Director	1993 - 1994
Northeast Publishing Co., Burlington, VT	
Art Director	1984 - 1993
Putnam Press, New York, NY	
Computer Graphics Designer	1982 - 1983
CBC Adventures, New York, NY	
Assistant Art Director/Designer	1978 - 1982
Farrah Books, New York,	
Graphic Designer	1975 - 1977
Mallets Bay Productions, St. Louis, MO	

* EDUCATION/SPECIALIZED TRAINING*

Bachelor of Arts Degree (*Art*) - <u>Summa Cum Laude</u>
Technical Institute, Stowe, VT

<u>Training in:</u>
Multi-Media Design; Web Design
Art College of Manhattan, Manhattan, NY

ACHIEVEMENTS

Art Directing & Conceptualization

Coordinated/redesigned covers of Edgar Beldof's 12 volume anthology of young adult books. Set deadlines; hired 5 illustrators with similar styles to accomplish artistic continuity; created series logo for brand identity; selected color combinations to create individual volume distinction; illustrated "dummies" for aggressive market promotion. Project's success put a fresh look to familiar works which increased sales.

Designed book cover for *The Golden Children* as Art Director for major publisher. Conceptualized cover scene; hired illustrator; established deadlines; critiqued illustration; created final layout; prepared/submitted mock-up for promotional catalog; prepared final mechanicals for separation; reviewed color proofs; approved/selected final product. Book was chosen by <u>Magazines and Cloth</u> as one of the "25 Best Book Covers of 1990".

Illustrated/directed design process for books by author/poet Maga Strand. Researched/reviewed covers and content; conceived, sketched/presented ideas; designed author's logo; created title type, layout and mechanicals for each book; developed marketing/sales comprehensives; reviewed, revised/approved proofs/covers. The contemporary look for her popular books increased visibility and strengthened sales.

Project Planning/Oversight

Fashioned new look/illustrations for covers of dated romance novels. Oversaw development of juvenile imprints; reviewed cover/interior layouts; conceived/created visual content/logos; hired, contracted and supervised illustrators, photographers/handletterers; participated in weekly concept/production meetings; delivered mechanicals; provided materials for promotions/marketing; evaluated, revised/approved product. Won recognition in 6 <u>Gathering of Artists Shows,</u> 5 <u>Original Art Shows for Children's Artists,</u> and by <u>Magazines and Cloth</u> as one of "The 25 Best Book Covers", which resulted in promotion to division Art Director.

Established systems/procedures for licenser movie/TV tie-ins, mass-market series/celebrity biographies for art department. Upgraded illustrations; reviewed/determined multi-book project needs; hired illustrators; conceptualized covers/interior scenes; directed designers; evaluated layouts with editors; created title type/logos; approved/revised illustrations/proofs; liaised with creative & art departments; retouched designs as required; critiqued final books. Met all production, sales/distribution deadlines tied into movie/ TV release dates.

Art Editing/Quality Control

Designed children's book for client. Created storyboard; scanned art prints; selected type, font/size; created/selected borders, type colors/placement; presented/revised designs for customer; prepared mechanicals; input/printed final design proofs accompanied by electronic file documentation; approved galley proofs. As <u>Mother Magazine's</u> choice for "Best Book of 1995", client's market share/sales increased.

Organized/oversaw trade/hardcover imprint for value-priced publisher. Created visual book identity; designed type; interviewed/hired designers/illustrators; directed department staff illustrators/packagers and paper engineers; collaborated with licensers/co-publishers; established/ maintained budgets/schedules; conducted bi-weekly department meetings; attended marketing/production sessions; developed promotional materials; evaluated performances; checked proofs; assessed artistic impact of final product. Many books were reviewed in trade/consumer publications, giving the company entrance into the upscale market.

Created visual character for new book company with inflexible deadline, no manuscripts/illustrators. Troubleshot graphics; hired/supervised design staff, conceived/sketched covers; selected models; directed and styled photo sessions; checked /evaluated proofs/final product. Within 4 months, completed first book list which launched at Christmas, surpassed all sales expectations with numerous items on back order.

AWARDS, MEMBERSHIPS/AFFILIATIONS

Society of Artists Annual Exhibitions

Maxie Mouse, 1985; *Peaches and Cream*, 1986
Felicity James, 1987; *My Pony, My Friend*, 1989; *Notes for Nancy*, 1990
Yours Truly, Benjamin Pierce, 1992; *Sister of the Sun*, 1993

Original Art Show for Children's Illustrations

All Dolled Up, 1990; *Me and My Shadow*, 1992
Sandy B. Lion, 1994

Magazines and Cloth

One of 25 Best Book Covers of 1990: *The Golden Children*

Mothers Magazine

Choice for Best Book, 1995: *Rainbow Colors*

Memberships & Affiliations

Society of Female Managers * Black Women Illustrators
Association for the Self-Employed * Wellington MacUsers Group
CDC Black Employees Association * Stowe University National Alumni Association
American Museum of Natural History * Museum of Modem Art

COMPUTER SKILLS

Illustrator
Photoshop
QuarkXpress
Dreamweaver
Director
TypeStyler
Microsoft Word

PORTFOLIO/REFERENCES

Will Be Given Upon Request

APPENDIX

BERNARD HALDANE ASSOCIATES NETWORK

As we noted previously, self-directed career books can help you become more effective with your job search. They outline useful principles, suggest effective strategies, and explain how you and others can achieve your own job and career success. That's our purpose in writing this and other books in the "Haldane's Best" series. We believe you can benefit greatly from the methods we have developed over the years and used successfully with thousands of our clients.

We know the Haldane methods work because our clients are real cases of success that go far beyond the anecdotal. Indeed, our files are filled with unsolicited testimonials from former clients who have shared their insights into what really worked—evidence of our effectiveness in delivering what we promise our clients. We've shared some of these testimonials throughout the text of this book. What especially pleases us as career professionals is the fact that we've helped change the lives of so many people who have gone on to renewed career success. They discovered new opportunities that were a perfect fit for their particular interests, skills, and abilities. By focusing on their strengths and identifying their motivated skills and abilities, they were able to chart new and exciting career directions.

But our clients didn't achieve success overnight nor on their own. They worked with a structure, a schedule, and a vision of what they wanted to do next with their lives. Most important of all, they worked with a Career Advisor who helped them every step of the way. What we and other career specialists have learned over the years is no real secret, but it's worth repeating: most job seekers can benefit tremendously by working with a trained and experienced career professional who helps them complete each step of the career management process.

Our methods are not quick and easy, nor do they come naturally to most people—especially if you want to make the right career move. Many of our clients come to us

> ### Client Feedback
>
> *"You cannot ask questions of a book. You cannot get feedback on what to do from a book. And most of all, no book can help you with a job hunting campaign designed specifically for you. This is where Haldane comes in."*
> —J.A.C.
>
> *"I felt I could read a book or two on resumes and the world would beat a path to my door. What you did was to provide a step-by-step process for developing an effective marketing campaign."*
> —W.G.S.

after several weeks and months of frustrated efforts in conducting their own job search. Some tried doing everything according to the books, but they soon discovered that the books are only as good as the actions and outcomes that follow. What they most needed, and later appreciated, was a career professional whom they could work with in completing the critical assessment work (Success Factor Analysis) and in relating that key data to all other stages in their job search, from resume and letter writing to networking and interviewing. Using the proprietary Career Strategy 2000 electronic system, they gained access to a huge database of opportunities and employers. Once our clients decide to "do it the Haldane way" with a Career Advisor, they get surprising results. Again and again their testimonials emphasize the importance of completing Success Factor Analysis, developing a Haldane objective, networking, writing focused resumes and "T" letters, and interviewing and negotiating salary according to Haldane principles. Most important of all, they point out the value of having someone there—a Haldane Career Advisor—to guide them through the psychological ups and downs that often come with the highly ego-involved and rejection-ridden job finding process.

There's a season for everything, be it reading a self-directed career book or contacting a career professional for assistance. We've shared with you our insights and strategies by writing this book. Now it's up to you to take the next step. What you do next may make a critical difference in your career and your life. You may well discover your dream job on your own because you organized a Haldane-principled job search. If and when you feel you could benefit from the assistance of a career professional, please consider the Haldane network of Career Advisors. They have an exceptional track record of success based upon the methods outlined in this and other books in the "Haldane's Best" series. For your convenience, we've listed, along with contact information, the more than 80 offices that make up the Haldane network in the United States, Canada, and the United Kingdom. You can contact the office nearest you for more information and arrange for a free consultation. Please visit our Web site for additional information on Bernard Haldane Associates:

www.jobhunting.com

Bernard Haldane Associates Offices

United States

ALABAMA:

10 Inverness Parkway, Suite 125
Birmingham, AL 35242
(205) 991-9134; Fax (205) 991-7164
bhaadm@aol.com

4725 Whitesburg Dr.; Suite 202
Huntsville, AL 35801
(256) 880-9500; Fax (256) 880-9522
bhahts@aol.com

ARIZONA:

3101 N. Central Avenue, Suite 1560
Phoenix, AZ 85012
(602) 248-8893; Fax (602) 248-8987
bhaphoenix@aol.com

5151 E. Broadway, Suite 390
Tucson, AZ 85711
(520) 790-2767; Fax (520) 790-2992
bha@azstarnet.com

CALIFORNIA:

1801 Avenue of the Stars, Suite 1011
Los Angeles, CA 90067
(310) 203-0955; Fax (310) 203-0933
careers@haldane.com

8801 Folsom Blvd., Suite 100
Sacramento, CA 95826
(916) 381-5094; Fax (916) 381-6506
haldane@job-hunting.com

8880 Rio San Diego Drive, Suite 300
San Diego, CA 92108
(619) 299-1424; Fax (619) 299-5340
sdbha@yahoo.com

388 Market Street, Suite 1600
San Francisco, CA 94111
(415) 391-8087; Fax (415) 391-4009
haldane@job-hunting.com

181 Metro Drive, Suite 410
San Jose, CA 95110-1346
(408) 437-9200; Fax (408) 437-1300
haldane@job-hunting.com

Pacific Plaza, Suite 220
1340 Treat Blvd.
Walnut Creek, CA 94596
(925) 945-0776; Fax (925) 939-3764
haldane@job-hunting.com

COLORADO:

The Registry, 1113 Spruce Street
Boulder, CO 80302
(303) 571-1757; Fax (303) 825-5900
jobhunt@haldane.com

Plaza of the Rockies,
111 S. Tejon Street, Suite 610
Colorado Springs, CO 80903-2263
(719) 634-8000; Fax (719) 635-8008
jobhunt@haldane.com

1625 Broadway, #2550
Denver, CO 80202
(303) 825-5700; Fax (303) 825-5900
jobhunt@haldane.com

Denver Technological Center
8400 E. Prentice Ave., Suite 301
Englewood, CO 80111
(303) 793-3800, Fax (303) 793-3040
jobhunt@haldane.com

Poudre Valley Center
1075 W. Horsetooth Road, Suite 204
Fort Collins, CO 80526
(970) 223-5459; Fax (970) 226-2757
jobhunt@haldane.com

CONNECTICUT:

State House Square
Six Central Row
Hartford, CT 06103-2701
(860) 247-7500; Fax (860) 247-1213
hartford@haldane.com

FLORIDA:

6622 Southpoint Dr. So., Suite 340
Jacksonville, FL 32216
(904) 296-6802; Fax (904) 296-3506
haldane340@msn.com

901 North Lake Destiny Drive, Suite 379
Maitland, FL 32751 **(Orlando)**
(407) 660-8323; Fax (407) 660-2434
bhaorlando@aol.com

5100 W. Kennedy Blvd., Suite 425
Tampa, FL 33609
(813) 287-1393; Fax (813) 289-4125
haldane@worldnet.att.net

GEORGIA:

4170 Ashford Dunwoody Road, Suite 575
Atlanta, GA 30319
(404) 255-3184; Fax (404) 250-1165
haldane@mindspring.com

ILLINOIS:

One Magnificent Mile
980 N. Michigan Ave., Suite 1400
Chicago, IL 60611
(312) 214-4920; Fax (312) 214-7674
jobs@bhaldane.com

One Tower Lane, Suite 1700
Oakbrook Terrace, IL 60181
(630) 573-2923; Fax (630) 574-7048
jobs@bhaldane.com

1901 N. Roselle Road, Suite 800
Schaumburg, IL 60195
(847) 490-6454; Fax (847) 490-6529
jobs@bhaldane.com

INDIANA:

8888 Keystone Crossing, Suite 1675
Indianapolis, IN 46240
(317) 846-6062; Fax (317) 846-6354
bha_indy_admn@worldnet.att.net

IOWA:

6165 NW 86th Street
Johnston, IA 50131 **(Des Moines)**
(515) 727-1623; Fax (515) 727-1673
jobs@bhaldane.com

KANSAS:

7007 College Blvd., Suite 727
Overland Park, KS 66211
(913) 327-0300; Fax (913) 327-7067
kchaldane@qni.com

2024 N. Woodlawn, Suite 402
Wichita, KS 67208
(316) 687-5333; Fax (316) 689-6924
bhaldane@swbell.net

KENTUCKY:

330 E. Main Street, Suite 200
Lexington, KY 40507
(606) 255-2163; Fax (606) 231-0737
bha_lex_admn@worldnet.att.net

9100 Shelbyville Rd., Suite 280
Louisville, KY 40222
(502) 326-5121; Fax (502) 426-5348
bha_louis_admn@worldnet.att.net

MAINE:

477 Congress Street, 5th Floor
Portland, ME 04101-3406
(207) 772-1700; Fax (207) 772-7117
jobhunting@haldane.com

MASSACHUSETTS:

277 Dartmouth St.
Boston, MA 02116-2800
(617) 247-2500; Fax (617) 247-7171
jobhunting@haldane.com

10 Mechanic Street
Worcester, MA 01608
(508) 767-0100; Fax (508) 767-0300
jobhunting@haldane.com

MICHIGAN:

5777 West Maple Rd., Suite 190
West Bloomfield, MI 48322 **(Detroit)**
(248) 737-4700; Fax (248) 737-4789
bhadet@coast.net

MINNESOTA:

3433 Broadway St., N.E., Suite 440
Minneapolis, MN 55413
(612) 378-0600; Fax (612) 378-9225
jobs@bhaldane.com

MISSOURI:

680 Craig Road, Suite 400
St. Louis, MO 63141
(314) 991-5444; Fax (314) 991-5207
careers@haldanestl.com

NEBRASKA:

12020 Shamrock Plaza, Suite 200
Omaha, NE 68154
(402) 330-9461; Fax (402) 330-9847
omaha@haldanestl.com

NEW HAMPSHIRE:

20 Trafalgar Square, Suite 452
Nashua, NH 03063
(603) 886-4200; Fax (603) 886-4242
jobhunting@haldane.com

NEW JERSEY:

The Atrium, E. 80 Route 4, Suite 110
Paramus, NJ 07652
(201) 587-9898; Fax (201) 587-9119
jobs@bhaldane.com

100 Princeton Overlook Center, Suite 100
Princeton, NJ 08540
(609) 987-0400; Fax (609) 987-0011
jobs@bhaldane.com

NEW YORK:

80 State Street, 11th Floor
Albany, NY 12207

(518) 447-1000; Fax (518) 447-0011
jobhunting@haldane.com

838 Crosskey Office Park
Fairport, NY 14450 **(Rochester)**
(716) 425-0550; Fax (716) 425-0554
haldane@frontiernet.net

261 Madison Avenue, Suite 1504
New York, NY 10016
(212) 490-7799; Fax (212) 490-1712
jobs@bhaldane.com

300 International Drive, Suite 213
Williamsville, NY 14221 **(Buffalo)**
(716) 626-3400; Fax (716) 626-3402
jobhunting@haldane.com

NORTH CAROLINA:

6100 Fairview Road, Suite 355
Charlotte, NC 28210
(704) 643-5959; Fax (704) 556-1674
charlotte@haldanestl.com

4011 West Chase Blvd., Suite 210
Raleigh, NC 27607
(919) 546-9759; Fax (919) 546-9766
raleigh@haldanestl.com

OHIO:

3250 W. Market Street, Suite 307
Akron, OH 44333
(330) 867-7889; Fax (330) 867-7874
gcmg_hq@worldnet.att.net

625 Eden Park Drive, Suite 775
Cincinnati, OH 45202
(513) 621-4440; Fax (513) 562-8943
bha_cincy_admn@worldnet.att.net

6500 Rockside Rd., Suite 180
Cleveland, OH 44131
(216) 447-0166 ; Fax (216) 447-0015
bha_clev_admn@worldnet.att.net

111 West Rich Street, Suite 480
Columbus, OH 43215
(614) 224-2322; Fax (614) 224-2333
bha_colb_admn@worldnet.att.net

Fifth Third Center
110 N. Main Street, Suite 1280
Dayton, OH 45402
(937) 224-5279; Fax (937) 224-5284
bha_dayton_admn@worldnet.att.net

3131 Executive Parkway, Suite 300
Toledo, OH 43606
(419) 535-3898; Fax (419) 531-4771
bhadet@coast.net

OKLAHOMA:

3030 NW Expressway, Suite 727
Oklahoma City, OK 73112
(405) 948-7668; Fax (405) 948-7869
bhaokc@telepath.com

7060 South Yale, Suite 707
Tulsa, OK 74136
(918) 491-9151; Fax (918) 491-9153
haldane@gorilla.net

OREGON:

1221 S.W. Yamhill, Suite 124
Portland, OR 97205
(503) 295-5926; Fax (503) 295-2639
bhacareers@aol.com

PENNSYLVANIA:

Parkview Tower
1150 First Avenue, Suite 385
King of Prussia, PA 19404 **(Philadelphia)**
(610) 491-9050; Fax (610) 491-9080
jobs@bhaldane.com

Three Gateway Center, 18 East
401 Liberty Avenue
Pittsburgh, PA 15222
(412) 263-5627; Fax (412) 263-2027
bhapittspa@aol.com

RHODE ISLAND:

1400 Bank Boston Plaza
Providence, RI 02903
(401) 461-9900; Fax (401) 461-0099
providence@haldane.com

SOUTH CAROLINA:

5000 Thurmond Mall, Suite 106
Columbia, SC 29201
(803) 799-9155; Fax (803) 799-9163
columbia@haldanestl.com

TENNESSEE:

7610 Gleason Drive, Suite 301
Knoxville, TN 37919
(423) 690-6767; Fax (423) 690-3990
bhaknox@worldnet.att.net

1661 International Drive, Suite 400
Memphis, TN 38120
(901) 820-4420; Fax (901) 818-3064
memphis@haldanestl.com

424 Church Street, Suite 1625
Nashville, TN 37219
(615) 742-8440; Fax (615) 742-8445
jobs@bhaldane.com

TEXAS:

Park Central VII, 12750 Merit Dr., Ste. 200
Dallas, TX 75251
(972) 503-4100; (Fax) 972-503-4445
bhadfw@ont.com

UTAH:

215 South State Street, Suite 200
Salt Lake City, UT 84111
(801) 355-4242; Fax (801) 355-3238
bhajobs@worldnet.att.net

VIRGINIA:

2101 Wilson Blvd., Suite 950
Arlington, VA 22201 **(DC)**
(703) 516-9122; Fax (703) 812-3001
jobs@bhaldane.com

6800 Paragon Place, Suite 106
Richmond, VA 23230
(804) 282-0470; Fax (804) 282-1983
jobs@bhaldane.com

WASHINGTON:

10900 N.E. 8th St., Suite 1122
Bellevue, WA 98004 **(Seattle)**
(425) 462-7308; Fax (425) 462-9670
careerspnw@aol.com

West 818 Riverside Drive, Suite 320
Spokane, WA 99201
(509) 325-7650; Fax (509) 325-7655
careersspo@aol.com

Tacoma Security Building
917 Pacific Avenue, Suite 400
Tacoma,WA 98402
(253) 383-8757; Fax (253) 383-0887
careersadv@aol.com

WISCONSIN:

4351 West College Ave., Suite 215
Appleton, WI 54914
(920) 831-7820; Fax (920) 831-7831
bhaappletn@aol.com

15800 W. Bluemound Road, Suite 320
Brookfield, WI 53005 **(Milwaukee)**
(414) 797-8055; Fax (414) 797-9002
bhamilw@aol.com

5315 Wall Street, Suite 220
Madison, WI 53718
(608) 246-2100; Fax (608) 246-2031
bhamadison@aol.com

Canada:

3027 Harvester Rd., Suite 105
Burlington, Ontario, Canada L7N 3G7
(905) 681-0180; Fax (905) 681-0181
haldane@bserv.com

One London Place,
255 Queens Avenue, Suite 2150
London, Ontario, Canada N6A 5R8
(519) 439-2580; Fax (519) 439-2587
bhaldane@ican.net

1250 Blvd. Rene-Levesque Ouest, Suite 2335
Montreal, Quebec, Canada H3B 4W8
(514) 938-0578; Fax (514) 938-9165
700617@ican.net

Manulife Place
55 Metcalfe Street, Suite 1460
Ottawa, Ontario, Canada K1P 6L5
(613) 234-2530; Fax (613) 234-2560
687131@ican.net

One Financial Place
One Adelaide Street East, Suite 2201
Toronto, Ontario, Canada M5C 2V9
(416) 363-9241; Fax (416) 363-9246
bhatoronto@aol.com

IBM Tower, Suite 1800
701 West Georgia Street
Vancouver, British Columbia V7Y 1C6
(604) 609-6661; Fax (604) 609-2638
bha@portal.ca

United Kingdom:

Cornwall Court
19 Cornwall Street
Birmingham 3 2DY UK
011-44-1212-243192; Fax 011-44-1212-005775
bhanorth@aol.com

2440 The Quadrant
Aztec West
Almondsbury, **Bristol** BS32 4AQ UK
011-44-1454-878506; Fax 011-44-1454-878606
temp@haldane.co.uk

Marcol House
289/293 Regent Street
London W1R 7PD UK
011-44-1712-909100; Fax 011-44-1712-909109
bha@haldane.co.uk

82 King Street
Manchester M2 4QW UK
011-44-1619-358070;
(Fax) 011-44-1619-358217
bhanorth@aol.com

INDEX